# Foundations of Artificial Intelligence in Finance

This book discusses the financial impact of artificial intelligence (AI) on the finance and business sectors. By providing readers with comprehensive insights, real-world case studies, and expert discussions, it delves into various applications of AI in finance, including NLP for financial document analysis, predictive analytics, explainable AI, and blockchain integration. Covering a range of topics, from simplifying financial documents to predicting stock market trends and ensuring ethical investing, this book is crucial to effectively bridge the gap between technical AI concepts and practical applications, making it suitable for both specialists and non-specialists.

- In-depth discussions focus on the potential impact of AI on sustainable investments, exploring how these technologies may shape the future of finance.
- Emphasizes the ethical implications of AI in finance, addressing the responsible use of these technologies and the importance of regulatory compliance.
- Each chapter includes practical case studies that illustrate the effective use of AI in the financial industry, providing readers with relatable insights into its applications.
- Aids non-specialists in comprehending complex AI concepts and demonstrates how AI can act as a smart assistant in solving intricate financial and business problems.
- Leverage AI for informed decision-making, risk management, and sustainable investments, making it a pivotal reference for navigating the rapidly evolving financial landscape.

The book is for professionals, data scientists, investors, policymakers, and anyone interested in understanding how AI can transform financial practices.

**AI Applications and Case Studies for Business**

*Foundations of Artificial Intelligence in Finance: Insights for Practitioners with Applications and Case Studies*
Edited By Syed Hasan Jafar, Hemachandran K, Donkor Nawaah, Raul Villamarin Rodriguez

# Foundations of Artificial Intelligence in Finance

## Insights for Practitioners with Applications and Case Studies

Edited By
Syed Hasan Jafar
Hemachandran K
Donkor Nawaah
Raul Villamarin Rodriguez

CRC Press
Taylor & Francis Group
Boca Raton London New York

CRC Press is an imprint of the
Taylor & Francis Group, an **informa** business
A CHAPMAN & HALL BOOK

Designed Cover Image: Shutterstock Image: 2434550923

First edition published 2026
by CRC Press
2385 NW Executive Center Drive, Suite 320, Boca Raton FL 33431

and by CRC Press
4 Park Square, Milton Park, Abingdon, Oxon, OX14 4RN

*CRC Press is an imprint of Taylor & Francis Group, LLC*



ISBN: 978-1-041-01033-3 (hbk)
ISBN: 978-1-041-00787-6 (pbk)
ISBN: 978-1-003-61164-6 (ebk)

DOI: 10.1201/9781003611646

Typeset in Times
by KnowledgeWorks Global Ltd.

# Contents

# Preface

The financial industry is in the process of being completely revolutionized. Amidst the shifting landscape of global volatility, growing regulatory demands, and the unprecedented abundance of data, artificial intelligence (AI) has emerged as a key force. "Foundations of Artificial Intelligence in Finance: Insights for Practitioners, with Applications and Case Studies" tackles this change with urgency, clarity, and depth. This volume brings together a diverse set of voices from academics, technologists, and practitioners to share perspectives: not merely on the fundamentals of AI but its use in finance. It builds on the buzz, looking ahead to the foundational architecture, analytics, and ethical imperatives of implementing AI throughout the Financial System.

Through 22 carefully curated chapters, the book covers real-world applications of key AI technology like machine learning, deep learning, natural language processing, and robotic process automation. It engages with the latest applications including AI-powered credit scoring, green finance, algorithmic trading, fraud detection, and more, while also addressing crucial conversations about explainability, governance, and inclusivity. This is a book of practice rather than only concepts. Every chapter is supported by real-world case studies and use cases that demonstrate how AI is actively changing institutional and systemic frameworks for asset management, compliance, ESG analysis, and decision-making. By doing this, it gives readers the ability to distinguish between the revolutionary potential of AI and its ethical or technical limitations.

Contributions from the United Kingdom, the United States, India, Germany, Ghana, Switzerland, Nigeria, and beyond, enhance this book's global reach and multidisciplinary viewpoint. This global scope guarantees that the conversation is not limited to a single market structure or regulatory framework but rather addresses a growingly integrated financial community. This book is for those practitioners, academics, and advanced students who want not just a theoretical understanding of AI but a pragmatic knowledge of how to use it to solve the financial problems of tomorrow. It is just as much a call to action: to embrace smart systems with rigour, with responsibility, with relevance. This book is intended to be a guide and an enabler: for learning, for change, and for impact, in a world where speed, scale, and intelligence are the hallmark of competitive advantage.

# Biography

**Syed Hasan Jafar**

Syed Hasan, an Associate Dean and Area Chair of Finance, is a multifaceted professional with a strong presence in the finance industry and academia. With expertise in equity and derivative research, capital markets, technical and fundamental analysis, Hasan's insights are sought after by leading platforms such as CNBC, AajTak, BizTak, and The Economic Times: BFSI. As a media speaker, Hasan bridges the gap between complex financial concepts and the wider audience, making finance more accessible. His leadership at Woxsen University and prominence in the finance world reflect his dedication to advancing education and sharing knowledge with others.

**Hemachandran K**

Hemachandran K is a distinguished professional, holding multiple prestigious positions in academia and research. He serves as the Director of the AI Research Centre and as an Associate Dean at Woxsen University. Additionally, he holds the Zita Zoltay Paprika Chair Professorship and the Course5i Chair Professorship, alongside his role as Professor and Area Chair in the Analytics Department at Woxsen University. Dr. Hemachandran is deeply involved in shaping the future of AI, evident through his role as an ATL Mentor of Change and his work on AI 2030 initiatives. Based in Hyderabad, India, his contributions to education and research are significant and far-reaching.

**Donkor Nawaah**

Donkor Nawaah is an Assistant Professor and Head of Accounting and Fintech Department at Woxsen University's School of Business, where he brings over 17 years of expertise in accounting and finance to foster next-generation business education. A dedicated educator and seasoned researcher, Dr. Donkor is committed to advancing the fields of financial reporting, corporate finance, and sustainability, with a particular focus on impactful, real-world applications. His work spans curriculum innovation, corporate governance, and ethical practices, all aimed at equipping students with the skills and insights needed to navigate today's complex financial landscapes. Through his leadership and research, Prof. Donkor actively shapes a forward-thinking academic environment, instilling in students a robust foundation in finance coupled with a commitment to ethical and sustainable practices.

**Raul Villamarin Rodriguez**

Raul Villamarin Rodriguez, serving as the Vice President at Woxsen University, is a cognitive technologist and advocate for new age higher education. With expertise in cognitive and behavioural psychology, Rodriguez is at the forefront of innovative approaches to learning and development. His role involves spearheading initiatives that integrate cutting-edge technology with educational practices to enhance student outcomes. As a thought leader in the field, Rodriguez is dedicated to pushing the boundaries of traditional education and fostering cognitive growth in students. His contributions to Woxsen University underscore his commitment to shaping the future of higher education through transformative methodologies.

# List of Contributors

**Dominic Acharic**
Department of Management Studies, University of Mines and Technology
Tarkwa, Ghana

**Mahesh Admankar**
School of Liberal Arts & Humanities, Woxsen University
Hyderabad, Telangana, India

**Cornelius Adorm-Takyi**
Department of Accounting, University of Cape Coast
Cape Coast, Ghana

**Marella Anvitha**
School of Business, Woxsen University
Hyderabad, Telangana, India

**Fredrick Appiah Asare**
Department of Accounting, University of Cape Coast (UCC)
Cape Coast, Ghana

**Prince Yeboah Asare**
Department of Business and Social Sciences Education, University of Cape Coast
Cape Coast, Ghana

**Leticia Bosu**
Lecturer, Department of Business and Social Sciences Education, University of Cape Coast
Cape Coast, Ghana

**Prashant Subhash Chougule**
School of Business, Woxsen University
Hyderabad, Telangana, India

**Kotagiri Sai Deepak**
School of Business, Woxsen University
Hyderabad, Telangana, India

**Reginald Djimateya**
Department of Entrepreneurship and Business Sciences, University of Energy and Natural Resources
Sunyani, Ghana, West Africa

**Dzisenu Dziedzorm**
780th Military Intelligence Brigade, Fort George G. Meade,
Maryland, United States

**Rajan Gupta**
School of Business, Woxsen University
Hyderabad, Telangana, India

**Wilson E. Herbert**
Department of Banking & Finance, Federal University Otuoke
Bayelsa State, Nigeria

**Uvesh Husain**
Mazoon College
Muscat, Oman

**Syed Hasan Jafar**
Department of Finance, Woxsen University
Hyderabad, Telangana, India

**Solomon Jeresa**
Huddersfield Business School, University of Huddersfield
Huddersfield, United Kingdom.

**Hemachandran K**
Department of Analytics, Woxsen University
Hyderabad, Telangana, India

**Murage Jane Karuana**
Swiss School of Business and Management
Geneva, Switzerland

**Joseph Tufuor Kwarteng**
Department of Business and Social Sciences Education, University of Cape Coast
Cape Coast, Ghana

**Rockson Mintah**
Department of Accounting and Finance, Faculty of Business Studies, Accra Technical University,
Accra, Ghana

**Ch Siddharth Nanda**
School of Business, Woxsen University,
Hyderabad, Telangana, India

**Dharmavarapu Naveen Kumar**
School of Business, Woxsen University
Hyderabad, Telangana, India

**Donkor Nawaah**
Department of Accounting and Fintech, Woxsen University
Hyderabad, Telangana, India

**Maureen N. Nwala**
Department of Banking & Finance, Nasarawa State University
Keffi, Nasarawa State, Nigeria

**R. V. Palanivel**
Berlin School of Business and Innovation
Berlin, Germany

**Ch. Purnachander**
Department of Commerce, Osmania University,
Hyderabad, Telangana, India

**Michael Ayikwei Quarshie**
Department of Entrepreneurship and Business Sciences, University of Energy and Natural Resources
Sunyani, Ghana

**Afzalur Rahman**
Department of Finance, Woxsen University
Hyderabad, Telangana, India

**M. V. Samba Shiva Rao**
School of Business, Woxsen University
Hyderabad, Telangana, India

**Mukundamgari Rishik Reddy**
Mahindra University, School of Management
Hyderabad, Telangana, India

**Sudeshna Sani**
Department of Business Analytics, School of Business, Woxsen University
Hyderabad, Telangana, India

**Muneer Shaik**
Mahindra University, School of Management
Hyderabad, Telangana, India

**Sujit Singh**
School of Business, Woxsen University
Hyderabad, Telangana, India

**Sruthi Sivakumar**
School of Business, Woxsen University
Hyderabad, Telangana, India

**Mulukalapally Susruth**
School of Business, SR University
Warangal, Telangana, India

**Emmanuel Asare Tettey**
Peduase Valley Resort, Ankama Close, Peduase, Aburi, Eastern Region
Ghana

# 1 Introduction to AI in Finance

## *Foundational Concepts and Emerging Challenges*

*Afzalur Rahman, Sruthi Sivakumar, Uvesh Husain, and Sujit Singh*

## 1.1 INTRODUCTION

Artificial intelligence (AI) is transforming the global financial services industry by increasing the efficacy, accuracy, and customisation of financial goods and services. Organisations can make better use of large datasets, identify trends, automate decision-making, and streamline operational procedures by leveraging AI tools, particularly machine learning (ML), deep learning (DL), and natural language processing (NLP) [1–4]. As a result, significant advancements have been made in areas such as fraud detection, asset management, credit rating, and client contact. AI-driven systems have been used more and more by FinTech companies and financial institutions in recent years to provide specialised services, lower transaction costs, and better manage risks.

For example, the AI-based lending platform Upstart stated that, at the same default rate, its models approve 27% more loans than conventional credit assessment systems [5]. Similar to this, robo-advisory services like Wealthfront and Betterment use AI-powered algorithms to provide individualised, reasonably priced investing advice with little assistance from humans [6]. The use of AI in financial decision-making presents serious ethical, legal, and technological issues in spite of its advantages. Regulators and scholars have focused on issues such as algorithmic opacity, possible bias in training data, lack of interpretability, and data privacy concerns [7–10]. As an example, the European Union, in its General Data Protection Regulation (GDPR), implements the principles of algorithmic transparency and non-discrimination [11]. This chapter makes a systematic and critical exploration of the backgrounds, applications, and the future of AI in Finance. It combines results from academic research and industrial practice to analyse the application of AI for solving real-life specific financial challenges like risk assessment, fraud detection and prevention, and regulatory compliance. We focus on new developments, such as new explainable AI (XAI) innovations, adversarial ML, and multimodal data analysis that are rising stars in the domains of financial technology [12, 13]. Moreover, the chapter beholds a systematic review of 162 peer-reviewed papers, to chart existing areas of research while

DOI: 10.1201/9781003611646-1

highlighting major areas that deserve attention. This chapter provides a bibliometric and thematic analysis that reveals the applied use of AI in various financial contexts and identifies areas for future investigation. Bridging theory and practice, it aims to provide researchers with a detailed manifesto for future research and practitioners with a practical guide to the process of adopting AI.

## 1.2 OBJECTIVES FOR THE CHAPTER

The following objectives are intended to be accomplished by this chapter.

### 1.2.1 Introducing AI's Function in Finance

To provide an overview of the history and core concepts of AI and discuss how it is revolutionising the finance industry by enabling automation and data-driven innovation.

### 1.2.2 Examining Fundamental AI Developments in Finance

To analyse and illustrate how DL, ML, automated robotic procedures, and language processing algorithms are among the major advancements impacting AI in the financial industry and how they are changing financial operations.

### 1.2.3 Examining Research Gaps and Trends

To conduct a thorough bibliographic examination of the current body of research in AI-driven finance, identifying key themes, new trends, and unexplored areas.

### 1.2.4 Overcoming Obstacles and Ethical Concerns

One of the important constraints while addressing ethical issues such as algorithmic bias and fairness is data accessibility, model interpretability, and regulatory compliance which can greatly hinder algorithm implementation.

### 1.2.5 Outlining Techniques for Successful Execution

To offer practical recommendations that guide researchers and practitioners in responsibly utilising AI technology to solve critical problems across compliance, fraud detection, credit scoring, and more.

## 1.3 THEORETICAL FRAMEWORK: FAT (FAIRNESS, ACCOUNTABILITY, AND TRANSPARENCY)

This chapter employs the Fairness, Accountability, and Transparency (FAT) framework to conduct a critical analysis of AI design in the financial sector. FAT is originating out of the computer science and data ethics communities that provide a novel holistic set of principles for judging the ethical and social consequences of AI technologies [14, 15]. Thus, FAT offers a clear and problem-structured exploratory pathway to examine how AI-enabled solutions can increase the potential for innovation while also generating additional difficulties within the multi-layer contexts of the financial domain:

a. *Fairness*: Fairness becomes crucial in areas like credit scores, loan approvals, and fraud detection to make sure AI systems do not promote bad behaviour. Examples include such drawbacks of biased training data that are harmful or discriminatory towards certain demographic groups [16, 17].
b. *Accountability*: Demands precise procedures to determine who is responsible for judgments made by AI. In financial situations, where algorithmic results can have a big impact on consumers and markets, this is especially important [18].
c. *Transparency*: Promotes the explainability of AI models, particularly in situations where decisions have significant consequences. For audit and compliance purposes, authorities are putting more and more pressure on financial institutions to offer interpretable AI tools, such as XAI [19, 20].

By aligning with these principles, the chapter evaluates:

a. The use of core AI technologies (ML, DL, NLP, etc.) in fields such as fraud detection, credit risk modelling, and customer service;
b. The relevance of existing research gaps to concerns of fairness and accountability (e.g., adversarial robustness, multimodal learning);
c. Responsible innovation and ethical regulation of the broader societal implications of AI in finance.

As a result, and beyond its theoretical capacity, the FAT framework has a normative stand that may be analysed through the balancing of innovation versus risk that are essential ingredients to the continuity of the financial ecosystem in accepting AI.

## 1.4 AI IN FINANCE

AI is changing the landscape of the financial service industry throughout the world with personalised financial services, immediate and on-spot decision-making, and better operational efficiency [21, 22]. Various methods that fall under the umbrella of AI, such as ML, NLP, robotic process automation (RPA), and DL, are increasingly being deployed in banking, insurance, asset management, and the regulation of these industries [23, 24].

### 1.4.1 Importance of AI in Modern Financial Systems

Current financial systems require adaptive risk management, quick decision-making, and real-time data processing. These needs are well-met by AI technologies, which automate difficult processes and extract useful information from massive databases. For example:

a. *Detection of Fraud*: ML algorithms can detect suspicious activity and identify abnormal patterns in transactions in milliseconds for fraud detection [25].
b. *Sensitisation for Credit Risk*: AI models enhance credit assessment by leveraging behavioural indicators in addition to traditional sources of data [26, 27].
c. *Management of Portfolio*: AI Robo-advisors deliver tailored investment recommendations as per the risk profile and financial objectives of the clients [28, 29].
d. *Financial Forecasting*: Time series models driven by DL have predicted market trends with lesser level of accuracy [30, 31].
e. *RegTech and Compliance*: AI technologies enable regulatory reporting and ensure compliance with regulations via live transaction monitoring [32].

These applications demonstrate how AI can be applied to enhancing service quality and efficiencies while reducing financial exposure.

### 1.4.2 Core AI Technologies Used in Finance

AI in finance is underpinned by a confluence of complementary technologies:

a. *Machine Learning (ML)*: Covers supervised, unsupervised, and reinforcement learning. Such techniques have been extensively adopted for risk analytics, pricing models and predictive analytics for market movements [25].
b. *Natural Language Processing (NLP)*: Enables one to analyse unstructured textual data like earnings reports, news articles, customer service transcripts, etc. NLP models can identify the sentiment, extract important financial metrics, and flag violations of regulations [26, 30].
c. *Robotic Process Automation (RPA)*: Automates high-frequency, rules-based processes like KYC verification, transaction processing, and compliance documentation. This improves operational efficiency and lowers manual errors [33, 34].
d. *Deep Learning (DL)*: Model complex patterns using convolutional neural networks (CNNs) and long short-term memory (LSTM). DL is very popular in high-frequency trading, financial time series prediction, and fraud analytics [11, 23, 29].

While each of these technologies has its individual function, they are typically used within the larger AI architectures for complete financial automation and decision-making interdependencies.

### 1.4.3 AI and Data in Finance

The performance of AI models in finance relies on data quality, diversity, and relevance. Financial institutions generally work with a mix of structured and unstructured datasets:

a. *Market Data*: Time series information of asset costs, interest rates, and monetary signs;
b. *Customer Data*: Transaction history, demographics, and behavioural insights;
c. *Textual Data*: Collected from newsfeeds, social media, analyst reports, and earnings calls;
d. *Alternative Data*: Data from more traditional sources that are not typically utilised for hedge fund strategies, including satellite imagery, web traffic, or mobile phone usage.

Combining these several heterogeneous streams of data also improves the accuracy of predictions and means that decisions are made with context-aware assumptions. At the same time, it brings up concerns regarding some aspects of the FAT framework we explored above; data governance, privacy, and model transparency, among others. Additionally, both academic and industrial studies highlight the increasing necessity for bibliometric analysis to comprehend the shifting research directions. While mapping citation networks, keyword streams, and author collaboration sheds light on novel research nooks and technology impediments in AI-driven finance [6, 35].

## 1.5 METHODOLOGY

The chapter is a bibliometric and regression paper of the related literature with "AI in Finance". Scopus database was chosen for broad multidisciplinary, and comprehensive peer-reviewed literature. With this advanced search query, we obtained the bibliometric data of 4,290 papers as follows: TITLE-ABS-KEY ("Finance" AND ("AI" OR "Machine Learning" OR "Artificial Intelligence" OR "Deep Learning")) AND (LIMIT-TO (DOCTYPE, "ar") OR LIMIT-TO (DOCTYPE, "ch") OR LIMIT-TO (DOCTYPE, "bk")) AND (LIMIT-TO (LANGUAGE, "English")).

The bibliometric analysis was conducted to look at the patterns of temporal trend, topic modelling, and co-citation analysis. The selection process led to a sample of 162 articles with more than 100 citations (per Scopus records) for in-depth analysis from the full dataset. This threshold was selected to yield a comprehensive capture of influential publications. However it carries the limitation of exclusion of recent, but uncited, studies in the past few years. Future researchers might mitigate this issue by merging highly cited sequences with newer works. LDA topic modelling, co-citation network, and temporal trend analyses were performed on the selected articles to extract representative themes, research clusters, and thematic evolution over time. These techniques enabled the derivation of key themes, the interrelations between different themes, and the evolution of themes over the field.

### 1.5.1 Key Insights from Topical Analysis

a. Prevailing Research Themes: Applications of AI in finance and AI methodologies for financial time series forecasting account for most research, highlighting AI's transformative importance in the sector of finance.
b. *Applications of Artificial Intelligence in Finance*: This sub-theme discusses the applications of AI in finance field [25, 27], including the effects of AI on portfolio management, credit evaluation, risk recovery, and financial inclusion.
c. *Emerging Issues*: XAI and AI in FinTech are the recent trends of the moment and match the increasing attention given to trust and accountability, as well as the advent of a new financial Envision 2021, 2022 technologies [2].
d. *AI to Fight Financial Crime*: Financial crime and risk environments are becoming more complex at a faster rate than ever seen before, and AI-personalised fraud detection, and risk assessment, is still a key research direction.

## 1.6 THEMATIC ANALYSIS

### 1.6.1 Applications of AI in Finance

AI has found many applications in finance and influences portfolio management, credit scoring, risk detection, and financial inclusion [21, 34]. Artificial neural network, expert systems, and hybrid intelligent systems are among the most common of these techniques to execute the tasks such as bankruptcy prediction and market forecasting. The FinTech and AI convergence is gradually transforming traditional banking through innovations such as robo-advisors and peer-to-peer lending platforms.

### 1.6.2 Artificial Intelligence Methods for Financial Time Series Forecasting

Different DL architectures (like CNN, Recurrent Neural Network (RNN), and LSTM networks) have also been shown to outperform traditional ML methods in financial time series modelling [11]. Recently, attention mechanisms and hybrid models that mix AIs with traditional econometric methods, including the GARCH models, have been proposed to improve forecasting performance.

### 1.6.3 Explainable AI (XAI) in Finance

AI systems that are interpretable have gained utmost importance now, particularly due to the inherent need for accountability and transparency in regulated financial environments [2]. While understanding how AI makes certain decisions is necessary for risk management, fraud detection, and credit scoring, some methods that do not rely on particular model structures, like Shapley-based explanation methods, can offer valuable explainability with respect to how the decisions are derived [16].

### 1.6.4 Using Artificial Intelligence for Fraud Detection and Risk Preparation

AI has controlled most of the world since it is utilised as a weapon for credit rating, bankruptcy activation, and financial fraud detection purposes. Support Vector Machines and ensembles, other ML classifiers, are not affected by the data imbalance and high dimensionality issues seen in financial datasets [13]. The fusion of numerical data with a significant amount of textual data (financial report) enhances detection capabilities [22].

### 1.6.5 Artificial intelligence and Financial Technology (FinTech)

By enabling new projects like robo-advisory tools, crowdfunding websites, and high-frequency trading infrastructures, AI is changing the FinTech scene [26, 33]. Additionally, the research suggests that AI will eventually become coupled more directly with blockchain and quantum computing as a means of delivering secure, transparent, and efficient financial services.

## 1.7 TRENDS OVER TIME

Temporal analysis shows a consistent upward trajectory of AI application in finance over the past 10 years. Over time, advanced AI methods started to displace more traditional models of financial forecasting. XAI rise indicates regulation pressure and limited system transparency. FinTech and AI integration is a novel fast developing research frontier [2, 25].

## 1.8 RESEARCH GAPS AND FUTURE OPPORTUNITIES

a. *Comprehensive Comparative Evaluations*: While many studies exist on individual AI methods, systematic comparative assessments remain limited, hindering clarity on optimal AI techniques for specific financial tasks.
b. *Multimodal Data Integration*: Current research predominantly focuses on numerical data, with opportunities to incorporate textual (news, social media) and other modalities (audio, images) for enhanced model accuracy.
c. *Data Quality and Privacy Challenges*: Addressing data imbalance, privacy, and scarcity through methods like few-shot learning, data augmentation, and federated learning is critical to improve AI model robustness.
d. *Advancements in Explainable AI*: More domain-specific and robust XAI techniques are needed to boost interpretability and trust in AI-driven financial decisions.
e. *Financial Inclusion and Sustainability*: Little is known about how AI affects financial inclusion and sustainable finance in society, especially in emerging nations.
f. *Quantum Computing Applications*: While quantum computing has the potential to revolutionise financial calculations, there is more exploration to be done to establish its scalability and practical use.

g. *Security and Adversarial Robustness*: As AI becomes prevalent in critical financial systems, there is a need to develop adversarial robust AI models.

## 1.9 IMPLEMENTATION AND FUTURE DIRECTIONS

While quantum computing may revolutionise financial data processing, it warrants further research to make its practical implications clearer. Simultaneously, an increase in the use of AI only causes the potential of malicious attacks to be higher, thus requiring making AI systems that are secure and reliable. At the nexus of AI and FinTech innovation is the combined application of AI with blockchain, cloud computing, and IoT financial products. Ethical considerations such as reduction of bias, accountability, and transparency are still essential to enabling more sustainable use of AI [8, 12, 18]. Collaboration between finance professionals and AI researchers will be key to develop creative and reliable AI solutions.

## 1.10 CONCLUSION

This chapter describes how quickly AI changes shape and how profoundly it can disrupt financial services. Financial performance prediction, portfolio optimisation, credit rating, fraud detection, and financial inclusion are just a few of the many application areas for these. While reinforcement and DL techniques are cutting edge in terms of traditional forecasting, recently reinforcement is augmenting the forecasting features well, and the XAI is bypassing the transparency and trust roadblocks. AI being switched onto FinTech is prompting these new ways of gaining access to financial markets. By bringing to bear academic and industry-related literature and exposing gaps and areas for future work here, this manuscript is both practical in nature and will, thus, appeal to both academics and industry researchers. Connecting new theory and practical initiatives to make AI risk a mind in a box, aid strategic resurgence and enable a more effective final decision in finance. Future research work should focus on integrating multimodal data, improving data quality, increasing explainability, and examining the societal impact of AI in finance.

## REFERENCES

1. Arrieta AB, Díaz-Rodríguez N, Del Ser J, Bennetot A, Tabik S, Barbado A et al. Explainable Artificial Intelligence (XAI): Concepts, taxonomies, opportunities and challenges toward responsible AI. *Inf Fusion*. 2020;58:82–115. https://doi.org/10.1016/j.inffus.2019.12.012
2. Brynjolfsson E, McAfee A. *Machine, platform, crowd: Harnessing our digital future*. New York: W. W. Norton & Company; 2017.
3. Bussmann N, Giudici P, Marinelli D, Papenbrock J. Explainable AI in FinTech risk management. *Front Artif Intell*. 2020;3:26. https://doi.org/10.3389/frai.2020.00026
4. Quarshie MA, Djimatey R, Akhtar S, Nawaah D. Maximizing financial efficiency through technological synergy: Unleashing ICT for enhanced cash management in SMEs. *J Int Counc Small Bus*. 2025:1–31.
5. Upstart. *Upstart annual impact report* [Internet]. 2022 [cited 2025 June 1]. Available from: https://www.upstart.com/about/impact

6. Sironi P. *FinTech innovation: From robo-advisors to goal-based investing and gamification.* Hoboken: Wiley; 2016.
7. European Commission. *Proposal for a regulation on a European approach for artificial intelligence* [Internet]. 2021 [cited 2025 June 1]. Available from: https://eur-lex.europa.eu/legal-content/EN/TXT/?uri=CELEX:52021PC0206
8. Hurley M, Adebayo J. Credit scoring in the era of big data. *Yale J Law Technol.* 2017;18(1):148–216.
9. Malik MY, Jafar SH, Dixit A. Efficiency analysis and macroeconomic determinants of non-tax revenues: Evidence from special category states of India. *Indian Econ J.* 2025. https://doi.org/10.1177/00194662251330385
10. Quarshie MA, Akhtar S, Nawaah D. Barriers to breakthroughs: The crucial role of support services in advancing accounting practices, financial literacy and performance in disability-led SMEs. *Qual Quant.* 2025;59:955–977. https://doi.org/10.1007/s11135-024-02050-1
11. European Parliament and Council. Regulation (EU) 2016/679 of the European Parliament and of the Council. General Data Protection Regulation (GDPR). *Off J Eur Union.* 2016;119:1–88.
12. Chen X, Huang Q, Wang H, Jiang H. A survey on machine learning for financial services. *Neurocomputing.* 2021;460:1–17. https://doi.org/10.1016/j.neucom.2021.06.088
13. Barocas S, Hardt M, Narayanan A. *Fairness and machine learning* [Internet]. 2019 [cited 2025 June 1]. Available from: http://fairmlbook.org
14. Mittelstadt BD, Allo P, Taddeo M, Wachter S, Floridi L. The ethics of algorithms: Mapping the debate. *Big Data Soc.* 2016;3(2):1–21. https://doi.org/10.1177/2053951716679679
15. Jafar SH, Oyedele OM, Nawaah D, Bolanle AS. Exploring leadership challenges for adoption of digital innovation and sustainability. In: *Innovation ecosystems and sustainable technologies.* Bingley: Emerald Publishing Limited; 2025. p. 253–69.
16. Hemachandran K, Rodriguez RV, editors. *Artificial intelligence for business: An implementation guide containing practical and industry-specific case studies.* Boca Raton: CRC Press; 2023.
17. Hemachandran K, Rodriguez RV, editors. *The business of the metaverse: How to maintain the human element within this new business reality.* Boca Raton: CRC Press; 2023.
18. Hemachandran K, Rodriguez RV, Toshniwal R, Junaid M, Shaw L. Performance analysis of different classification algorithms for bank loan sectors. In: *Intelligent sustainable systems: Proceedings of ICISS 2021.* Singapore: Springer Singapore; 2021. p. 191–202.
19. Deloitte. *AI in financial services: Balancing innovation and risk* [Internet]. 2020 [cited 2025 June 1]. Available from: https://www2.deloitte.com
20. Hemachandran K, George PM, Rodriguez RV, Kulkarni RM, Roy S. Performance analysis of k-nearest neighbour classification algorithms for bank loan sectors. In: *Smart intelligent computing and communication technology.* Amsterdam: IOS Press; 2021. p. 9–13.
21. Jafar SH. Financial applications of Gaussian processes and Bayesian optimization. In: *Bayesian reasoning and Gaussian processes for machine learning applications.* Boca Raton: Chapman and Hall/CRC; 2022. p. 111–22.
22. Jafar SH, Akhtar S, Johl SK. AI in insurance. In: *Artificial intelligence for business.* New York: Productivity Press; 2023. p. 164–73.
23. Salim M, Khan PA, Jalil NA, Johl SK, Jafar SH, Irfan F et al. Fusion of blockchain and sustainable development goals: A bibliometric analysis for future trends. *KnE Soc Sci.* 2023:633–54.
24. Arner DW, Barberis J, Buckley RP. FinTech, RegTech and the reconceptualization of financial regulation. *Nw J Int Law Bus.* 2017;37(3):371–413.

25. Krauss C, Do XA, Huck N. Deep neural networks, gradient-boosted trees, random forests: Statistical arbitrage on the S&P 500. *Eur J Oper Res*. 2017;259(2):689–702.
26. Loughran T, McDonald B. When is a liability not a liability? Textual analysis, dictionaries, and 10-Ks. *J Finance*. 2011;66(1):35–65.
27. EY. *The rise of RPA in financial services* [Internet]. 2020 [cited 2025 June 1]. Available from: https://www.ey.com
28. Fischer T, Krauss C. Deep learning with long short-term memory networks for financial market predictions. *Eur J Oper Res*. 2018;270(2):654–69. https://doi.org/10.1016/j.ejor.2017.11.054
29. Jafar SH, Kashid AU, Ghosh S, Srividhya S, Sharma D, Bodhankar A. An enhanced performance optimization of ATM networks for cross-border money transfers. In: *2024 15th Int Conf Comput Commun Netw Technol (ICCCNT)*. New York: IEEE; 2024. p. 1–5.
30. Nawaah D, Asare PY, Quarshie MA. Climate finance and natural capital: Linking global initiatives with local impact. In: *Climate neutrality through smart eco-innovation and environmental sustainability*. Cham: Springer Nature Switzerland; 2025. p. 317–32.
31. Jafar SH, Dhandhukia V, Kumar GB. Application of artificial intelligence in banking: A review. In: *Machine learning for business analytics*. Boca Raton, Florida: CRC Press (Taylor & Francis Group); 2022. p. 145–51.
32. Jafar SH, Hemachandran K, El-Chaarani H, Moturi S, Gupta N, editors. *Artificial intelligence for capital markets*. Boca Raton: CRC Press; 2023.
33. Floridi L, Cowls J, King T, Taddeo M. How to design AI for social good: Seven essential factors. *Sci Eng Ethics*. 2018;26(4):1771–96. https://doi.org/10.1007/s11948-020-00213-5
34. El Abiad Z, Abraham R, El-Chaarani H, Skaf Y, Binsaddig RO, Jafar SH. The impact of CEO characteristics on the financial performance of family businesses listed in the Euronext Exchange. *J Risk Financ Manag*. 2024;17(3):129.
35. Morgan JP. *Big data and AI strategies: Machine learning and alternative data approaches to investing*. New York: J.P. Morgan; 2017.

# 2 Framework for Responsible AI Adoption in Fintech

*Syed Hasan Jafar*

## 2.1 INTRODUCTION

Massive and unprecedented changes have been observed in the fintech field primarily due to the introduction and use of artificial intelligence (AI) [1, 2]. AI enables financial institutions to improve efficiency, automate processes, and create value for their corporate and retail clients. One of the main benefits of the technology to the world of fintech, is the ability of AI to increase operational efficiency by automating complex and routine processes, reducing human process dependencies, and considerably reducing operational costs [3]. AI solutions have enhanced several business processes for financial institutions including the transaction processing, credit rating, risk management, and customer service. The use of AI facilitates fintech companies to deliver personalized and customized consumer experiences [4]. With the most recent AI techniques such as machine learning (ML) and natural language processing (NLP), financial service organizations can analyse huge amounts of customer data and achieve actionable insights. These and many more solutions allow a deep understanding of individuals that can help businesses leverage the financial products, offer customized financial consultancy, and use AI-enabled chatbots for providing timely service to customers. Predictive analytics, yet another prominent use case of AI, has also further improved the consumer experience by anticipated client needs, providing them with contextual financial solutions and even predicting early signs of financial distress [5]. Ultimately, this leads to a strategy that is more focused on the customer, building brand loyalty, trust, and happiness. In addition to its customer experience enhancement, AI has also revolutionized risk and compliance management by financial institutions [6–8].

From algorithmic trading to automated wealth management, real-time fraud detection to risk assessment, AI systems have enabled such services. AI has been utilized in various usages to accelerate the process of finding fraudulent transactions while enhancing accuracy, finetune investment strategies via data-driven trading algorithms [9] and offer better techniques for checking borrowers' extent of credit risk. These intelligent innovations have not only enhanced financial performance but also contributed to the security and stability of the financial system. But, when it comes to the AI implementation in the finance sector, few hurdles have arisen. AI brings with it numerous ethical concerns such as data privacy, algorithm bias

DOI: 10.1201/9781003611646-2

problem in decision-making and black-box nature of complex AI models. Complex nature of AI technology and rapid advancement of technology imply challenges and uncertainty for fintech because the development of regulatory frameworks has not kept pace with technological advancement [10, 11]. Accountability is vital to maintain public trust and also comply with the regulation in the AI-based decision-making pathways.

### 2.1.1 The Role of AI in Fintech

AI enhancements have readily benefited a diverse range of new fintech-related fields, such as lending, fraud detection, digital banking, and payment systems, even regulatory compliance [12, 13]. Applications which utilize AI-based approaches apply computation intelligence and data analytics to improving risk assessment, automating repetitive processes, and enhancing decision-making. Several key domains are influencing AI:

a. *Credit Scoring and Lending with AI*: Traditional credit scoring models leverage historical data to evaluate the creditworthiness of individuals. AI models, on the other hand, combine data from other sources such as transaction history, social media activity, and behavioural analytics to more accurately assess the creditworthiness of borrowers. AI-based lending systems can analyse spending habits [14], job history, and even smartphone usage patterns to expand access to credit to individuals with little or no credit history and promote financial inclusion.
b. *AI-Powered Fraud Detection Systems*: Fraud Detection Systems: AI-powered detection systems deploy behavioural biometrics, pattern recognition, and anomaly detection, in order to create broad-based detection measures to scrutinize financial transactions on a real-time basis with the aim of recognizing malicious activity. They analyse user behaviour data, device fingerprints, and geolocation data to monitor for potentially harmful transactions in real-time before they can impact finances. An AI-tool not only assists customers and institution in preventing potential financial losses but also features an exceptional deep learning model that detects real activity from false [15–17].
c. *AI in Customized Financial Services*: Automated investment advice or robo-advisors use AI to merge customer preferences, risk profile, and market movement to offer suitable investments in an automatic manner. Such AI advisers will tailor its financial recommendations according to the individual needs of the clients and optimizing risk allocation and portfolio management. Furthermore, AI chatbots enhance customer service by addressing inquiries, offering on-demand support and suggesting information on insurance rates and financial planning [1].
d. *Regulatory Compliance and AI*: Regulatory technology (RegTech) uses AI to help financial firms comply with changing requirements. AI systems assist with real-time transaction monitoring, regulatory reporting, and anti-money laundering (AML) compliance. Ultimately, these solutions

will support transparency and accountability in financial transactions by identifying unusual transactions, standardizing compliance processes, and reducing the risk of regulatory violations.

### 2.1.2 Challenges in AI Adoption in Fintech

AI has the potential to change the way fintech operates. However, various challenges exist on its adoption path including ethical and regulatory challenges along with many other operational hurdles. Key challenges include:

a. *AI Decision-Making Bias*: AI algorithms, especially those related to credit scoring and lending, have proven to be biased with respect to race, gender, and socioeconomic factors [18]. Such biases are often based on the skewed training data, which in the case of financial data may not be wholly unbiased, as the historical finance trends evolve in the backdrop of different systemic disparities. As a result, lending decisions based on AI may unintentionally replicate discriminatory practices, restricting financial access for marginalized populations.
b. *Absence of Transparency of Algorithms*: A lot of fintech rely on "black-box" AI models, which can render AI-driven financial decisions opaque and not easy to interpret and explain. This opacity begs questions of accountability; customers and regulators alike are unable to identify the grounds on which these credit approvals, investment recommendations and risk assessments are made.
c. *AI Driven Fintech Solutions*: Require massive amounts of customer data to operate. Therefore, the same data is vulnerable to be leaked or hacked into. Yet, the collection and processing of data come with privacy implications, including unauthorized access, data leakage, and other misuse of personal data. Financial agencies want to make use of stable cybersecurity measures to protect the consumer data in addition to being compliant with global data protection guidelines.
d. *Regulatory Uncertainty*: While many countries have regulatory frameworks in place, they often lack adequate specific regulation of AI in general or in a specific context such as fintech [19, 20]. Absence of clarity in policies leads to disparate level of AI governance making it a compliance hurdle for the financial institutions. Regulatory uncertainty, on the other hand, clogs innovation, making firms question if offering AI-led financial services is legally allowed.
e. *AI Market Manipulation Risk*: This means some market traders operate with almost full-powered trading algorithms assisted by AI, especially in the HFT, which can also lead to distortion in the financial market [21]. Thus, the absence of regulation wreaking havoc on AI trading strategies can result in fast price changes which could also raise the chance of market volatility spikes or financial instability. To be successful in doing so, fintech firms must adopt the responsible AI frameworks that emphasize fairness, transparency, accountability, and compliance, on AI-enabled financial services platforms.

## 2.2 LITERATURE REVIEW/THEORETICAL FRAMEWORK

### 2.2.1 Principles of Responsible AI in Fintech

To create an ethical fintech AI framework, it should essentially be emphasized on the basics of fair access to loans, compliance with regulatory guidelines and transparency. Key principles include:

a. *Fairness and Bias Mitigation*: AI models have to be trained on more than one or two datasets to avoid biases in credit scoring, lending, and insurance underwriting [13, 14, 22]. Mitigation of discriminatory AI through bias detection algorithms, fairness-aware ML models and human observation.
b. *Explainability and Transparency (XAI)*: Explainable AI (XAI) methods make AI-powered decisions more understandable and interpretable for financial institutions [23]. Auditable—customers, regulators, and stakeholders can evaluate and verify financial decisions with transparent AI models, promoting accountability.
c. *Data Privacy and Security*: AI needs to comply with applicable data protection laws, including GDPR in Europe and CCPA in California [4, 24]. Such regulations make sure that the customer data is dealt with safely as well as truthfully.
d. *Regulatory Compliance and Accountability*: Various AI fintech applications must comply with financial regulations such as AML laws, fraud prevention policies, digital lending guidelines, etc. [25]. Financial institutions are also advised to mitigate legal risk with appropriate compliance frameworks for the use of AI.
e. *AI Ethics and Human Oversight*: Although AI can help us with automating financial decision-making, we should also be careful to determine the rule underneath this to avoid mistakes that would not make a good influence towards customers. AI should be designed in a way that human intervention will be possible where required, so that responsible decision-making can be carried out [26].

### 2.2.2 AI Governance in Fintech

This is supported by a few theoretical models for responsible AI governance in the fintech context:

a. *AI Risk Management Framework*: Provided by the U.S. National Institute of Standards and Technology (NIST), the framework describes risk assessment methodologies applicable to AI-enabled financial systems, focusing on security, fairness, and accountability [7, 20].
b. *AI Act in the European Union*: An EU proposal would create a risk-based framework for governing AI in the banking, insurance, and wealth

management sectors and mandate compliance with ethical AI principles and standards [27].

c. *FATF AI Compliance Framework*: This international framework applies to the use of AI to know your customer (KYC), AML compliance, fraud detection, and regulatory reporting, and offers guidance on responsible deployment of AI in financial services [28].

### 2.2.3 Global Trends: Fintech Adoption of AI

From region to region, AI-powered fintech innovations are revolutionizing financial services:

a. *United States*: Companies like Betterment and Wealth front use ML-based robo-advisors for basic investment vehicles [29]. AI is used by Canada's largest banks in fraud detection to protect payment transactions [30].
b. *Europe*: The European Central Bank (ECB) requires the explainability of AI so that financial institutions implement fair lending and investment decision-making frameworks that are driven by AI [31].
c. *Asia*: Smart digital loans by Ant Financial and WeBank in China based on AI credit risk assessment. The Reserve Bank of India (RBI) encourages the use of AI for regulatory compliance and risk management in India [18].
d. *Africa*: Fintech's in Nigeria and Kenya leverage AI-enabled credit scoring to expand financial access [32].
e. *South America*: Brazil Nubank and Mexico Fintech Ecosystem offer AI applications for fraud detection, risk management and services in digital banking [33].

## 2.3 AI BIAS, FAIRNESS, AND ETHICAL LENDING PRACTICES IN FINTECH

AI-dependent fintech applications are bound to cause a lot of harm to financial inclusion and ethical decision-making through algorithmic bias. Credit scoring, lending, and insurance underwriting AI models are trained on historical financial data that tends to reflect society [9, 34, 35]. Unchecked, these biases can lead to discriminatory lending, financial exclusion, and borderline unethical credit assessments. Quality of training data is one of the leading causes of bias. If historical discrimination has played a role in financial decisions, an AI model will learn from this practice, continuing to withhold credit or imposing penalties on marginalized groups. A further challenge is the transparency issues with AI decision-making, or the so-called "black box" issue, that makes it hard to understand why a certain credit decision was made and why financial services were denied [6, 36]. Practical AI solutions can address algorithmic bias with investment in bias-detection measures to make AI models more transparent and ensuring training datasets are diverse and representative. AI bills of rights should require explainability in AI-based financial decisions and receptors for appeal.

AI brings efficiency and accuracy to the fintech industry but should be used cautiously [37]. There is a risk of entrenching systemic inequalities if there are no (or insufficient) safeguards. To build trust and create equitable financial outcomes for all, it is important to ensure that fairness, accountability, and transparency is implemented in AI models.

### 2.3.1 Sources of AI Bias in Fintech

Training Data Bias—AI models trained on historical lending data have the potential to learn and replicate biases against people from low-income groups, people from racial minorities, or people from yet underrepresented communities [38]. It is about trying to select some non-traditional features in AI credit scoring models such as social media behaviour and digital footprints features, which would raise ethical concerns as this sort of feature selection bias may impose systemic discrimination. Many of the decision-making algorithms deployed by fintech companies are black-box models, which cannot be audited or explained in terms of the AI-generated lending decisions. In some AI-led lending platforms, indirect variables (for example, ZIP codes, education history) are used that are associated with race or socioeconomic status [39], and such proxy features often get carried with the model to make biased decisions such as the credit score of consumers. In 2021, for example, a US fintech lender came under regulatory scrutiny when its AI credit-scoring model turned down minority applicants at extremely high rates [40]. In much the same fashion, a study on AI-based lending in EU found that automated mortgage decisions favoured high income borrowers, contributing to greater financial inequality [7].

#### 2.3.1.1 Reducing Bias with Ethical Frameworks for AI

For fairness and ethical lending practice to take place, fintech firms must bring in:

Regular audits should identify discrimination and unfairness that may arise through the use of AI models used in Lending—Bias Audits in AI Lending models.

a. *Explainable AI (XAI) for Credit Decisions*: Even as XAI-based lending platforms provide credit approvals and rejections, these models should explain credit approval and rejection so that customers understand why they were served a credit card.
b. *Diverse Examples in AI Training Data*: AI models should be trained on examples that represent diverse socioeconomic groups, gender distribution, and geographical locations [24, 41].
c. *Create Regulatory Oversight for Fairness of AI*: Governments and fintech regulators should implement and enforce AI governance standards in order to have fintech companies conform to some ethical lending practices [42].

### 2.3.2 Data Privacy, Security, and AI Governance in Fintech

Concerns regarding data privacy, security issues, and AI-driven cyberattacks are raised by the fintech industry's heavy reliance on AI-driven data processing. Financial institutions retain highly sensitive client data, including financial transactions, personal identities, biometric information, and credit histories, making them great targets for assaults.

#### 2.3.2.1 AI-Powered Cybersecurity Risks in Fintech

a. *AI-Driven Phishing and Fraud*: Cybercriminals use AI-generated deepfake voices, phishing scams, and social engineering attacks to exploit fintech systems [39].
b. *Data Breaches in AI Models*: AI-powered fraud detection tools store massive datasets, making them vulnerable to hacking, data leaks, and identity theft.
c. *Unauthorized AI Data Collection*: Some fintech firms use AI-driven analytics to track customer spending behaviour's, location data, and online transactions, raising concerns over consumer privacy rights [34].
d. *AI in Digital Identity Theft*: Fraud threats have increased as a result of the deployment of sophisticated AI methods, such as deepfake AI and biometric spoofing, to get beyond KYC verification processes [25].

For instance, a significant AI-driven fraud assault occurred in 2022 at a European digital bank, resulting in millions of dollars in damages as thieves created fictitious accounts using fictitious identities [5]. Similar to this, online lending platforms in Latin America saw a 40% increase in AI-driven identity fraud instances, underscoring the urgent need for more robust AI governance regulations [3].

#### 2.3.2.2 AI Governance Models for Fintech Security

Fintech companies must have strong AI governance frameworks in place to reduce the security risks associated with AI. These frameworks should include:

a. *AI-Driven Threat Detection Systems*: Which use ML models to identify and stop phishing attempts, fraudulent transactions, and AI-powered cyberthreats instantly.
b. *Privacy-Enhancing AI Techniques*: To safeguard consumer data while AI is processing, fintech platforms should use federated learning and differentiated privacy models.
c. *Compliance with Data Protection Legislation*: Fintech must abide by the CCPA (California), GDPR (Europe), and new AI privacy legislation in Asia and Africa [42].
d. *Biometric Authentication for Secure AI Transactions*: To improve digital identity protection, AI-powered finance services should employ biometric encryption, multi-factor authentication, and face recognition security.

AI-powered biometric security features, for example, have been included into financial platforms in India to guard against illegal access and safeguard online transactions [10, 19]. Strong AI governance in data security allows fintech companies to strike a balance between innovation and customer safety.

## 2.4 FUTURE TRENDS AND POLICY IMPLICATIONS

### 2.4.1 The Future of Responsible AI in Fintech

As AI develops further, the following factors will influence the responsible adoption of AI in fintech going forward:

a. *Blockchain and AI Integration for Transparent Financial Transactions*: Blockchain technology will improve AI-driven financial security by guaranteeing tamper-proof records of lending histories and banking transactions.
b. *Quantum AI for Financial Risk Prediction*: High-frequency trading tactics, fraud detection, and market risk assessment will all be transformed by quantum-powered AI models.
c. *Decentralized AI for Peer-to-Peer Fintech Lending*: AI-powered DeFi models will make transparent, algorithm-based lending possible without the need for middlemen.
d. *Regulatory Sandboxes for AI Innovation in Fintech*: Prior to completely approving new AI-driven fintech models, governments will set up AI testing environments [8].

These new developments will change fintech governance, guaranteeing ethical AI development while safeguarding the interests of customers and the stability of the financial system.

### 2.4.2 Policy Recommendations for Responsible AI in Fintech

Financial authorities, fintech companies, and AI developers must put the following into practice to guarantee the responsible usage of AI:

a. *Global AI Fintech Standards*: International cooperation will be necessary to develop consistently applied AI laws that ensure responsible AI adoption across all markets.
b. *AI Audit Mandates*: To ensure AI lending and fraud detection systems remain unbiased and fair, fintech companies need to be required to conduct regular AI bias audits.
c. *Fintech Decision Making Need Explainable Artificial Intelligence (XAI)*: AI models deployed for loan automation, investment recommendations, and credit approvals must be able to provide understandable explanations for financial decisions [27].
d. *AI Governance Boards in Financial Institutions*: Banks and fintech companies should establish AI oversight boards to monitor AI-powered financial services for ethical AI compliance.

The integration of these policy recommendations could enable policies that allow responsible deployment of AI in fintech businesses, which ensures similar regulation, transparency, and fairness in AI-enhanced financial services [39].

## 2.5 CONCLUSION

The fintech industry is undergoing a transformation with the adoption of AI for various functions that include Digital banking, lending, investment services, and fraud detection. On the other hand, AI-driven fintech solutions can also lead to bias, privacy, security, and regulatory violations without proper AI governance. This shows that the structure of fintech responsible AI deployment should primarily be focused on fairness, data privacy, security, ethical AI governance, and regulatory compliance. The future of AI in fintech is going to be influenced by explainable AI, integration with blockchain technologies, and mutual recognition of AI regulatory frameworks among nations, which will ensure a fair, transparent, and sustainable fintech field.

## REFERENCES

1. El Abiad Z, Abraham R, ElChaarani H, Skaf Y, Binsaddig RO, Jafar SH. The impact of CEO characteristics on the financial performance of family businesses listed in the Euronext Exchange. *J Risk Financ Manag.* 2024;17(3):129.
2. Jafar SH, Hemachandran K, ElChaarani H, Moturi S, Gupta N, editors. *Artificial intelligence for capital markets.* CRC Press; 2023.
3. Jafar SH, Akhtar S, Johl SK. AI in insurance. In: *Artificial intelligence for business.* Productivity Press; 2023. p. 164–73.
4. Ridzuan NN, Masri M, Anshari M, Fitriyani NL, Syafrudin M. AI in the financial sector: The line between innovation, regulation, and ethical responsibility. *Information.* 2024;15(8):432.
5. Hemachandran K, Rodriguez RV, Toshniwal R, Junaid M, Shaw L. Performance analysis of different classification algorithms for bank loan sectors. In: *Intelligent sustainable systems: Proceedings of ICISS 2021.* Springer Singapore; 2021. p. 191–202.
6. Javed AR, Ahmed W, Pandya S, Maddikunta PKR, Alazab M, Gadekallu TR. A survey of explainable artificial intelligence for smart cities. *Electronics.* 2023; 12(4):1020.
7. Malik MY, Jafar SH, Dixit A. Efficiency analysis and macroeconomic determinants of non-tax revenues: Evidence from special category states of India. *Indian Econ J.* 2025. https://doi.org/10.1177/00194662251330385
8. Johora FT, Hasan R, Farabi SF, Alam MZ, Sarkar MI, Al Mahmud MA. AI advances: Enhancing Banking security with fraud detection. In: *2024 First Int Conf on Technological Innovations and Advance Computing (TIACOMP).* IEEE; 2024. p. 289–94.
9. Omokhoa HE, Odionu CS, Azubuike C, Sule AK. AI-powered fintech innovations for credit scoring, debt recovery, and financial access in microfinance and SMEs. *Gulf J Adv Bus Res.* 2024;2(6):411–22.
10. Adamyk B, Benson V, Adamyk O, Liashenko O. Risk management in DeFi: Analyses of the innovative tools and platforms for tracking DeFi transactions. *J Risk Financ Manag.* 2025;18(1):38.

11. Booth J, Metz DW, Tarkhanyan DA, Cheruvu S. Machine learning security and trustworthiness. In: *Demystifying intelligent multimode security systems.* Apress; 2023. p. 137–222.
12. Cao L. AI in finance: Challenges, techniques, and opportunities. *ACM Comput Surv.* 2022;55(3):1–38.
13. Faheem MA. AI-driven risk-assessment models: Revolutionizing credit scoring and default prediction. *Iconic Res Eng J.* 2021;5(3):177–86.
14. Hemachandran K, Rodriguez RV, editors. *Artificial intelligence for business: An implementation guide containing practical and industry-specific case studies.* CRC Press; 2023.
15. Kavitha M, Hanumanthu KD, Sai ON, Chandrashekhar G, Sugandha S. The role of artificial intelligence in financial decision-making. *J Mark Soc Res.* 2025;2:189–98.
16. Hemachandran K, George PM, Rodriguez RV, Kulkarni RM, Roy S. Performance analysis of k-nearest-neighbour classification algorithms for bank loan sectors. In: *Smart intelligent computing and communication technology.* IOS Press; 2021. p. 9–13.
17. Kotovskaia A. Financial technology in global context: Risks and opportunities. In: *Finance, growth and democracy.* Springer; 2024. p. 247–62.
18. Salim M, Khan PA, Jalil NA, Johl SK, Jfar SH, Irfan F, Khan M. Fusion of blockchain and SDGs: A bibliometric analysis. *KnE Soc Sci.* 2023:633–54.
19. Jafar SH. Financial applications of Gaussian processes and Bayesian optimization. In: *Bayesian reasoning and Gaussian processes for machine learning applications.* Chapman & Hall/CRC; 2022. p. 111–22.
20. Khan R, Taqi M, Afzal A. Deepfakes in finance: Unravelling the threat landscape and detection challenges. In: *Navigating the world of deepfake technology.* IGI Global; 2024. p. 91–120.
21. Jafar SH, Dhandhukia V, Kumar GB. Application of artificial intelligence in banking: A review. In: *Machine learning for business analytics.* Productivity Press; 2022. p. 145–51.
22. Almada M. Human intervention in automated decision-making: Toward the construction of contestable systems. In: *Proc 17th Int Conf on AI and Law.* Association for Computing Machinery (ACM); 2019. p. 2–11.
23. Jafar SH, Kashid AU, Ghosh S, Srividhya S, Sharma D, Bodhankar A. An enhanced performance optimization of ATM networks for cross-border money transfers. In: *2024 15th Int Conf on Computing Communication and Networking Technologies (ICCCNT).* IEEE; 2024. p. 1–5.
24. Bernanke BS, Gertler M. Inside the black box: The credit channel of monetary policy transmission. *J Econ Perspect.* 1995;9(4):27–48.
25. Kandpal V, Ozili PK, Jeyanthi PM, Ranjan D, Chandra D. Regulation of the fintech industry. In: *Digital finance and metaverse in banking.* Emerald; 2025. p. 181–98.
26. Kaur G. Trust the machine and embrace artificial intelligence to combat money-laundering activities. In: *Computational intelligence for modern business systems.* Springer; 2023. p. 63–81.
27. Barrett C. Are the EU GDPR and the California CCPA becoming the de facto global standards for data privacy and protection? *Scitech Lawyer.* 2019;15(3):24–29.
28. Komandla V, Chilkuri B. AI and data analytics in personalizing fintech online account-opening processes. *Educ Res (IJMCER).* 2019;3(3):1–11.
29. Kong Y, Nie Y, Dong X, Mulvey JM, Poor HV, Wen Q, Zohren S. Large language models for financial and investment management: Applications and benchmarks. *J Portf Manag.* 2024;51(2):162–210.
30. Buocz T, Pfotenhauer S, Eisenberger I. Regulatory sandboxes in the AI Act: Reconciling innovation and safety? *Law Innov Technol.* 2023;15(2):357–89.

31. Kothandapani HP. Social implications of algorithmic decision-making in housing finance. *J Knowl Learn Sci Technol.* 2025;4(1):78–97.
32. Nawaah D, Asare PY, Quarshie MA. Climate finance and natural capital. In: *Climate neutrality through smart eco-innovation and environmental sustainability.* Springer; 2025. p. 317–32.
33. Mishra AK, Tyagi AK, RichaPatra SR. Introduction to ML and AI in banking and finance. In: *Applications of blockchain technology and artificial intelligence.* Springer; 2024. p. 239–90.
34. Truby J, Brown R, Dahdal A. Banking on AI: Mandating a proactive approach to AI regulation. *Law Financ Mark Rev.* 2020;14(2):110–20.
35. Chawla N, Kumar B. Ecommerce and consumer protection in India. *J Bus Ethics.* 2022;180(2):581–604.
36. Quarshie MA, Akhtar S, Nawaah D. Barriers to breakthroughs: The crucial role of support services in advancing accounting practices, financial literacy, and performance in disability-led SMEs. *Qual Quant.* 2025;59(Suppl 2), 955–77.
37. Quarshie MA, Djimatey R, Akhtar S, Nawaah D. Maximizing financial efficiency through technological synergy: Unleashing ICT for enhanced cash management in SMEs. *J Int Counc Small Bus.* 2025:1–31.
38. Raza A. The application of artificial intelligence in credit-risk evaluation. *Cent Manag Sci Res.* 2025;3(2):240–51.
39. Torrie V, Payette D. AI governance frameworks for the banking sector. In: *Artificial intelligence in finance.* Edward Elgar Publishing; 2023. p. 114–41.
40. Rolando B, Mulyono H. Managing risks in fintech: AI-based risk management. *Econ Bus J (ECBIS).* 2024;2(3):249–68.
41. Shafik W. Security, privacy, and trust in fintech. In: *FinTech and financial inclusion.* Routledge; 2025. p. 216–33.
42. D'Silva D, Filková Z, Packer F, Tiwari S. The design of digital financial infrastructure: Lessons from India. *BIS Papers.* 2019;(106):1–39.

# 3 Exploring Explainable AI (XAI)

## *Implications for Transparency in Financial Decision-Making*

*Hemachandran K*

## 3.1 INTRODUCTION

Artificial intelligence (AI) in finance is a disruptive technology that has global institutions rethink about decision-making and processes [1]. In the last decades of years, AI has advanced from an add-on tool to one of the cornerstones of financial services, automating complex tasks such as credit risk evaluation, fraud identification, algorithmic trading, and investment portfolio management [2]. AI has not only changed the landscape of the public and private sector financial systems but also force institutions to move beyond early intuition and decision-making based on human actors to data driven, algorithm driven financial system. The underlying rationale is that financial models are increasingly using AI models as a supplement to human decision-making in high stakes environments with higher transparency and speed as compared to human performance. Without a doubt, one of the most revolutionary aspects of AI is its ability to assimilate, process, and analyse vast amounts of structured and unstructured financial data [3, 4]. Financial data today arrive at such high speed and in large volumes that traditional data analysis techniques, pegged to human scaling factors, no longer scale. In contrast, AI models employ machine learning and deep learning algorithms to spot trends, relationships, and outliers that may go unnoticed by human analysts [5]. All of this provides a significant computational advantage to financial institutions resulting in improved financial decision-making in terms of accuracy, consistency, and efficiency. Automated credit scoring systems are being used by banks and lending institutions to determine a potential borrower's creditworthiness, which includes the analysis of historical credit data, social media activity, transaction histories, and alternative data sources [6]. In the same manner, AI-based algorithmic systems can execute a trade in milliseconds, placing tens of thousands of trades in a single day as well as adapt to market changes in real-time and find the near-optimal investment strategy based on sophisticated predictive models [7–9]. AI-enabled innovations have therefore resulted in considerable


DOI: 10.1201/9781003611646-3

benefits across the financial sector, such as increased operational efficiency, cost reduction, and risk reduction.

However, great opportunity comes with great challenges and ethical concerns in finance regarding the widespread adoption of AI despite the prospect of more efficiency and accuracy. AI also exposes us to massive risks of lack of transparency, accountability, and equity. An emerging literature has highlighted the opaque nature of many AI models wherein the decision-making process is a black-box even to the developers and operators of these systems [10]. The problem is that these black-box systems are based on complex neural networks and high-dimensional computations that provide little insight into how the actual decision was made for a particular case. The absence of interpretability poses a vital obstacle to regulatory oversight, auditing, and validation. In sectors like finance, where decisions have direct consequences as they impact consumers credit availability, investment stability and, in general, financial inclusion, shall be seen as socially and ethically undesirable when there is opacity in the decision-making mechanism. The dangers of unexplainable AI models are no abstract concept; they are already real-world problems as we see with improper financial applications. A notable instance was that of a major Australian financial institution whose AI-based loan approval system approved loans for middle-high income earners, while rejecting significantly more applicants from lower income brackets [2]. The system did not explain well at all why patterns of rejections took place, and this brought their users to the public eye, eventually resulting in some backlash, legal proceedings against the university, and severe reputational hit on the institution. This case highlights the risks of entrenching historical biases in AI systems, and the potential ethical and legal consequences of inadequate transparency and accountability. Similarly, a 2023 study by Reserve Bank of India (RBI) highlighted that the AI-based fraud observance system flagged a transaction as suspicious if a consumer deposited a lot of money into his bank account without any history of a big deposit, leading to the suspension of real consumers' accounts and monetary loss [11]. These examples underscore the extent to which training data, model specification, and operational flaws can convert AI models into problem magnets that consumer distrust and regulatory penalties will erode. The paradigm of Explainable Artificial Intelligence (XAI) has been designed to mitigate these challenges in the context of responsible AI in financial services. The main aim of XAI is to generate the predictions which are not only correct but also give some explanation of the prediction which are human-interpretable. XAI seeks to unlock the "black box" of AI models by explaining the reasons behind decisions made by AI which will allow financial professionals, regulators, and impacted stakeholders to understand why AI makes the decisions it does. Such interpretability becomes especially important for financial decision-making, where non-negotiable transparency and accountability are essential because of the potential outcomes for consumers and markets as a whole. XAI has the potential to bridge the gap between the advantages of AI and good practices from ethical and responsible AI. XAI also leads decisions made more visible, which in turn fosters increased confidence in the financial sector between institutions and their clients, helps mitigate the risk of potential regulatory non-compliance, and helps reduce discrimination and bias. In addition, XAI allows financial practitioners to properly audit the AI systems, to find (and fix) the source of error, and to iterate on the model effectiveness over time. As regulations evolve, XAI is being seen as a key component in ensuring that automated systems will conform with new legal and ethical requirement, such as privacy, fairness, and non-discrimination principles [12]. It should be noted that the introduction of XAI does not mean a compromise between accuracy and interpretability. However, recent advancements in the field have demonstrated high predictive performance of AI models along with a decent level of explainability sufficient to fulfil regulatory and ethical requirements [13]. They include model distillation, feature attribution methods, and fundamentally interpretable models, each of which provides some compromise between level of complexity and transparency that is interesting. Hence, broadly, AI has transformed decision-making in finance, providing invaluable assistance in making them quicker, more precise, and responsive to market shifts, but has also created significant problems around transparency, equity, bias, and accountability.

## 3.2 THEORETICAL FRAMEWORK

### 3.2.1 The Foundations of Explainable AI (XAI)

XAI in financial systems is an emerging issue of scholarly concern due to implications for performance, accountability, and trust. To enhance the interpretability of AI Model, a number of methodological approaches have been defined each of which represents a particular manner of bringing clarity to complex algorithms [14, 15]. Among these methods, Shapley Additive Explanations (SHAP) has gained immense popularity due to its provision of relevance scores for separate input features, thus illustrating the relative importance of each variable in a comprehensive way and its wise application in mission-critical financial use cases. Local Interpretable Model-Agnostic Explanations (LIME) also have the same end goal and try to imitate the behaviour of otherwise black-box models, generating locally accurate and human interpretable approximations of decision boundaries [16]. However, counterfactual explanations take this a step further by showing scenarios in which decisions can lead to different outcomes, so not only do they help end users to understand how a prediction is made but also why certain predictions occur. Regulatory and ethical requirements have also significantly driven the increasing adoption of XAI methods among financial systems [17]. Across jurisdictions, regulators have explicitly required AI-based financial systems to be interpretable to ensure that such systems do not unfairly discriminate [18]. Such increasing focus on openness is now central to regulatory expectation and is impacting how financial institutions are seeking to operationalise the technology into their businesses. For instance, non-transparent decision-making procedures can undermine consumer confidence, exacerbate our already existing bias, and hold together the structural inequalities, resulting in ethical issues that have been mentioned about XAI [19]. In support of the emerging common ground regarding the importance of explainability there is also empirical evidence. Banking institutions employing XAI models are in a better position to augment stakeholder and customer confidence and mitigate legal risk. Companies which have adopted XAI system have shown gain in client retention and consumer confidence. A fair and transparent AI-driven financial product could lead to a 20% increase in customer loyalty [20]. The results exemplify the potential of explainability to drive a new competitive advantage in an increasingly data-centric financial market while reinforcing preliminary commercial justification for XAI adoption. Despite these promising developments, the integration of explainability into AI-based financial decision-making is by no means a straightforward process. The goals of interpretability and forecast accuracy remain mutually exclusive at a broad level. The outputs of a model are rendered in a way that is more digestible using XAI methods. However, critics argue that prioritising interpretability features often results in a loss in predictive power which is especially important in risk assessment, fraud detection, and credit scoring [21]. Simplified models can miss the entirety of complexity of financial data, resulting in suboptimal forecasts that could put institutional objectives and consumer welfare at risk [3]. On the other hand, advocates of XAI deny that the trade-off is either inevitable or universal, pointing to new methodological advances in post-hoc interpretability methods and hybrid models seeking equilibrium between accuracy and interpretability [22, 23]. Consequently, the XAI debate in financial circumstances is an ongoing and mirrors bigger unaddressed questions about the appropriate balance between technological expertise, ethical responsibility, and legal compliance.

## 3.3 APPLICATIONS OF XAI IN FINANCIAL DECISION-MAKING

### 3.3.1 Credit Scoring and Loan Approvals

Modern lending processes have been considerably transformed with AI-driven credit score and loan approval systems by analysing large and diverse datasets to dynamically assess borrowers' creditworthiness [24, 25]. Traditional ways of measuring credit rely on a limited set of unchangeable factors such as debt-to-income ratios, income levels, and effective credit history. In contrast, AI models leverage unobserved behavioural markers, transaction patterns, and additional data sources to provide more granular predictions of default risk [26, 27]. While these enhancements have undoubtedly boosted predictive power and operational efficiency, the opacity of these systems has created significant accountability and fairness concerns among regulators, consumers, and financial institutions alike. One of the key arguments to incorporate XAI into credit assessment relates to its capability to identify and mitigate algorithmic bias. If AI models are trained on historical data that reproduce existing institutional or social biases, they risk perpetuating biased lending outcomes [6]. XAI's ability to assess how a small number of input variables may have affected the overall credit decisions for individuals means that financial organisations can investigate whether certain protected features (such as gender, race, or location) have a disproportionate impact on model outcomes. To pinpoint such biases and then counteract them is of utmost importance, as discrimination in lending not only diminishes customer trust but also exposes the lenders to legal and reputational risks.

Moreover, the importance of XAI in credit scoring systems is being increased with changes in regulatory environments [28]. Regulatory authorities in various countries, including the European Union, RBI, and Central Bank of Kenya (CBK), among others have also formalised demands for greater transparency and explainability in AI-powered financial decision-making. Some existing laws, such as the European AI Act (2023) and India's Fair Lending Guidelines (2023) directly demand financial companies to provide straightforward explanations for automated loan decisions [29, 30]. As a result, a push for explainability is more of a regulatory requirement than a technical one. In India, an XAI-based credit risk assessment methodology was deployed by HDFC Bank, providing applicants with transparent explanations for loan approvals and denials. By allowing customers to understand what the key factors are affecting credit decisions, the bank experienced higher customer satisfaction and fewer complaints with loan results. Likewise, to enhance the transparency of its consumer credit score and large-scale loan approval processes, Kenya's Safaricom integrated XAI methodologies into its M-Pesa platform, which provides a mobile-based micro-loan [31]. By utilising machine learning to elucidate microloan decisions according to consumers spending patterns and transaction histories, Safaricom successfully mitigate customer complaints and enhance borrower confidence. These examples highlight the role of XAI in credit scoring to improve institutional credibility, enhance consumer trust in AI-powered financial services, and simplify regulatory compliance. To ensure that AI-based financial decisions align with institutional objectives and societal expectations, XAI becomes an essential enabler for the responsible use of AI-based approaches in credit scoring and lending by providing transparency and interpretability, thereby helping to mitigate fairness, regulatory, and consumer understanding-related issues.

### 3.3.2 2 Fraud Detection and Risk Management

AI-powered fraud detection system can analyse financial records at large scale to detect anomalies, identify potentially suspicious transactions, and spot signs of a fraud [17]. Traditional fraud detection techniques, on the other hand, usually depend on rule-based algorithms, which commonly generate high false positive rates, misclassifying valid transactions as fraudulent and so resulting in unhappy customers [1, 32]. Although AI models improve fraud detection accuracy, they are frequently uninterpretable, making it difficult to comprehend or justify a transaction that has been reported. Today, AI-based fraud-detecting systems play a crucial role in modern financial security, allowing financial records on a large scale to analyse irregularities from genuine to fraudulent activity [7, 33]. Soon to provide you with an upper hand in the way they provide prediction of financial fraud or money laundering by detecting the underlying patterns and some of the subtle anomalies, through large datasets that such systems can detect. AI-driven approaches differ from traditional approaches, which typically use rule-based techniques, in that they create adaptive methods for detecting fraud by learning from past data and adapting with performance, allowing the methods to evolve with fraudulent behaviour. Limitations of traditional fraud detection techniques. Traditional fraud detection techniques are still widely used but have several limitations. This results in a high number of false positives because the rule-based algorithm is wrong most of the time in classifying a real transaction as an illegitimate one. As a result, operational inefficiencies arise, and customer trust and satisfaction are also undermined as legitimate transactional communication is frequently stopped in its tracks or delayed without adequately documented reasons. Examples of the immutability of these legacy systems have also proven their susceptibility to changing fraud typologies, necessitating adaptive solutions. Although AI models offer higher accuracy: Minimising false positives and detecting novel fraud trends, they come with their own issues. Top concerns include the explainability (or lack thereof). Many AI systems operate in a "black box" way, making it impossible to explain what caused a financial institution to flag a given transaction. The absence of transparency makes it difficult for affected customers and regulators who demand simple, understandable explanations and justifications for why fraud decisions have been made, and it jeopardises the compliance of organisations [34]. Striking a fair trade-off between the accuracy of detection and the interpretability of the AI, is the evergreen challenge for deploying AI solutions for fraud detection.

### 3.3.3 3 Algorithmic Trading and Investment Strategies

High-frequency trading (HFT), also referred to as algorithmic trading, this type of trading utilises AI-driven systems that deploy trades in the market in microseconds based on complex financial algorithm models. They are created to maximise profits and limit risks by analysing the market data and discovering trading opportunities very quickly [35]. But, although the model used would allow for quick calculations, the black-box nature of this type of AI raises serious issues. This opacity has the potential of creating tenuous market disruptions, flash crashes to be preventable and the development of unbalance market of advantage that can devalue the market conditions [36, 37]. The importance of XAI in algorithmic trading is on the rise owing to escalating regulatory, operational, and market pressures [10]. As a result, it has become imperative for regulatory authorities around the world to focus on the explainability of AI-powered trading systems to mitigate market manipulation and ensure fairness in the marketplace. To meet these expectations, a few financial institutions implemented and executed models that not only perform trades better but also explain which trading decision was taken and why [38, 39], achieving higher compliance scores for the financial regulations. XAI is essential for risk management, in addition to other regulatory considerations. To manage and control financial risks associated with investments, traders and fund managers need transparency on the rationale for AI-induced trades. Knowing the logic behind individual trading decisions can allow authorities to recognise systemic weaknesses, and to modify strategies in advance to avoid financial crises. Finally, institutional investors are more and more moving to use trading models that provide transparent and interpretable investment signals. This contributes to less speculation and more confidence among market players. Early realisation of XAI can be observed in algorithmic trading implementations of XAI [17, 40]. Bank A use concrete examples where it had introduced explainable trading models with improvements to its investment decision-making and algorithmic errors [27]. Others have already started to allow institutional investors to audit their AI-generated investment strategies, gaining investor confidence with more regulatory adherence to financial markets [24, 31, 41]. Such developments reflect the role of XAI in algorithmic trading in promoting stability, transparency, and accountability in the financial markets, thus mitigating the risks of the black box nature of AI systems.

## 3.4 FUTURE TRENDS AND POLICY IMPLICATIONS

### 3.4.1 Emerging Trends in XAI for Financial Decision-Making

Several trends are shaping the future of XAI adoption in financial decision-making:

a. *Hybrid AI Models*: To enhance AI-driven financial forecasting, financial institutions are implementing hybrid AI models that strike a compromise between predictability and transparency [8, 42].
b. *Blockchain-based Transparency*: By generating tamperproof AI decision records, blockchain, and XAI are being combined to improve financial auditability.
c. *Regulatory Expansion*: Around the world, governments are announcing stricter rules for AI transparency of what is included in the system that needs to be explained and justifiable [43].

### 3.4.2 Policy Recommendations

The following guidelines should be implemented by financial regulators and organisations to guarantee the efficient and responsible use of XAI:

a. *XAI Guidelines*: To guarantee uniformity in AI-powered financial decision-making, regulatory agencies should set up international explainability requirements.
b. *Mandatory AI Audits*: To find any biases and hazards, financial services organisations that use AI should audit their algorithms every year.
c. *Consumer Education Initiatives*: Financial institutions need to educate their customers on how AI-based decisions work.

These regulations may assist financial institutions to enhance ethical AI stewardship in financial markets, reduce financial risk, and enhance accountability [24, 35].

## 3.5 CONCLUSION

XAI is revolutionising decision-making in finance by enhancing transparency, reducing algorithmic bias, and meeting regulatory compliance. The practical applications of XAI such as algorithmic trading, fraud detection, and credit scoring are assisting financial institutions in enhancing risk management, gaining customer confidence, and adhering to global AI regulations. XAI adoption is encumbered with several challenges such as controlling the cost of AI transparency, compliance irregularities, and balancing interpretability with predictive power. The efficient use of XAI in the realm of the financial system requires consolidation of effort from financial institutions, legislatures, and AI developers to build standardised frameworks, enact regulations that ensure AI accountability and create initiatives for AI literacy. More importantly, this is how the financial sector can leverage the power of AI, whilst still maintaining its fair and responsible decision-making.

## REFERENCES


1. Rahman MM, Terano HJ, Rahman MN, Salamzadeh A, Rahaman MS. ChatGPT and academic research: A review and recommendations based on practical examples. *J Educ Manag Dev Stud.* 2023;3(1):1–12.
2. El Abiad Z, Abraham R, El-Chaarani H, Skaf Y, Binsaddig RO, Jafar SH. The impact of CEO characteristics on the financial performance of family businesses listed in the Euronext Exchange. *J Risk Financ Manag.* 2024;17(3):129.
3. Jafar SH, Dhandhukia V, Kumar GB. Application of artificial intelligence in banking: A review. In: *Machine learning for business analytics.* Productivity Press; 2022. p. 145–51.
4. Ridzuan NN, Masri M, Anshari M, Fitriyani NL, Syafrudin M. AI in the financial sector: The line between innovation, regulation, and ethical responsibility. *Information.* 2024;15(8):432.
5. Ali SM. Containment, primacy, flux: Systemic transitional fluidity. In: *Asia-Pacific security dynamics.* Springer; 2025. p. 235–321.
6. Andrae S. Fairness and bias in machine learning models for credit decisions. In: *Machine learning and modeling techniques in financial data science.* IGI Global; 2025. p. 1–24.
7. Aziz LAR, Andriansyah Y. The role of artificial intelligence in modern banking. *Rev Contemp Bus Anal.* 2023;6(1):110–32.
8. Budacu D. The impact of artificial intelligence on hybrid conflicts in the 21st century. *Studia Securitatis.* 2024;18(2):87–108.
9. Collins J, Ketter W, Sadeh N. Pushing the limits of rational agents: The trading agent competition for supply chain management. *AI Mag.* 2010;31(2):63.
10. Ekundayo F. Economic implications of AI-driven financial markets: Challenges and opportunities in big data integration. *Int J Sci Res Arch.* 2024;13:1500–15.
11. Faheem MA. AI-driven risk assessment models. *Iconic Res Eng J.* 2021;5(3):177–86.
12. Felzmann H, Fosch-Villaronga E, Lutz C, Tamò-Larrieux A. Towards transparency by design for artificial intelligence. *Sci Eng Ethics.* 2020;26(6):3333–61.
13. Gerlein EA, McGinnity M, Belatreche A, Coleman S. Evaluating machine learning classification for financial trading. *Expert Syst Appl.* 2016;54:193–207.
14. Hassija V, Chamola V, Mahapatra A, et al. Interpreting black-box models: A review. *Cogn Comput.* 2024;16(1):45–74.
15. Hemachandran K, Rodriguez RV, editors. *Artificial intelligence for business.* CRC Press; 2023.
16. Hemachandran K, Rodriguez RV, editors. *The business of the metaverse.* CRC Press; 2023.
17. Hemachandran K, George PM, Rodriguez RV, et al. Performance analysis of k-nearest neighbour classification algorithms. In: *Smart intelligent computing and communication technology.* IOS Press; 2021. p. 9–13.
18. Hemachandran K, Rodriguez RV, Toshniwal R, et al. Performance analysis of different classification algorithms. In: *Intelligent sustainable systems: ICISS 2021.* Springer; 2021. p. 191–202.
19. Hohnen P, Ulfstjerne MA, Krabbe M. Assessing creditworthiness in the age of big data. *J Extreme Anthropol.* 2021;5(1):29–55.
20. Jafar SH. Financial applications of Gaussian processes and Bayesian optimization. In: *Bayesian reasoning and Gaussian processes.* CRC Press; 2022. p. 111–22.
21. Jafar SH, Akhtar S, Johl SK. AI in insurance. In: *Artificial intelligence for business.* Productivity Press; 2023. p. 164–73.
22. Jafar SH, Hemachandran K, El-Chaarani H, et al., editors. *Artificial intelligence for capital markets.* CRC Press; 2023.

23. Jafar SH, Kashid AU, Ghosh S, et al. ATM optimization for cross-border money transfers. In: *2024 15th Int Conf on Computing Communication and Networking Technologies (ICCCNT)*. IEEE; 2024. p. 1–5.
24. Kavitha M, Hanumanthu KD, Sai ON, et al. The role of artificial intelligence in financial decision-making. *J Mark Soc Res*. 2025;2:189–98.
25. Kumar N, Agarwal P, Gupta G, et al. AI-driven financial forecasting. In: *Intelligent optimization techniques for business analytics*. IGI Global; 2024. p. 146–70.
26. Malik MY, Jafar SH, Dixit A. Efficiency analysis and macroeconomic determinants of non-tax revenues. *Indian Econ J*. 2025. https://doi.org/10.1177/00194662251330385
27. Mer A, Singhal K, Virdi AS. The role of artificial intelligence in banking and stock market trading. In: *Finance analytics in business*. Emerald Publishing Limited; 2024. p. 175–98.
28. Nawaah D, Asare PY, Quarshie MA. Climate finance and natural capital. In: *Climate neutrality through smart eco-innovation and environmental sustainability*. Springer; 2025. p. 317–32.
29. Nguyen DK, Sermpinis G, Stasinakis C. Big data, AI, and ML in fintech. *Eur Financ Manag*. 2023;29(2):517–48.
30. Ohana JJ, Ohana S, Benhamou E, et al. Explainable AI (XAI) models for financial markets. In: *Explainable and transparent AI and multi-agent systems*. Springer; 2021. p. 189–207.
31. Porwal PD. Ethics and laws in financial AI. In: *Generative artificial intelligence in finance*. John Wiley & Sons, Inc.; 2025. p. 283–98.
32. Quarshie MA, Akhtar S, Nawaah D. Barriers to breakthroughs. *Qual Quant*. 2025;59:1–23.
33. Quarshie MA, Djimatey R, Akhtar S, Nawaah D. Maximizing financial efficiency. *J Int Counc Small Bus*. 2025:1–31.
34. Rahman MM, Terano HJ, Rahman MN, et al. ChatGPT and academic research. *J Educ Manag Dev Stud*. 2023;3(1):1–12.
35. Rahmani FM, Zohuri B. The impact of AI on financial institutions. *J Eng Appl Sci Technol*. 2023;5(6):2–6.
36. Rawal A, McCoy J, Rawat DB, et al. Trustworthy XAI: Status, challenges, and perspectives. *IEEE Trans Artif Intell*. 2021;3(6):852–66.
37. Raza A. AI in credit risk evaluation. *Cent Manag Sci Res*. 2025;3(2):240–51.
38. Ridzuan NN, Masri M, Anshari M, et al. AI in the financial sector. *Information*. 2024;15(8):432.
39. Santoso A, Surya Y. Edge-based AI systems. *Q J Emerg Technol Innov*. 2024; 9(2):104–32.
40. Schwarcz D. Transparency opaque: Understanding insurance consumer protection. *UCLA Law Rev*. 2013;61:394.
41. Wischmeyer T. Artificial intelligence and transparency. In: *Regulating artificial intelligence*. Springer; 2019. p. 75–101.
42. Yamaguti Mondego D. The use of AI in Australian cloud-based payments. [Doctoral dissertation]. CQUniversity; 2024.
43. Jafar SH, Oyedele OM, Nawaah D, Bolanle AS. Exploring leadership challenges for adoption of digital innovation and sustainability. In: *Innovation ecosystems and sustainable technologies*. Emerald Publishing Limited; 2025. p. 253–69.

# 4 Implementing Robotic Process Automation (RPA) for Financial Operations

*Solomon Jeresa*

## 4.1 INTRODUCTION

### 4.1.1 The Need for Automation in Financial Operations

Financial institutions process millions of transactions on a daily basis ranging from everyday banking services, investments, risk, and regulatory reporting [1]. These activities need a high level of accuracy, efficiency, and a high adherence to stringent financial audits. However, traditional manual processes become resource-intensive, inefficient, and error-prone. Research [2, 3] has shown that, operational activities are occupying 80% of the time of financial institutions, limiting their time for strategic decision-making, customer engagement, and innovation. The complexity of financial regulations only adds to the confusion. Thousands of global financial institutions are being challenged with fiercer compliance regimes by enforcement bodies such as the European Central Bank (ECB), the US Securities and Exchange Commission (SEC), the UK's Financial Conduct Authority (FCA), and others. Non-compliance with laws like General Data Protection Regulation (GDPR), Basel III, and Anti-Money Laundering (AML) regulations can lead to high monetary fines, damaged company reputation, and loss of investor confidence [4]. Robotic process automation (RPA) allows financial institutions to automate high-volume, rules-based jobs in a scalable, cost-effective manner. RPA enables organizations to improve operational efficiency, compliance, and accuracy in finance. Automation in transaction verification, fraud detection, client onboarding, and compliance reporting has helped the FinTech firms to not only drive efficiency and cost benefits but also liberate the bandwidth on other value driven strategic activities [5–7].

### 4.1.2 Key Drivers of Robotic Process Automation Adoption in Finance

There are numerous associated factors like enhanced cost savings, efficient compliance with regulations, higher accuracy levels, along with a scalability cycle that are encouraging the adoption of RPA to be adopted in the financial functions.

#### 4.1.2.1 Cost Reduction and Operational Efficiency

The main reason financial institutions have been embracing RPA is the promise of substantial savings. In a study commissioned by PricewaterhouseCoopers (PwC) in 2003, it was reported that financial organizations that have adopted RPA have cut

DOI: 10.1201/9781003611646-4 

down 25% to 50% of their operating expenses [8, 9]. Most of this drop can be attributed to the automation of processes that used to require a lot of human engagement. For example, customer onboarding, transaction validation, and compliance checks, all financial-related processes, can be fully automated, minimizing rampant human work and associated costs due to errors, reworks, and delays. Moreover, robots performing RPA are 24/7 active with no fatigue, assuring transaction processing, and better customer service. This capability would especially be useful for global financial firms that conduct transactions across time zones and require real-time financial processing.

#### 4.1.2.2 Compliance with Regulatory Requirements

Due to increased global regulatory attention, financial institutions are becoming increasingly concerned about regulatory compliance [10–12]. Compliance procedures generally involve dealing with the massive amounts of data, conducting audits, generating reports, and undertaking risk assessments. Regulatory compliance depends on RPA, which automates fraud detection, trail management, and Data reconciliation. By automating some processes, financial organizations can lower the risk of falling out of compliance and ensure large-scale uniformity with financial standards. For example, the Central Bank of Kenya (CBK) lowered 20% of compliance costs and improved the detection of rules by deploying an AML system powered by RPA. Moreover, automation allows financial organizations to adhere to evolving regulations promptly as well. RPA solutions quickly adapt to evolving financial regulations and compliance standards ensuring organizations remain compliant with little to no manual intervention.

#### 4.1.2.3 Improved Accuracy and Reduction in Human Errors

Accuracy is crucial as even a small error in data entry, calculations, or reconciliations can lead to significant financial losses and tarnish reputation [13, 14]. Manual processes are highly susceptible to human error, especially when large volumes of financial data are involved [15]. RPA automates processes that involve a lot of data which lowers human error and thus guarantees consistency, accuracy, and reliability. In the case of ICICI Bank of India, for example, after establishing transactional reconciliation through RPA, the financial aberrations were reduced by 95% resulting in enhanced operational reliability of the organization [16]. Automation further enhances your fraud detection proficiency by recognizing suspicious transactions and monitoring financial operations in real-time. Unlike traditional fraud detection methods which are rigid and rule-based, RPA can adapt to new fraud patterns, expanding the financial security and protecting organizations from financial crimes.

#### 4.1.2.4 Scalability and Business Growth

As financial institutions expand service offerings and global presence, they require scalable systems that can absorb increasing volumes of transactions without a commensurable increase in operating expenses [17, 18]. RPA makes this scalability feasible as financial institutions can quickly scale activity without corresponding increases in headcount for processing high transaction volumes. As an example, Banco do Brasil S.A. integrated the RPA into its investment processing processes allowing to step up operations by 35% with no labour growth [1, 19, 20]. As repetitive financial processes get automated, institutions can then allocate human resources to more strategic activities such as risk management, investment planning, and client advisory.

### 4.1.3 The Role of Artificial Intelligence and Machine Learning in Enhancing Robotic Process Automation

Traditional RPA systems are based on predefined rule-based automation and hence, are limited in how they can manage complex decision-making processes and unstructured data. The integration of artificial intelligence (AI) and machine learning (ML) has advanced RPA from a simple rule-based execution to intelligent automation. Using RPA with AI and ML, financial organizations can do the following:

a. *Assimilate Data from Non-Structured Sources*: Organizations have a plethora of non-structured sources like financial records, consumer and regulatory reports, from which RPA bots with AI capabilities can assimilate value. Customer service automation with Natural Language Processing (NLP) enables bots to interpret the raw text data entered by the customer and reply accordingly.
b. *Time History Analysis*: ML algorithms can detect fraudulent patterns and forecast fraudulent transactions and potential business risks based on historical transaction data. The AI-driven RPA gets better results as the time passes through learning from the new data which is assigned to it.
c. *Automated Processes*: AI-enabled RPA systems automatically adjust the compliance process as per the changing financial regulations; ultimately reducing risks of being non-compliance. The results of a study commissioned by Deloitte [21, 22] report that financial institutions that had implemented RPA and AI amalgamated led to the reduction of processing times by another 40% than institutions that had only used automation technology by itself. With the perfect blend of RPA, AI, and ML, hyperautomation is emerging as the big-picture strategy that brings together different automation technologies to automate entire financial operations from end to end. RPA in financial services has, in fact, established a shift in paradigm for how financial institutions transact, comply, and operate. Automating repetitive rule-driven processes allows financial institutions to cut costs, increase accuracy, and boost regulatory compliance.

While RPA is a driving force in the finance function, the combination of RPA with AI and ML facilitates autonomous and intelligent decision-making, predictive and prescriptive analytics, and real-time financial automation. With the continued digitization of financial institutions, RPA will be an essential technology to maintain innovation, enhance the integrated risk control framework and ultimately achieve sustainable business expediency. Nonetheless, commitment from financial institutions to resolve the staffing redundancy, cybersecurity threats and ethical AI governance is critical in order for the technology to reach its potential. However, if carried out prudently and strategically enough, RPA can represent a net benefit to financial institutions. Thus, a robust, transparent, and equitable financial system.

## 4.2 EVOLUTION OF ROBOTIC PROCESS AUTOMATION IN FINANCIAL OPERATIONS

RPA is a software technology that strengthens humans as they perform digital work [23]. Although finance has been experimenting with automation for decades, many of the early automation tools relied heavily on scripts and often complemented traditional backend adjustments [24–26]. Such approaches, while capable of automating certain processes, were inflexible, expensive, and offered limited capacity to dynamically manage unstructured financial data. In the 2010s, RPA came along and changed the nature of financial automation, enabling a much more flexible, less technical approach. RPA is different from traditional systems because it simply works at a user interface level which means it can work with existing applications in the same way a human worker does without needing to make any major changes to the whole system. The non-invasiveness of RPA is a huge linear feature, helping financial institutions implement RPA on different systems to automate intelligent workflows without affecting core banking or financial systems [27]. In the pursuit of better efficiency, financial institutions are shifting towards AI-driven RPA and complementing it with ML, NLP, and predictive analytics to offer a higher degree of automation. Today, this evolution has led to the emergence of hyper-automation concepts, in which financial organizations converge end-to-end automation approaches to lower the human participation in decision-making or eliminate it. Hyper-automation adopts new tools and allows institutions to capitalize on the real-time improvement of fraud detection, risk assessment, and regulatory compliance [28].

### 4.2.1 Theoretical Models Underpinning Robotic Process Automation Adoption in Financial Institutions

The acceptance, use, and strategic importance of RPA in financial operations are explained by a number of theoretical models. These models shed light on the reasons behind automation in financial institutions as well as its difficulties and long-term effects.

#### 4.2.1.1 Technology Acceptance Model (TAM)

Davis [15] developed the Technology Acceptance Model (TAM), which is a popular framework for describing how businesses embrace new technology. Technology adoption is influenced by two main variables, according to TAM:

a. *Perceived Usefulness*: How much technology enhances productivity, efficiency, and company results.

b. *Perceived Ease of Use*: The degree to which a technology is easy to use and fits in with current processes.

RPA is becoming more and more popular in financial organizations due to its ability to drastically cut processing times (by as much as 60%), eliminate human error, and improve adherence to financial laws [14, 29]. However, to overcome opposition to automation and fully reap its benefits, successful deployment necessitates investment in organizational alignment, staff training, and change management methods.

#### 4.2.1.2 Resource-Based View (RBV)

An organization's competitive advantage, according to Barney's [13, 30] Resource-Based View (RBV) thesis, is derived from its capacity to obtain and employ distinctive technology resources. RPA is a strategic tool used by financial organizations to boost competitiveness through the following:

a. By automating risk assessments, client onboarding, and transaction processing, operating expenses can be decreased.
b. Enabling fraud detection, automated loan approvals, and real-time transaction verification would speed up service delivery.
c. Enhancing compliance and fraud detection using AI-powered bots that examine vast amounts of financial data and more accurately identify irregularities.

By reducing the need for manual labour, improving process accuracy in high-risk financial activities, and simplifying operational procedures, banks and investment businesses who embrace RPA early on have a technical advantage over rivals.

#### 4.2.1.3 Institutional Theory

According to DiMaggio and Powell [24], organizations do not use new technologies only to gain a competitive advantage, but also to comply with coercive, mimetic, and normative pressures stemming from regulatory authorities, professional bodies, and customers (i.e., institutions), to which they are continuously exposed. There are three main institutional reasons for the widespread adoption of RPA among financial institutions:

a. *Regulatory Compliance Requirements*: Financial institutions are required to comply with strict regulatory frameworks, including the Foreign Account Tax Compliance Act (FATCA), Basel III, the GDPR, and AML regulations. By guaranteeing accurate and timely reporting and lowering compliance risks, RPA helps financial organizations to satisfy these regulatory obligations [31, 32].
b. *Industry Best Practices*: Prominent international financial organizations have established standards for automation, encouraging others to use RPA in order to stay competitive. To improve operational efficiency and stay

relevant in the business, rivals must adopt cutting-edge automation technologies as market leaders do.

c. *Customer Expectations*: With the rise in usage of digital banking, users are now expecting seamless financial services; auto fraud detection, instant loan approvals, and 24/7 customer support. With these ever-increasing expectations, RPA is a critical capability to help financial services deliver customer-centricity speed, accuracy, and efficiency.
d. In all, these theory-based models show that adoption motivations for RPA within financial institutions are both technology feasibility and strategic advantage-related. These frameworks offer a detailed insight into how and why organizations are automating to achieve the most amount of efficiency, compliance, and competitiveness from their automation.

## 4.3 ROLE OF RPA IN FINANCIAL OPERATIONS

RPA ensures organizational efficiency by eliminating redundant tasks and reducing human and compliance errors and improving compliance with regulatory requirements in financial institutions. The financial functions have RPA implemented in almost all its functions starting from banking services, compliance reporting, risk assessment, etc.

### 4.3.1 Banking Automation

Financial institutions process millions of transactions daily which require a low process time and simultaneously, the organization must also comply with all the regulations [33–36]. RPA will contribute towards banking operations in key areas of:

a. *Customer Onboarding*: Robots automate identity and document verification to not only ensure compliance with KYC regulations but also dramatically reduce KYC onboarding time.
b. *Loan Processing*: Automated workflows cut manual document verification to help with quick loan approvals and a better customer experience with quick decision-making.
c. *Security*: Automation through RPA powered by AI improves security by constantly monitoring transaction patterns, finding deviations from the norm, and reducing the potential of fraud.

### 4.3.2 Compliance and Regulatory Reporting

Financial Institutions are required to adhere to complex regulations [37–40] such as Basel III capital requirements, GDPR standards, among others. This calls for extensive data analysis followed by correct reporting on potential violations and constant monitoring to eradicate all possibilities of financial malpractice in compliance processes. In this regard, the role of RPA in Enhancing Regulatory Compliance includes:

a. *Automation of Risk Assessment*: Based on regulatory compliance, RPA bots scan through transactions as they happen in real-time and identify fraud.
b. *Efficiency in Regulatory Reporting*: Automated reporting systems facilitate financial disclosures, increased transparency, and the avoidance of manual errors.
c. *Better Audit and Internal Control*: RPA minimizes the regulatory penalty by ensuring accurate documentation and meeting the criteria for an Audit.

## 4.4 FUTURE TRENDS AND POLICY CONSIDERATIONS

### 4.4.1 Emerging Trends in RPA for Financial Services

Financial automation development is driven by technical developments that enhance the capabilities of RPA. Key trends that will shape the future of RPA include:

a. *Hyper-Automation*: The combination of RPA, AI, and ML to build fully automated financial decision-making engines.
b. *Blockchain-based RPA*: It figures out financial transactions with smart contracts via RPA that are safe and unhackable.
c. *Cognitive Automation*: AI-powered RPA systems can learn from past patterns to predict financial risk and optimize overall operational efficiency.

### 4.4.2 Policy Recommendations for Effective RPA Implementation

To fully maximize the benefits of RPA, while remaining ethical and legal, financial officials and institutions should take the following tactical steps:

a. *Harmonization of Automation Regulations*: Global regulatory entities need to introduce standards for RPA compliance so that there is uniform implementation and governance of RPA across the financial institutions.
b. *Changing and Upgrading Workforce*: Organizations must invest in retraining programs to give employees the skills to manage AI-powered automation systems.
c. *Cybersecurity and Data Protection Measures*: Crafting strong regulatory monitoring to protect the financial system from automation-induced cyber-threats and data breaches.

## 4.5 CONCLUSION

RPA is revolutionizing the finance industry by improving regulatory compliance, reducing costs, and enhancing productivity. By providing automation of critical processes, financial organizations may be able to improve risk management, streamline banking services, and elevate the accuracy and clarity of compliance reporting. To reap the most benefits from RPA, financial institutions should bolster cybersecurity, embed next-gen, AI-powered automation, and dynamically adapt to evolving regulations. While the financial industry evolves towards hyper-automation, RPA will continue to play a critical role in driving innovation, operational resilience, and longevity.

## REFERENCES


1. Jafar SH. Financial applications of Gaussian processes and Bayesian optimization. In: *Bayesian reasoning and Gaussian processes for machine learning applications.* Boca Raton, FL: Chapman & Hall/CRC; 2022. p. 111–22.
2. Jednak D, Jednak J. Operational risk management in financial institutions. *Management.* 2013;66:66–80.
3. Hatzakis ED, Nair SK, Pinedo M. Operations in financial services—An overview. *Prod Oper Manag.* 2010;19(6):633–64.
4. Ozioko AC. Preventive strategies for financial institutions: Compliance and legal implications. *Multi Discipl Res Dev J Int.* 2024;5(1):86–107.
5. George JG. Leveraging enterprise agile and platform modernization in the FinTech AI revolution: A path to harmonized data and infrastructure. *Int Res J Mod Eng Technol Sci.* 2024;6(4):88–94.
6. Quarshie MA, Akhtar S, Nawaah D. Barriers to breakthroughs: The crucial role of support services in advancing accounting practices, financial literacy, and performance in disability led SMEs. *Qual Quant.* 2025;5:1–23.
7. Bayya AK. Implementing AI driven transaction security protocols and automation in next gen FinTech solutions. *Asian J Math Comput Res.* 2025;32(1):104–32.
8. Rechtman YM. Can robotic process automation improve quality control in audits? *CPA J.* 2021;91(8/9):69–72.
9. Şen Y. Auditors' perceptions of artificial intelligence: Evidence from global audit companies [master's thesis]. İzmir (Turkey): İzmir Ekonomi Üniversitesi; 2023.
10. Davies H, Green D. *Global financial regulation: The essential guide.* Rev ed. Hoboken (NJ): John Wiley & Sons; 2013.
11. Hemachandran K, Rodriguez RV, editors. *Artificial intelligence for business: An implementation guide containing practical and industry specific case studies.* Boca Raton (FL): CRC Press; 2023.
12. Jafar SH, Akhtar S, Johl SK. AI in insurance. In: Hemachandran K, Rodriguez RV, editors. *Artificial intelligence for business.* Boca Raton (FL): Productivity Press; 2023. p. 164–73.
13. Barney J. Firm resources and sustained competitive advantage. *J Manag.* 1991;17(1): 99–120. https://doi.org/10.1177/014920639101700108
14. Jafar SH, Hemachandran K, El Chaarani H, Moturi S, Gupta N, editors. *Artificial intelligence for capital markets.* Boca Raton (FL): CRC Press; 2023.
15. Davis FD. Perceived usefulness, perceived ease of use, and user acceptance of information technology. *MIS Q.* 1989;13(3):319–40. https://doi.org/10.2307/249008
16. Reserve Bank of India. Financial stability report – July 2023 [Internet]. Mumbai: RBI; 2023 [cited June 2, 2025]. Report No.: 27. Available from: https://www.rbi.org.in/Scripts/BS_PressReleaseDisplay.aspx?prid=55889
17. Hancock D, Humphrey DB, Wilcox JA. Cost reductions in electronic payments: The roles of consolidation, economies of scale, and technical change. *J Bank Finance.* 1999; 23(2–4):391–421.
18. Jafar SH, Kashid AU, Ghosh S, Srividhya S, Sharma D, Bodhankar A. An enhanced performance optimization of ATM networks for cross border money transfers. In: *2024 15th International Conference on Computing Communication and Networking Technologies (ICCCNT).* Piscataway, New Jersey: IEEE; 2024. p. 1–5.

19. Adorno ODA. *Business process changes on the implementation of artificial intelligence [dissertation].* São Paulo: Universidade de São Paulo; 2020.
20. Odilla F. *The digitalisation of anti corruption in Brazil: Scandals, reforms, and innovation.* Abingdon: Taylor & Francis; 2025. p. 152.
21. Redko K, Zaletska I, Chyrva H. Comprehensive modernization and innovative development of the SMART economy of the future. *Futur Econ Law.* 2023;3(1):72–98.
22. Hemachandran K, George PM, Rodriguez RV, Kulkarni RM, Roy S. Performance analysis of k nearest neighbour classification algorithms for bank loan sectors. In: *Smart intelligent computing and communication technology.* Amsterdam: IOS Press; 2021. p. 9–13.
23. PricewaterhouseCoopers. The power of robotic process automation: How RPA is transforming business operations [Internet]. PwC; 2023 [cited June 2, 2025]. Available from: https://www.pwc.com/
24. DiMaggio PJ, Powell WW. The iron cage revisited: Institutional isomorphism and collective rationality in organizational fields. *Am Sociol Rev.* 1983;48:147–60.
25. Hemachandran K, Rodriguez RV, editors. *The business of the metaverse: How to maintain the human element within this new business reality.* Boca Raton (FL): CRC Press; 2023.
26. Salim M, Khan PA, Jalil NA, Johl SK, Jafar SH, Irfan F, Khan M. Fusion of blockchain and sustainable development goals: A bibliometric analysis for future trends. *KnE Soc Sci.* 2023:633–54.
27. Hemachandran K, Rodriguez RV, Toshniwal R, Junaid M, Shaw L. Performance analysis of different classification algorithms for bank loan sectors. In: *Intelligent sustainable systems: Proceedings of ICISS 2021.* Singapore: Springer; 2021. p. 191–202.
28. Pramod D. Robotic process automation for industry: Adoption status, benefits, challenges and research agenda. *Benchmarking Int J.* 2022;29(5):1562–86.
29. Quarshie MA, Djimatey R, Akhtar S, Nawaah D. Maximizing financial efficiency through technological synergy: Unleashing ICT for enhanced cash management in SMEs. *J Int Counc Small Bus.* 2025:1–31.
30. Siderska J. Robotic process automation—A driver of digital transformation? *Eng Manag Prod Serv.* 2020;12(2):21–31.
31. Villar AS, Khan N. Robotic process automation in Banking industry: A case study on Deutsche Bank. *J Bank Financ Technol.* 2021;5(1):71–86.
32. Policepatil S, Sharma J, Kumar B, Singh D, Pramanik S, Gupta A, Mahabub BS. Financial sector hyper-automation: Transforming Banking and investing procedures. In: *Examining global regulations during the rise of Fintech.* Hershey (PA): IGI Global; 2025. p. 299–318.
33. Jafar SH, Dhandhukia V, Kumar GB. Application of artificial intelligence in banking: A review. In: *Machine learning for business analytics.* Productivity Press; 2022. p. 145–51.
34. Jafar SH, Oyedele OM, Nawaah D, Bolanle AS. Exploring leadership challenges for adoption of digital innovation and sustainability. In: *Innovation ecosystems and sustainable technologies.* Bingley: Emerald Publishing; 2025. p. 253–69.
35. Malik MY, Jafar SH, Dixit A. Efficiency analysis and macroeconomic determinants of non tax revenues: Evidence from special category states of India. *Indian Econ J.* 2025. https://doi.org/10.1177/00194662251330385
36. Nawaah D, Asare PY, Quarshie MA. Climate finance and natural capital: Linking global initiatives with local impact. In: *Climate neutrality through smart eco innovation and environmental sustainability.* Cham: Springer; 2025. p. 317–32.
37. Prorokowski L, Prorokowski H. Organisation of compliance across financial institutions. *J Invest Compliance.* 2014;15(1):65–76.

38. World Bank. *World development report 2003: Sustainable development in a dynamic world—Transforming institutions, growth, and quality of life.* Washington (DC): Oxford University Press; 2003. Available from: https://openknowledge.worldbank.org/handle/10986/5985
39. Deloitte. Global RPA survey: Scaling intelligent automation [Internet]. Deloitte Insights; 2023 [cited June 2, 2025]. Available from: https://www2.deloitte.com
40. El Abiad Z, Abraham R, El Chaarani H, Skaf Y, Binsaddig RO, Jafar SH. The impact of CEO characteristics on the financial performance of family businesses listed in the Euronext Exchange. *J Risk Financ Manag.* 2024;17(3):129.

# 5 Leveraging Natural Language Processing (NLP) in Financial Customer Service

## *Enhancing User Experience*

*Rajan Gupta and Sudeshna Sani*

## 5.1 INTRODUCTION

### 5.1.1 The Rise of AI in Financial Customer Service

Over the past few decades, the financial industry had been relying a lot on human-driven approaches when it comes to handling customer care-related inquiries, transactions, and resolving customer issues [1–3]. However, with digital being at the core of banking and financial services, customer demands are now shifting to a need for immediate, omnipresent customer support, self-service at the fingertips, and personalization, all driving impact through behavioural insights [4–6]. In this evolution, financial institutions have been piloting AI-powered automation, mostly via Natural Language Processing (NLP)-based automation to deliver smart, real-time consumer interactions. NLP allows organizations to process information in various languages and provides human-like responses in any linguistic manner, which is how it helps organizations enhance productivity, engagement and the quality of service rendered to customers [7]. In several financial companies, AI-based chatbots and assistant can work out complicated questions and emotions along with carrying out the transactional component, which enhances consumer satisfaction and brand to patron loyalty. In this chapter, we analyse some of the key drivers of the adoption of NLP in financial services including the need for real-time personalized service, cost reduction as well as fraud prevention. Building on models like Unified Theory of Acceptance and Use of Technology (UTAUT) and the Customer Experience (CX) Framework, it examines the impact of NLP on the CX through accessibility, accuracy, and personalization. It covers the practical, such as chatbots, sentiment analysis, multilingual tools as well as real-world case studies and new trends.

### 5.1.2 Key Drivers of NLP Adoption in Financial Services

Several factors underpinned the rise of NLP in financial services.

DOI: 10.1201/9781003611646-5

#### 5.1.2.1 Customer Demand for Real-Time and Personalized Services

In the fast-paced world of today, customers want timely responses and personalized service. The presence of technology has made methods such as waiting on hold for customer service or making the physical trip to a bank branch obsolete [8]. NLP-powered chatbots and virtual assistants deliver scalable on-demand contextual support that works in a 24×7 economy [9, 10]. They can quickly resolve complex issues, offer personal guidance, and analyse transaction histories. It is a step-up towards AI-supported customer support for a better client experience where solutions are faster, more accurate and more personalized.

#### 5.1.2.2 Cost Reduction and Operational Efficiency

In the past, financial institutions relied on large customer support teams to answer queries, leading to expensive labour and scaling challenges [11, 12]. Through NLP-based automation, the financial services industry will automate banking services while keeping the service quality on par thereby reducing operational cost for banks and FinTechs. Automation is also capable of managing routine queries, improving human agent well-being by allowing them to focus on more complex tasks. Transitioning to NLP improves efficiency overall through providing a better service and lowering labour costs while simultaneously boosting productivity and precision.

#### 5.1.2.3 Fraud Prevention and Sentiment Analysis

In this fast-paced world, customers expect personalized attention and fast responses [13]. We live in an increasingly digital-first world and the old-school customer service tactics like holding on the line to speak to a bank teller are no longer an option. NLP chatbots and virtual assistants help scale 24×7, contextual support to meet these ever-increasing demands. They can easily guide users through complicated issues, provide personalized assistance, and investigate transactions. AI allows for this transition through the comprehension of consumers and tailoring accurate responses, improving customer satisfaction.

### 5.1.3 The Role of NLP in Enhancing Customer Experience

Unlike simply automating processes, the objective of NLP within financial services is to create a smarter, more customer-centric function [14]. It makes them more accessible and faster and more tailored services.

#### 5.1.3.1 Personalized Interactions

NLP systems can tailor finance advice to a consumer by analysing consumer behaviour and previous interactions to recommend products and to notify consumers about potential issues such as upcoming payments, frauds, etc. [15]. Such a high degree of customization translates into a happier client and better relationships.

#### 5.1.3.2 Increased Efficiency and Accuracy

By removing repetitive processes, NLP automations reduce human error and improve response times [16, 17]. Such fast service, reliable data and regular communication improve service and compliance quality, which is of benefit to consumers.

#### 5.1.3.3 Enhanced Accessibility

Through NLP-based solutions, banking has become easier and more diverse by adapting a voice-based banking service, a multi-lingual assistant to help with queries, and a more organic and natural style of communication through AI. These features will enable financial services to be as accessible as possible, including their multilingual capability or for people with disabilities. When it comes to revamping the customer service experience for financial institutions, NLP is enveloping the wrestle indispensable as they further embracing the technologies to make customer service richer, swifter and customer centric [18]. AI enables an unrivalled ability to understand and respond to human language, revolutionary to banking and establishing new standards for customer support.

## 5.2 UNDERSTANDING NLP IN FINANCIAL CUSTOMER SERVICE

NLP is a subfield of artificial intelligence (AI) that enables computers to understand, interpret, and generate human language. NLP has changed the way customers interact with banks and financial facility providers enabling a far greater rate of process automation while maintaining the same level of customer effective engagement. NLP-driven applications in financial services include:

a. *Chatbots and Virtual Assistants*: AI-powered banking assistants that handle routine customer queries, guide users through transactions, and provide instant support.
b. *Speech-to-Text Processing*: AI-powered tools provide voice-based customer-service solutions and deliver seamless interactions for users having disabilities or those who feel easy by verbally placing requests.
c. *Sentiment Analysis*: AI-powered tools that analyse customer feedback, emails, and social media interactions to detect dissatisfaction, improving customer retention strategies.
d. *Fraud Detection*: NLP-based fraud prevention mechanisms that analyse conversational patterns, transaction histories, and behavioural data to identify suspicious activities.

These applications have taken service efficiency to the next level by providing better user experience, adaptive to instant transactions, and more personalized service delivery, which in turn reduces the operational costs and enhances CX. As long as financial institutions continually prioritize the implementation of AI, NLP is predicted to play an increasingly vital role in shaping the future of customer service delivery.

## 5.3 THEORETICAL MODELS SUPPORTING NLP ADOPTION IN FINANCIAL SERVICES

The application of NLP in financial services is supported by some theoretical frameworks of the adoption of AI-powered solutions and their usage by businesses and consumers explaining how and why businesses and consumers adopt AI-driven solutions. These include customer satisfaction, user behaviour and technology, which also explain what drives the uptake of NLP as per these models.

### 5.3.1 Unified Theory of Acceptance and Use of Technology (UTAUT)

Venkatesh et al. [19] developed the model of UTAUT. This model identifies four main determinants that drive the implementation of solutions based on NLP:

a. *Performance Expectancy*: Financial institutions spend money on NLP solutions primarily because they enhance client interaction, reduce response time, improve operational efficiency, and make delivery of services faster. Banks use NLP chatbots for 24/7 availability, which reduces human handling costs and improves service accuracy.
b. *Effort Expectancy*: User-friendliness is needed for adoption in NLP solutions. Their conversational, intuitive interfaces allow customers to engage with AI-powered chatbots and virtual assistants without any technical know-how and with little or no training.
c. *Social Influence*: Leading companies in the fintech and digital banking sectors are crucial in establishing benchmarks for AI-powered customer support. Other banks follow suit as top financial organizations use NLP technologies in order to stay competitive and satisfy client demands.
d. *Facilitating Conditions*: An environment that is favourable for the application of NLP in financial services has been established by the growth of cloud computing, big data analytics, and AI regulatory frameworks. Financial institutions now have the resources and technological assistance needed to successfully integrate NLP solutions thanks to growing investments in AI infrastructure.

By applying the UTAUT model, financial institutions can enhance their client engagement and operational efficiency by optimizing their strategies and gaining a deeper understanding of the reasons.

### 5.3.2 Customer Experience (CX) Framework

The impact of AI-driven interactions on customer satisfaction and engagement is highlighted by Meyer and Schwager's [20] CX Framework. Customers' and service providers' emotional, cognitive, and behavioural exchanges influence the CX, according to this theory. NLP-driven financial customer service enhances the CX in several ways:

a. *Minimizing Frustration*: AI chatbots provide immediate answers, reducing the frustration that accompanies long wait times for queries to be answered. This enhances customer satisfaction and builds loyalty for the brand itself.
b. *Better Personalization*: The recommendations that take advantage of NLP lead to a better consumer experience. AI could study transaction patterns,

purchasing habits, and previous dialogues to provide personalized financial advice and help clients receive individualized care.

c. *Increased Accessibility*: Solutions for multilingual NLP and technologies for speech recognition also provide access to a wider audience including people with disabilities and other people who want a dialogue in their native language when using financial services.

## 5.4 KEY APPLICATIONS OF NLP IN TRANSFORMING FINANCIAL CUSTOMER SERVICE

NLP has revolutionized financial customer service by allowing financial institutions to communicate better with their clients and giving these institutions the ability to deal with their requests and individualize their experience that they have with the financial institution [21–24]. Due to their heavy reliance on the human element of customer service, traditional financial services were often slow to respond, with long queues and inconsistent relationships with staff due to high operating costs. Within the provision of financial services, NLP is applied in multiple domains.

### 5.4.1 AI Chatbots for Banking Assistance

Chatbots are changing the way banks and fintech institutions serve financial customer care, as they are now performing transactions, automating responses, and provide real-time support. On the contrary, NLP chatbots understand user intent, process unstructured user queries, and provide more natural, human-like responses, as compared to traditional rule-based chatbots that work on a limited set of rules.

#### 5.4.1.1 Benefits of NLP-Based Chatbots in Financial Services

a. *Scalability*: With NLP-based chatbots, thousands of customers can be interacted with at the same time and a response to the queries can be given without requiring human agents.
b. *Round the Clock Availability*: Unlike human operators, AI chatbots are available all the time, which means that the connection and service availability with customers is largely improved.
c. *Chatbots for Banking Services*: With an AI-based chatbot, personalized recommendations and financial advice based on past interactions and transaction histories will ultimately increase customer satisfaction.

As in the case of HDFC Bank in India, where the bank introduced "Eva", a NLP-powered virtual assistant that addresses millions of consumer inquiries every year. This innovation reduced inquiry resolution time significantly leading to a huge productivity gain along with more than 85% customer satisfaction [24, 25]. Likewise, Safaricom's M-Pesa had deployed an NLP-powered chatbot in Kenya for functions such as fraud reporting, balance queries, and financial literacy in local languages. This is how we decreased the customer support workload and improved the accuracy of fraud reporting by 40% [26, 27].

### 5.4.2 Sentiment Analysis for Customer Insights

Sentiment analysis, one of the most important applications of NLP, can help financial firms to explore customer reviews, identify dissatisfaction, and predict service improvement opportunities [28–30]. By processing a vast amount of customer reviews, chat transcripts, and other social media interactions using NLP-powered sentiment analysis technologies, financial institutions can make better data-driven decisions to enhance CX.

#### 5.4.2.1 Benefits of Sentiment Analysis in Financial Services

a. *Pain-Point Identification*: The adoption of banking analytics enables financial institutions to identify recurring pain-points such as transaction delays or unexpected charges and take steps to overcome them in advance.
b. *Loyalty Programs Improvements*: Using sentiment analysis, financial organizations can make better compliant loyalty programs suitable for the consumer segments which can increase the customer retention data rate significantly.
c. *Brand Perception Monitoring*: NLP-powered sentiment analysis enables organizations to track sentiment trends, monitor public opinion, and adapt strategies to increase customer satisfaction.

For instance, to monitor its reviews on the Internet, Brazil's Banco do Brasil applied a sentiment analysis platform that identifies negative sentiment in less than a minute to allow customer support representatives to react proactively. As a result, customer satisfaction improved by 28% showcasing the role that sentiment analysis can have on financial services [1, 31].

### 5.4.3 Multilingual NLP for Global Banking Services

With financial organizations increasingly operating in multicultural, multilingual contexts, the demand for NLP-driven solutions that transcend language lines will only become more prevalent [2, 18, 32]. With multi-lingual NLP, banks can offer customer support in different languages and do multinational service for their client segment.

#### 5.4.3.1 Benefits of Multilingual NLP in Financial Services

a. *Improved Accessibility*: Multilingual NLP tools allow banks to connect with customers in a language that they are comfortable with, resulting in customer service that is not just robust but also convenient and user-friendly [33, 34].
b. *Better Customer Interaction*: By providing support in multiple languages in real time, banks can go for a better multichannel customer interaction and can also improve customer satisfaction and finally their loyalty [35].
c. *Better Global Reach*: Expansion in foreign markets allows financial institutions to be more certain that this basic service is not being withheld from consumers because of a language barrier [36, 37].

The case of Commonwealth Bank of Australia is an example of multilingual NLP in action and result. Commonwealth Bank of Australia developed a multilingual ATM-driven chatbot that is capable to help clients speaking Arabic, Mandarin, Hindi, and English [17]. This improvement helped the bank have a 22% greater customer engagement and made it easier for the bank to serve the large variety of immigrants from all over Australia. Similarly, multilingual chatbots help global financial corporations overcome the challenge of providing continuous client comfort across borders.

## 5.5 FUTURE TRENDS AND POLICY IMPLICATIONS

### 5.5.1 Future Trends in NLP for Financial Services

With trends like voice-based financial assistants embedded into systems like Alexa, Google Assistant, and Siri, NLP clients care of the financial advisor of the future seems inevitable. Emotion AI will allow chatbots to vary their responses according to customer emotion. The role of NLP in blockchain integration in various aspects like smart contracts security and fraud detection will make great use of it.

### 5.5.2 Policy Recommendations

With increasing adoption of NLP, policymakers will have to issue new regulations or provide groundbreaking laws that assure ethical use of AI for impartial interactions. Focusing on data privacy in the form of GDPR-compliant encryption, will not only make access and inclusivity much easier as well, but also give rise to greater multilingual and voice-based banking solutions as well.

## 5.6 CONCLUSION

NLP is reshaping the financial customer service industry, enabling faster, smarter, and more convenient communication. But financial institutions are not just increasing customer engagement with AI chatbots, sentiment analysis, and multilingual solutions, they are also reducing operational costs and enhancing fraud detection. As technology develops, governance around ethical AI and data privacy and innovation will play a vital part in both leveraging NLP for financial inclusion and well-being but also protecting these human outcomes. The future of banking will hinge on hyper-personalization, voice-activated banking assistants, and AI-enabled defence against fraud which together will enable personalized, convenient, secure, and customer-first financial ecosystems.

## REFERENCES

1. Harles R. *Human-driven experience: The battle for trust in the digital age.* Hoboken: John Wiley & Sons; 2022.
2. Quarshie MA, Akhtar S, Nawaah D. Barriers to breakthroughs: The crucial role of support services in advancing accounting practices, financial literacy and performance in disability-led SMEs. *Qual Quant.* 2025;59:1–23.

3. Tan TM, Saraniemi S. Trust in blockchain-enabled exchanges: Future directions in blockchain marketing. *J Acad Mark Sci.* 2023;51(4):914–39.
4. Jafar SH, Akhtar S, Johl SK. AI in insurance. In: *Artificial intelligence for business.* New York: Productivity Press; 2023. p. 164–73.
5. Mohanty A, Mohanty J, Lingam N, Mohanty S, Acharya A. Artificial intelligence transforming customer service management: Embracing the future. *Oriental Stud.* 2023;12:35–47.
6. Palm M. *Technologies of consumer labor: A history of self-service.* New York: Routledge; 2016.
7. Hemachandran K, Rodriguez RV, editors. *The business of the metaverse: How to maintain the human element within this new business reality.* Boca Raton: CRC Press; 2023.
8. Jafar SH. Financial applications of Gaussian processes and Bayesian optimization. In: *Bayesian reasoning and Gaussian processes for machine learning applications.* Boca Raton: Chapman and Hall/CRC; 2022. p. 111–22.
9. Vetrivel SC, Arun VP, Saravanan TP, Maheswari R. Harnessing AI for next-generation service marketing. In: *Integrating AI-driven technologies into service marketing.* Hershey: IGI Global; 2024. p. 265–98.
10. Gomber P, Kauffman RJ, Parker C, Weber BW. On the fintech revolution: Interpreting the forces of innovation, disruption, and transformation in financial services. *J Manag Inf Syst.* 2018;35(1):220–65.
11. Jafar SH, Dhandhukia V, Kumar GB. Application of artificial intelligence in banking: A review. In: *Machine learning for business analytics.* Productivity Press; 2022. p. 145–51.
12. Hemachandran K, George PM, Rodriguez RV, Kulkarni RM, Roy S. Performance analysis of k-nearest neighbour classification algorithms for bank loan sectors. In: *Smart intelligent computing and communication technology.* Amsterdam: IOS Press; 2021. p. 9–13.
13. Kannan S. The role of AI and machine learning in financial services: A neural network-based framework for predictive analytics and customer-centric innovations. *Migr Lett.* 2022;19(6):985–1000.
14. Temara S, Samanthapudi SV, Rohella P, Gupta K. Using AI and natural language processing to enhance consumer banking decision-making. In: *2024 Int Conf E-mobility, Power Control and Smart Syst (ICEMPS).* IEEE; 2024. p. 1–6.
15. Jafar SH, Hemachandran K, El-Chaarani H, Moturi S, Gupta N, editors. *Artificial intelligence for capital markets.* Boca Raton: CRC Press; 2023.
16. Sethu M, Kotla B, Russell D, Madadi M, Titu NA, Coble JB, et al. Application of artificial intelligence in detection and mitigation of human factor errors in nuclear power plants: A review. *Nucl Technol.* 2023;209(3):276–94.
17. El Abiad Z, Abraham R, El-Chaarani H, Skaf Y, Binsaddig RO, Jafar SH. The impact of CEO characteristics on the financial performance of family businesses listed in the Euronext Exchange. *J Risk Financ Manag.* 2024;17(3):129.
18. Hemachandran K, Rodriguez RV, Toshniwal R, Junaid M, Shaw L. Performance analysis of different classification algorithms for bank loan sectors. In: *Intell Sustain Syst: Proc ICISS 2021.* Singapore: Springer; 2021. p. 191–202.
19. Venkatesh V, Morris MG, Davis GB, Davis FD. User acceptance of information technology: Toward a unified view. *MIS Q.* 2003;27(3):425–78.
20. Meyer C, Schwager A. *Understanding customer experience.* Boston: Harvard Business Publishing; 2007.
21. Nawaah D, Asare PY, Quarshie MA. Climate finance and natural capital: Linking global initiatives with local impact. In: *Climate neutrality through smart eco-innovation and environmental sustainability.* Cham: Springer; 2025. p. 317–32.

22. Suresh DM, Vincent G, Vijai C, et al. Analyse customer behaviour and sentiment using NLP techniques to improve customer service and personalize banking experiences. *Educ Adm Theory Pract.* 2024;30(5):8802–13.
23. Xiao J, Wang J, Bao W, Deng T, Bi S. Application progress of natural language processing technology in financial research. *Financ Eng Risk Manag.* 2024;7(3):155–61.
24. Press Trust of India. HDFC Bank launches chatbot Eva for customer services [Internet]. *The Economic Times*; 2017 [cited June 2, 2025]. Available from: https://economictimes.indiatimes.com/industry/banking/finance/banking/hdfc-bank-launches-chatbot-eva-for-customer-services/articleshow/57481943.cms
25. Safaricom. Tracking Zuri: Safaricom's customer care chatbot [Internet]. 2022 [cited June 2, 2025]. Available from: https://newsroom.safaricom.co.ke/innovation/tracking-zuri-safaricoms-customer-care-chatbot/
26. Jafar SH, Kashid AU, Ghosh S, Srividhya S, Sharma D, Bodhankar A. An enhanced performance optimization of ATM networks for cross-border money transfers. In: *2024 15th Int Conf Comput Commun Netw Technol (ICCCNT).* IEEE; 2024. p. 1–5.
27. Kang D, Park Y. Measurement of customer satisfaction in mobile service: Sentiment analysis and VIKOR approach. *Expert Syst Appl.* 2014;41(4):1041–50.
28. Mittal D, Agrawal SR. Determining banking service attributes from online reviews: Text mining and sentiment analysis. *Int J Bank Mark.* 2022;40(3):558–77.
29 Banco do Brasil. 1Q24 Management Report [Internet]. 2024 [cited June 2, 2025]. Available from: https://www.marketscreener.com/quote/stock/BANCO-DO-BRASIL-S-A-6494540/news/Banco-do-Brasil-S-A-1Q24-Management-Report-46671033/
30. Dodda R, Maddhi S, Thuraab MS, Reddy AN, Chandra ASM. NLP-driven strategies for effective email spam detection: A performance evaluation. In: *2023 Int Conf Sustain Commun Netw Appl (ICSCNA).* IEEE; 2023. p. 275–9.
31. Malik MY, Jafar SH, Dixit A. Efficiency analysis and macroeconomic determinants of non-tax revenues: Evidence from special category states of India. *Indian Econ J.* 2025. https://doi.org/10.1177/00194662251330385
32. Kusum K, Ahmed A, Vivek V. Unsupervised translation of programming language—A survey paper. In: *2022 4th Int Conf Adv Comput Commun Control Netw (ICAC3N).* IEEE; 2022 Dec. p. 384–8.
33. Walsh T, Levy N, Bell G, Elliott A, Maclaurin J, Mareels I, Wood F. *The effective and ethical development of artificial intelligence: An opportunity to improve our wellbeing.* Canberra: Australian Council of Learned Academies (ACOLA); 2019.
34. Salim M, Khan PA, Jalil NA, Johl SK, Jafar SH, Irfan F, Khan M. Fusion of blockchain and sustainable development goals: A bibliometric analysis for future trends. *KnE Soc Sci.* 2023:633–54.
35. Hemachandran K, Rodriguez RV, editors. *Artificial intelligence for business: An implementation guide containing practical and industry-specific case studies.* Boca Raton: CRC Press; 2023.
36. Quarshie MA, Djimatey R, Akhtar S, Nawaah D. Maximizing financial efficiency through technological synergy: Unleashing ICT for enhanced cash management in SMEs. *J Int Counc Small Bus.* 2025:1–31.
37. Jafar SH, Oyedele OM, Nawaah D, Bolanle AS. Exploring leadership challenges for adoption of digital innovation and sustainability. In: *Innovation ecosystems and sustainable technologies.* Emerald Publishing Limited; 2025. p. 253–69.

# 6 Advanced NLP for Financial Document Analysis

## *Tools and Techniques*

*Prince Yeboah Asare*

## 6.1 INTRODUCTION

### 6.1.1 The Growing Importance of NLP in Financial Document Analysis

The environment in which investment firms, regulatory agencies, and financial institutions work is becoming more and more data-driven and compliance-intensive [1]. Legal contracts, investment prospectuses, risk assessment studies, and regulatory filings are just a few of the important papers that the financial industry depends on being processed methodically. Large volumes of unstructured financial data are contained in these papers; to make well-informed decisions, this data must be retrieved, examined, and verified [2]. Financial institutions have traditionally processed financial data using rule-based automation, human data input, and systems based on Structured Query Language (SQL) [3]. However, these approaches are ineffective when dealing with large-scale, multi-format financial information, labour-intensive, and prone to human mistake. Natural language processing (NLP) has revolutionized the analysis of financial documents through enabling automatic text extraction, highly intelligent document categorization, automatic risk flagging, and automatic fraud detection [4, 5]. Advanced NLP methods reduce human involvement and provide real-time data processing, thus making the system more efficient and exact. Financial workflows have adopted advanced NLP models, such as deep learning-based language models, optimized sentiment analysis, optical character recognition (OCR), and named entity recognition (NER), particularly to speed up inherently document-reliant processes. These technologies are excellent in making fraud detection systems even more efficient, they help in compliance monitoring, and they also help in leveraging risk assessment techniques.

Evidence of growing use of NLP in Finance study shows that 85% of global financial institutions have already invested in some kind of AI-powered document intelligence including NLP that is critical coverage for transaction verification, financial risk, and regulatory compliance [6, 7]. Case studies of projects conducted by financial institutions in Brazil, Australia, Kenya, and India are presented to highlight the ability of NLP-powered systems to automate compliance


DOI: 10.1201/9781003611646-6

reporting, detect anomalies, and ensure compliance with international financial regulations. NLP holds revolutionary promise for the analysis of unstructured data sources, but there are several challenges that prevent its widespread adoption in the analysis of financial documents. Some of the top issues include risks to data security, language challenges in processing multilingual financial documents, biases in AI models, and challenges integrating with legacy financial systems [8]. Addressing such challenges will require the continuous advancement of NLP techniques, a tightening of regulatory oversight, and the creation of explainable AI models that align with the norms of the financial sector. In the future, self-learning financial document intelligence systems, multilingual AI-driven financial processing, and the combination of blockchain technology with NLP will all contribute to increased automation and precision in financial operations [9–11]. NLP is a vital component of intelligent financial processes, guaranteeing effectiveness, compliance, and data-driven decision-making (DDDM). It is not only an auxiliary tool for financial institutions [12].

### 6.1.2 Key Drivers of NLP Adoption in Financial Document Processing

There are multiple factors that are propelling the demand of NLP for the analysis of financial documents specifically in the industries where timeliness, security, and compliance are of essence [13–15]. A major factor underpinning this is regulatory compliance and risk management. Because of stringent rules and regulations, financial establishments need to maintain very accurate records and report whenever necessary. Institutions must examine thousands of pages of legal and financial documents to ensure compliance with regulations like the Sarbanes-Oxley Act (SOX), the General Data Protection Regulation (GDPR), the Financial Action Task Force (FATF) guidelines, and the Third Basel Accord by the Basel Committee on Banking Supervision (Basel III). NLP makes this process much easier by identifying important compliance clauses, spotting policy violations, and confirming compliance with regulations. Central Bank of Kenya (CBK) has already been using support NLP-based compliance monitoring technology that helps regulatory analysts to audit millions of financial transactions in real time, with the technology reducing the manual monitoring workload of regulatory analysts by 40%. Besides the growing adoption of NLP, operational efficiency and cost reduction are other big drivers. Financial institutions process millions of documents over the course of a year, which may include loan agreements, risk declarations, credit assessments, transaction records, and so on [16, 17]. It is time-consuming and costly to manually process these documents. Solutions powered by NLP can classify, extract, and validate financial data autonomously, and cut the document processing time with a margin. For example, India's ICICI Bank used AI-driven document automation to automate the processing of 500 variable reports and cut the processing of financial reports from two weeks to three days, saving the bank millions in annual operation costs [18].

Moreover, as financial crimes are evolving into more complex schemes, fraud detection, and anomaly detection have moved into the spotlight among financial industry institutions [19, 20]. For example, NLP models can identify fraud patterns in financial documents by identifying anomalies in loan applications, risks of duplicate invoices, or detecting risk in the underlying transaction narrative. In Brazil, NLP-based Fraud Detection Models were integrated into the Ministry of Finance and used to detect tax filing and loan application irregularities reducing cases of financial fraud in the country by 25% in 2023. The last major driver is document globalization and multilingual document processing. With financial services going international, institutions need to translate documents into different languages. Most traditional translation tools fail when it comes to hardcore technical financial language, and this is where NLP-based multilingual models can be extremely useful; financial institutions across Australia are using multilingual NLP solutions that can translate and even vet financial documents for 15+ languages making all cross-border financial operations and regulatory compliance a breeze [21]. Documerge facilitates NLP and extract top tools for the financial activities of common practice, and with Financial Institutions seeking further automation, scalability, and security, NLP driven document intelligence is expected to become a solution for these manual financial workflows, where it becomes critical by ensuring compliance, cost reductions, and risk minimization scalable and secured to drive the future of money.

## 6.2 THEORETICAL FRAMEWORK

### 6.2.1 Understanding NLP in Financial Document Processing

NLP is an advanced technology for Artificial Intelligence (AI) machines to analyse the language and text part/process of human language generation. NLP is used for financial document analysis which automates the extraction of information, auditing for compliance, detection of anomalies in financial statements, and sentiment detection in corporate filings [22]. Financial documents are typically thick with numbers and legalese and provide other challenges which need specialized NLP techniques such as OCR, NER, and Sentiment and Text summarization [23]. McKinsey and Company in 2023 reported that NLP has increased decision-making speed by 65% for financial institutions [8, 24] where NLP was used to process documents, and these institutions experienced 30% fewer regulatory penalties because of improved monitoring of compliance content [25]. With an ever-increasing amount of financial data, the need for NLP to automate document-heavy workflows is becoming more crucial than ever before.

### 6.2.2 Theoretical Models Supporting NLP in Financial Analysis

#### 6.2.2.1 Information Extraction (IE) Theory

Based on the Information Extraction (IE) theory, this makes unstructured text amenable to transformation into structured, machine-readable outputs by an NLP-driven process [26, 27]. IE techniques are applied by financial firms in risk management, tax audits, and regulatory compliance [28], which allow it to identify errors, inconsistencies, and noncompliance issues before they become major problems.

#### 6.2.2.2 Data-Driven Decision-Making (DDDM) Model

The DDDM model highlights how strategic planning can be facilitated using AI-driven information derived from financial documents [29]. Banks and investor firms use NLP-driven sentiment analysis to understand market sentiment and forecast market trends from corporate earnings reports and investor filings [30].

## 6.3 APPLICATIONS OF NLP IN FINANCIAL DOCUMENT ANALYSIS

Given the immense volume of contracts, invoices, compliance reports, audit statements, transaction records, research reports, and all other documents that institutions operate on, the financial industry is inherently document intensive [31, 32]. Handling such documents manually is a time-consuming, expensive, and error-prone process. NLP-powered automation enables financial institutions to process, classify, and extract contextual understanding from structured and unstructured documents at an unprecedented scale financial organizations and institutions can incorporate advanced NLP models into their workflows to achieve legal compliance, risk and fraud detection, risk management, business operational efficiency, and much more. These are some of the key applications of NLP in financial document analysis that has become a gamechanger in the industry. These include text summarization for compressing lengthy reports, sentiment analysis for financial insights, NER for extracting important financial entities, OCR for digitizing documents, and text analytics for fraud detection. Every one of these NLP techniques is essential for turning unstructured financial documents into data that can be used.

### 6.3.1 Optical Character Recognition (OCR) for Financial Document Digitization

OCR, one of the most basic forms of applications of NLP to financial document processing, allowing machines to extract machine-readable text from scanned or image-based documents. For example, OCR is essential when digitizing paper financial records, such as invoices, receipts, tax filings, and loan applications, making it easier to store, retrieve, and analyse historical financial data [33]. OCR improves operational efficiencies and enables DDDM for financial institutions by converting unstructured documents into searchable and analysable formats. In the past, rapid progress in using a combination of AI-enhanced NLP models in OCR has resulted in major improvements in text recognition accuracy of even the most complex financial documents. Currently, modern OCR systems can efficiently read structured and semi-structured documents along with tables, hand-written text, and documents with multi-column layout. Moreover, AI-enhanced OCR can identify various fonts, layouts, and languages, establishing it as a crucial innovation for global financial institutions dealing with multiple document styles. AI-powered OCR systems have proved to significantly boost efficiency in document processing, help reduce errors, and automate compliance [34, 35]. Financial institutions deploying this technology have slashed processing times for loan applications, financial statements, and regulatory filings from manual data extraction to automated workflows [2, 36]. By reducing human errors, this shift also improves fraud detection and regulatory compliance as financial data is processed with a greater degree of accuracy. As more financial institutions embrace the new-age AI-powered OCR, this technology will indeed revolutionize the way financial operations are processed and become stronger backup for digital transformations.

#### 6.3.1.1 Named Entity Recognition (NER) for Automated Data Extraction

NER is one of the basic tasks of NLP, allowing financial institutions to identify and classify vital financial entities, specific to such unstructured documents. NER contributes to automating the processing and analysis of financial data by identifying and extracting company names, monetary values, transaction details, legal terms, and financial instruments [3]. This feature is especially ideal for industries with large amounts of financial documents, to lessen the amount of manual work while increasing accuracy and efficiency. NER vitally assists in auditing regulatory compliance by finding non-compliant clauses in regulatory filings and financial disclosures, enabling organizations to comply with evolving financial and legal requirements. By using automated identification of critical terms, financial institutions can ease the burden of monitoring compliance and decrease their regulatory risk. Likewise, investment companies use NER to analyse earning reports by mining quarterly statements to capture important financial figures which helps them in quicker decision-making ability and better portfolio management. NER has achieved significant advancements in financial work processes, risk management, fraud detection, transaction monitoring, and more. Ner-based systems have thus, helped institutions in reducing operational losses and compliance-related penalties greatly. Utilizing AI-powered entity recognition allows financial organizations to enforce regulatory scrutiny, increase accuracy in textual data, and develop the reliability of financial reports and processes. NER models are constantly improving, and the evolution with wider applicability in the financial automation space, continuing to underpin digital transformation efforts in the sector.

#### 6.3.1.2 Text Summarization for Financial Reports and Risk Analysis

Every day, financial institutions process huge amounts of data from financial statements, regulatory filings, and market reports. Manual review processes are slow at best, and at worst can miss things, needlessly delaying decision-making. Text summarization based on NLP solves this problem by summarizing long documents into smart, quick summaries that allow financial analysts to get an idea of the most important facts in minutes instead of hours. Recently, summarization models used deep learning methods like transformer-based architectures (e.g., BERT, GPT-4, T5, etc.) to produce text that is humans-friendly, preserves important financial information, and is context-aware [23]. These models driven by AI tools improve financial workflows through picking up larger trends, summarizing earnings reports, and breaking down complicated regulatory documents into more easily understood formats. This allows analysts to spend more time on high-level strategic decision-making, rather than document review. All kinds of financial institutions worldwide are pumping up their operations with the help of AI-powered summarization tools to make analysing financial documents quicker and save maximum time [16, 32]. They have been especially useful in compliance, where they help with flagging important legal provisions and breaking down regulatory updates. Likewise, investment banking will see improved ability to rapidly analyse quarterly earnings reports and market research as automated summarization speeds up response to market developments. In an ever-growing data driven financial market, text summarization technology will continue to be a big player in risk management, investment analysis, and compliance monitoring. From better decision-making to vastly improved operational efficiency AI-powered summarization dramatically reduces the cognitive load on financial professionals.

## 6.4 FUTURE TRENDS AND POLICY IMPLICATIONS

### 6.4.1 Future Trends in NLP for Financial Document Processing

Technological advancements in NLP are shaping the future of financial document processing in terms of automation, security, and multilingual processing capabilities [28]. As NLP models evolved, financial companies are increasingly adopting AI-powered document intelligence systems in replacing some manual processes for improving compliance and reducing fraud detection and transaction monitoring dependence on an ever-increasing overworked workforce. The combination of NLP and blockchain is perhaps one of the most exciting developments to create tamper-proof, verifiable, and permanent financial records. Accordingly, NLP systems based on blockchain help to provide transparency of contracts, invoices, and compliance documents by turning them into immutable and auditable reports which significantly minimize the likelihood of these types of documents being manipulated and thus falling prey to fraud. NLP allows Financial Institutions to leverage text analysis capabilities while Blockchain contributes through its secure technology to enhance transparency and integrity in document management processes. The third trend is the utilization of self-learning AI models which automatically update them to take in new financial regulations over time [16]. Such models use reinforcement learning (RL) algorithms to track changes in the financial legislation and policies, thus automating compliance, and compliance auditing with minimal to no human intervention. This new development not only eases one of the biggest regulatory burdens on financial institutions while also introducing higher accuracy in legal and compliance reviews. Similarly, multilingual NLP models are also changing the financial document processing, enabling the analysis of financial documents irrespective of language or nationality. As a simple financial service model, they enable support for cross-border transactions, international contracts, and geographically local regulatory needs [34] and thus continue the trend of globalizing financial services. NLP solutions can help financial institutions streamline operations, across multiple languages while revolutionizing efforts towards domestic and international financial regulatory compliance. In addition to these developments, AI-based NLP can prove to be a game-changing solution that has the potential to position itself into an integral part of the world of financial document processing, increasing productivity, enabling security, and enhancing regulatory compliance [23].

### 6.4.2 Policy Recommendations for NLP Adoption in Finance

As financial institutions show the positive adoption of more NLP-driven automation, the adoption of AI for processing financial documents can be made with clear regulatory frameworks to guide the responsible, safe, and transparent use [23]. Policymakers must address concerns over data privacy, algorithmic bias, and model explainability to the reliability and accountability of AI-driven financial systems [5]. At the core of these policy recommendations is the implementation of AI transparency regulations that require NLP models in financial institutions to follow disclosure requirements on how these models process and interpret financial documents. Explainability and auditability are key for trust in automation, especially as risks of biases and black-boxes in AI-based financial decision-making abound. This transparency that regulations would enforce would ensure institutions are held accountable, this can also include AI in terms of completion of a financial transaction, compliance monitoring, and risk assessments [3]. Then, governments must establish best class AI compliance processes and require the financial institutions to build, develop, and rollout NLP models compliant to world data protection laws and financial regulations such as GDPR, SOX, and Basel III. This regulation carefully demands compliance with these frameworks to keep AI-based financial document processing secure, bias-free, and lawfully compliant. In fact, regulators have now mandated the need for bias audits for AI applications impacting financial choices to ensure that NLP algorithms do not assimilate into the systems and end up propagating prejudicial norms around loan approval, fraud detection, and investment evaluation [23]. The enforcement of stringent governance policies can help financial institutions in minimizing the ethical risks and maximizing the promise of AI-backed financial automation [14]. Although NLP-based technologies will increase the efficiency and accuracy of processing financial documents [6], we will need a robust regulatory environment to ensure that innovations deliver value in a responsible and accountable manner amidst a rapidly evolving landscape.

## 6.5 CONCLUSION

NLP in Financial Document Analysis is changing the way financial institutions extract data, detect fraud, and monitor compliance. By leveraging advanced NLP techniques such as text summarization, sentiment analysis, NER and OCR, Financial Institutions analyse massive data volumes much faster, accurately, and securely than they would be able to do using human approaches. As financial institutions deploy AI-driven document automation, addressing important issues including data privacy, model openness, and the governance of ethical AI is critical. Ensuring that NLP systems operate fairly, securely, and in alignment with international financial norms will be essential for maintaining confidence and accountability in AI-assisted financial processes. Multilingual AI models for financial document processing, Blockchain-integrated financial intelligence, and hyper-automation powered by NLP will define this landscape in future. Ultimately, these technologies will enable financial institutions to operate more safely and intelligently in a secure, data-driven, and cognitive way by improving efficiency, risk management, and regulatory compliance. Overall, as AI technologies will keep on evolving, a greater degree of financial document analysis will be faced by them and will bring a change in the financial operations and decision-making.

## REFERENCES


1. Jafar SH, Akhtar S, Johl SK. AI in insurance. In: *Artificial intelligence for business*. Productivity Press; 2023. p. 164–73.
2. Angelo L. *Unlocking hidden value: A framework for transforming dark data in organizational decision-making*. SSRN. 2024. https://doi.org/10.2139/ssrn.5032778.
3. Palanivel K. Machine-learning architecture to financial service organizations. *Int J Comput Sci Eng*. 2019;7(11):85–104.
4. Oyewole AT, Adeoye OB, Addy WA, Okoye CC, Ofodile OC, Ugochukwu CE. Automating financial reporting with natural language processing: A review and case analysis. *World J Adv Res Rev*. 2024;21(3):575–89.
5. Jafar SH, Dhandhukia V, Kumar GB. Application of artificial intelligence in banking: A review. In: *Machine learning for business analytics*. Productivity Press; 2022. p. 145–51.
6. Singh KB, Aggarwal N, Devbrath D. Revolutionizing financial analysis and decision-making with AI-powered insights. *AIP Conf Proc*. 2025;3253:040003.
7. Garcia A, Adams J. Data-driven decision making: Leveraging analytics and AI for strategic advantage. *Res Stud Bus*. 2023;1(2):77–85.
8. Ghosh UK. Transformative AI applications in business decision-making: Advancing data-driven strategies and organizational intelligence. In: *AI-powered leadership*. IGI Global; 2025. p. 1–40.
9. Gunisity SR, Vandanapu MK. Evolving financial paradigms: The impact of intelligent document processing on accounting automation. *Int J Comput Eng Technol*. 2024;15(2):72–82.
10. Hemachandran K, Rodriguez RV, editors. *Artificial intelligence for business: An implementation guide containing practical and industry-specific case studies*. CRC Press; 2023.
11. Hemachandran K, Rodriguez RV, editors. *The business of the metaverse: How to maintain the human element within this new business reality*. CRC Press; 2023.
12. Hemachandran K, George PM, Rodriguez RV, Kulkarni RM, Roy S. Performance analysis of k-nearest-neighbour classification algorithms for bank-loan sectors. In: *Smart intelligent computing and communication technology*. IOS Press; 2021. p. 9–13.
13. Hemachandran K, Rodriguez RV, Toshniwal R, Junaid M, Shaw L. Performance analysis of different classification algorithms for bank-loan sectors. In: *Intelligent sustainable systems: Proceedings of ICISS 2021*. Springer; 2021. p. 191–202.
14. Islam T, Islam SM, Sarkar A, Obaidur A, Khan R, Paul R, Bari MS. Artificial intelligence in fraud detection and financial risk mitigation: Future directions and business applications. *Int J Multidiscip Res*. 2024;6:1–23.
15. Jafar SH. Financial applications of Gaussian processes and Bayesian optimization. In: *Bayesian reasoning and Gaussian processes for machine learning applications*. Chapman & Hall/CRC; 2022. p. 111–22.
16. Truby J, Brown R, Dahdal A. Banking on AI: Mandating a proactive approach to AI regulation in the financial sector. *Law Financ Mark Rev*. 2020;14(2):110–20.
17. Li C, Zhang Y, Yu H. Digitalization and the "Too Big to Fail" Dilemma: Mechanisms and asymmetric effects of banks' fintech innovation on total factor productivity. *Technol Econ Dev Econ*. 2024;30(2):464–88. https://doi.org/10.3846/tede.2024.21299

18. Jafar SH, Hemachandran K, ElChaarani H, Moturi S, Gupta N, editors. *Artificial intelligence for capital markets.* CRC Press; 2023.
19. Jafar SH, Kashid AU, Ghosh S, Srividhya S, Sharma D, Bodhankar A. An enhanced performance optimization of ATM networks for cross-border money transfers. In: *2024 15th Int Conf Comput Commun Netw Technol (ICCCNT).* IEEE; 2024. p. 1–5.
20. Jafar SH, Oyedele OM, Nawaah D, Bolanle AS. Exploring leadership challenges for adoption of digital innovation and sustainability. In: *Innovation ecosystems and sustainable technologies.* Emerald Publishing; 2025. p. 253–69.
21. Kalusivalingam AK, Sharma A, Patel N, Singh V. Enhancing corporate governance and compliance through AI: Implementing natural language processing and machine-learning algorithms. *Int J AI ML.* 2022;3(9).
22. Khan A. The role of artificial intelligence in financial decision-making. *Front Bus Finance.* 2024;1(1):59–75.
23. Kothandapani HP. AI-driven regulatory compliance: Transforming financial oversight through large language models and automation. *Emerg Sci Res.* 2025;3:12–24.
24. Lin P, Abney K, Bekey GA, editors. *Robot ethics: The ethical and social implications of robotics.* MIT Press; 2014.
25. Malik MY, Jafar SH, Dixit A. Efficiency analysis and macroeconomic determinants of nontax revenues: Evidence from special category states of India. *Indian Econ J.* 2025;3:12–24. https://doi.org/10.1177/00194662251330385.
26. Nawaah D, Asare PY, Quarshie MA. Climate finance and natural capital: Linking global initiatives with local impact. In: *Climate neutrality through smart eco-innovation and environmental sustainability.* Springer Nature Switzerland; 2025. p. 317–32.
27. Othayoth PK, Khanna S. Implementation of artificial intelligence and chatbot for the enhancement of new age banking systems: A systematic review. In: *Generative AI in FinTech.* 2025. p. 1–19.
28. Salim M, Khan PA, Jalil NA, Johl SK, Jafar SH, Irfan F, Khan M. Fusion of blockchain and sustainable development goals: A bibliometric analysis for future trends. *KnE Soc Sci.* 2023:633–54.
29. Pakhale K. Comprehensive overview of named entity recognition: Models, domain-specific applications, and challenges. *arXiv Preprint.* 2023. https://doi.org/10.48550/arXiv.2309.14084.
30. Quarshie MA, Akhtar S, Nawaah D. Barriers to breakthroughs: The crucial role of support services in advancing accounting practices, financial literacy, and performance in disability-led SMEs. *Qual Quant.* 2025;59:1–23.
31. Quarshie MA, Djimatey R, Akhtar S, Nawaah D. Maximizing financial efficiency through technological synergy: Unleashing ICT for enhanced cash management in SMEs. *J Int Counc Small Bus.* 2025:1–31.
32. El Abiad Z, Abraham R, ElChaarani H, Skaf Y, Binsaddig RO, Jafar SH. The impact of CEO characteristics on the financial performance of family businesses listed in the Euronext Exchange. *J Risk Financ Manag.* 2024;17(3):129.
33. Setiono R, Mues C, Baesens B. *Risk management and regulatory compliance: A datamining framework based on neural-network rule extraction.* ICIS Proc. 2006;7.
34. Schragger RC. Mobile capital, local economic regulation, and the democratic city. *Harv Law Rev.* 2009;123:482.
35. Sultana R. *Artificial intelligence for decision making in the era of big data evolution.* SSRN. 2024. https://doi.org/10.2139/ssrn.5056805.
36. Efunniyi CP, Abhulimen AO, Obiki-Osafiele AN, Osundare OS, Agu EE, Adeniran IA. Strengthening corporate governance and financial compliance: Enhancing accountability and transparency. *Finance Account Res J.* 2024;6(8):1597–616.

# 7 Predictive Analytics and AI in Credit Scoring

## *Transforming Lending Practices*

*Samba Shiva Rao, Dharmavarapu Naveen Kumar, and Marella Anvitha*

## 7.1 INTRODUCTION

Over the past few years, AI and predictive analytics have begun to radically transform the very fabric of financial services, creating a paradigm shift in credit scoring [1, 2]. Despite their long history of use, traditional credit scoring models which in general depend on logistic regression and utilize statistics such as historical repayment behaviour, credit utilization, and bureau scores have drawn an ever-increasing amount of criticism for their restricted forecasting ability, exclusion of a much larger population from mainstream credit pools, and potential for entrenched systemic bias [3, 4]. These limitations have led to an urgent demand for more versatile, data ponging, and context-oriented credit assessment methods [5]. Whereas traditional credit scoring was often based solely on data captured in the formal financial system, large digital financial footprints across emerging economies, especially in India, are now leading to rich alternative data sets (e.g., from smartphone metadata, social media, utility payments, and e-commerce), which can be used to assess creditworthiness in a much more holistic way. The data revolution is simultaneously occurring with developments in machine learning (ML), and AI, allowing for new generation credit scoring systems capable of processing vast amounts of high-dimensional, unstructured data in real time [6, 7].

Supervised and unsupervised learning algorithms are used in AI-based credit scoring models, including random forests, gradient boosting, and neural network models to reveal complex, potentially non-linear relationships between borrower characteristics and default risks [8–11]. Not only are these more accurate in predicting loan defaults, but they also have the capacity for adaptive learning – they can recalculate with incoming economic conditions and human behaviour. Thus, AI and predictive analytics mark a fundamental change from static, rule-based scoring systems towards adaptive, self-improving risk assessment systems.

Given this reality, financial inclusion has been regarded as one of the leading policy objectives, especially in developing countries, where a substantial share of the adult population is unbanked or underbanked. This alternative approach to credit

DOI: 10.1201/9781003611646-7

scoring may be able to expand access to credit to these populations by reducing reliance on traditional documentation of creditworthiness and integrating non-traditional indicators of creditworthiness [12]. We study leading fintech platforms like CASHe and Paytm (India), Ant Group (China), and Zest AI and Upstart (United States), which have spurred the use of AI in lending, showcasing varied operational designs, regulatory reactions, and social effects.

That said, implementing AI in credit scoring is fraught with ethical, regulatory, and operational challenges. Algorithmic bias, lack of explainability (the "black box" problem), data privacy, and regulatory compliance are still serious barriers to mass adoption. Concerns exist when credit decisions arise that impact vulnerable segments of the population, which reinforces the need for strong governance frameworks, transparency mechanisms, and regulatory oversight [13–19].

In this context, the chapter examines the extent to which predictive analytics and AI are revolutionizing the credit scoring practices around the world, based on use cases drawn from the United States, India, and China. Providing a multi-dimensional analysis which examines:

a. The development and structure of credit scoring models based on artificial intelligence (AI),
b. The consequences for financial inclusion, risk management, and loan availability,
c. Cross-jurisdictional regulatory reactions and ethical issues.

The chapter attempts to give academics, professionals, and policymakers a thorough grasp of the revolutionary potential, and inherent risks, of AI in credit scoring by synthesizing empirical research, real-world case studies, and comparative frameworks.

## 7.2 LITERATURE REVIEW

Models in traditional credit scoring are based on structured data, such as credit history data, income, and outstanding debt. These are the most common models such as logistic regression and discriminant analysis [20]. But these models often tend to underperform for thin-file or new-to-credit consumers. Compared to traditional scoring approaches, recent studies show that ML models are superior. For example, Baesens et al. [20] ML techniques provide significantly improved predictive accuracy over logistic regression, neural networks, and support vector machines. Lessmann et al. [21] compared existing ML classifiers and found that the credit scoring performance with ensemble methods (random forests and gradient boosting) was greatly improved. Alternative data-behavioural factors such as mobile phone usage, utility payments, and social media activity have been demonstrated to expand accessibility to financial services [22, 23]. Nonetheless, issues of fairness, transparency, and explainability have arisen [24], particularly with regulations such as the GDPR.

## 7.3 CONCEPTUAL FRAMEWORK AND THEORY

### 7.3.1 Theoretical Framework

Using an integrative theoretical framework based on behavioural finance, credit risk theory, and ML theory, this chapter provides a multifaceted explanation and improvement of credit scoring systems. Together, these theoretical foundations support the entire process of making credit decisions based on data.

#### 7.3.1.1 The Theory of Machine Learning

Complex, non-linear relationships in data can be detected computationally thanks to ML theory. Without being specifically coded for every situation, ML algorithms can learn from past data to make predictions or judgements on their own, as Domingos [25] emphasizes. ML makes it possible to find complex patterns in borrower behaviour, repayment history, and financial attributes that conventional linear models would miss in the context of credit scoring. To create flexible and data-rich credit evaluation systems, this theoretical framework supports the phases of feature engineering, model selection, and score production.

#### 7.3.1.2 Theory of Credit Risk

This framework incorporates ideas from the Basel Committee on Banking Supervision's [25] Credit Risk Theory to operationalize the credit scoring procedure. Credit risk is divided into three essential parts by this theory:

a. *Probability of Default (PD)*: The chance that a borrower will fail to fulfil their commitments.
b. *Loss Given Default (LGD)*: The percentage of exposure that is lost in the event of a default.
c. *Exposure at Default (EAD)*: The entire value exposed to loss at the moment of default.

Both the score-creation and decision-implementation stages are informed by these characteristics, which offer an organized method for measuring and controlling credit risk. Technical modelling can be brought into compliance with financial and regulatory risk standards by optimizing ML models trained on past loan data to estimate PD, LGD, and EAD.

#### 7.3.1.3 Behavioural Finance

Quantitative models are not sufficient if they do not account for human patterns of behaviour. Behavioural finance theory, especially by Kahneman and Tversky [26], introduces psychological factors (namely, cognitive biases, such as overconfidence and loss aversion, and anchoring) into decision-making processes. This is a necessary observation to understand borrower behaviour, particularly in many instances of default. When leveraged during the model feature engineering and post-decision monitoring phases, behavioural indicators increase model robustness and mitigate unanticipated risk emanating from the irrational behaviour of borrowers.

### 7.3.2 Conceptual Framework

To synthesize these theories into a cohesive process, the framework follows the logical sequence:

*Data Gathering → Feature Engineering → Model Selection → Score Creation → Decision Execution → Monitoring and Feedback*

a. *Data Gathering:* Entails compiling pertinent borrower data from the past and present.
b. *Feature Engineering*: Constructs meaningful variables from raw data by utilizing behavioural indicators and risk dimensions (PD, LGD, and EAD).
c. *Model Selection*: Uses ML techniques appropriate for high-dimensional, non-linear patterns.
d. *Score Creation*: Converts model results into risk ratings.
e. *Decision Execution*: Makes credit choices using these scores, either automatically or manually.
f. *Monitoring and Feedback*: Integrates real-world behavioural deviations and feedback loops to guarantee ongoing model improvement and risk calibration.

In such a multifaceted financial ecosystem, a unique theory cannot sufficiently explain the complexity of credit scoring, making this integrative framework essential. Human aspects are embedded in algorithmic systems (behavioural finance), regulatory compliance, and financial risk are mathematically binding (credit risk theory), and computing capacity and pattern recognition are delivered by ML. Together, they enable credit scoring systems to be theoretically sound and operationally feasible whilst being more ethical, accurate, and adaptive.

## 7.4 METHODOLOGY

Adopting a qualitative analytical approach based on secondary data, this chapter examines the changing direction of predictive analytics and AI in credit scoring. The analysis combines several lines of inquiry in order to capture both depth and breadth of understanding.

To synthesize the existing knowledge on ML and AI use in credit risk assessment, two steps of study selection were as follows first, we performed a systematic review of empirical and white papers. We performed a review of the literature, our focus being limited to peer-reviewed journal articles, industry publications, and technical reports from prominent financial institutions and technology firms.

Second, through case-based analysis of AI-enabled credit scoring platforms in different geographical and regulatory contexts, the study reveals that the limitation and enablement of regulatory options are tied to the interactions between the firm and its contextual landscape. More specifically, cases were taken from:

a. India (e.g., CASHe, Paytm),
b. China (e.g., Ant Group), and
c. United States (Zest AI, Upstart, etc.)

The selected cases are distinguished not only for their prominence but also for the novelty of the character of the credit risk modelling and the existence of public access data on their activities and results. Third, a novel comparative assessment framework was employed to assess AI-based models on three key domains of effectiveness:

a. Predictive Performance (accuracy, reduction in default rate),
b. Access (for underserved populations) is one of the financial inclusion outcomes, and
c. Ethics and regulations (Transparency, Fairness, and Compliance).

The main sources of original data for this work are peer-reviewed scholarly literature, regulatory reports from organizations like the Reserve Bank of India (RBI) and the Bank for International Settlements (BIS), and corporate filings, annual reports, and technology white papers of the firms being analysed. Careful implementation of this methodological triangulation adds to the credibility, transferability, and analytical rigour of the results described in the following section.

## 7.5 FINDINGS AND ANALYSIS

### 7.5.1 Higher Predictive Ability

Several empirical studies [27–30] showed that credit risk models based on ML algorithms have much higher predictive power than those based on traditional logistic regression or scorecard-type methods. This kind of "non-linear" risk assessment is used by platforms such as Zest AI and Upstart, which put together ensembles of hundreds of such variables; from educational background to live financial behaviour when making a loan decision. Traditional credit models would approve 27% fewer loans at the same level of default risk as compared with their ML-based system [31]. This implies that not only do the AI-driven models create greater access to credit but also have an equal or even better portfolio quality via more exact risk stratification.

### 7.5.2 Inclusiveness through the Use of Alternative Data

As a method based on such data, alternative data adoption in credit scoring has been widely identified as a game changer to address the lack of access to financial services in populations with low credit information availability, particularly in some emerging economies. Fintech platforms like CASHe and Tala have innovatively utilized non-traditional data sets – including smartphone metadata, communication patterns and mobile money transactions – to assess the creditworthiness of individuals with limited or no formal credit history in markets like India and Kenya. An Indian digital lending firm, CASHe employs a unique credit scoring method referred to as Social Loan Quotient (SLQ) based on behavioural indicators such as mobile app usage, social connectivity, income flow via UPI or wallets, and digital footprint data [32, 33]. It allows for in-depth analysis of gig workers, self-employed, and other non-salaried borrowers who are frequently shut out by traditional credit models. In a similar vein, Tala, which offers consumer loans in mainly Kenya, the Philippines, and Mexico, harnesses more than 10,000 data points from a borrower's smartphone, including text messages, call logs, geolocation, and device activity, to create predictive models that assess client solvency and set loan sizes and terms [34–36].

According to a BIS study [18], such alternative credit scoring mechanisms boost financial inclusion substantially. They discovered that by scoring new-to-credit individuals using alternative data, digital lenders could improve credit access for people and still retain low default rates. They enabled lenders to by-pass the conventional needs for credit score records or collateral, and offer quicker, cheaper credit score. To illustrate, they discovered mobile phone usage data was exceptionally telling of repayment behaviour, especially with low income and rural demographics. With fewer than 22% of adults in India holding a credit score with a bureau [37], alternative data presents a significant step towards closing structural credit gaps. Digital lenders have exploited this increasing complementary enabling environment in Aadhaar-based financial behaviour, mobile payments, and digital identity footprints to scale lending to the financially excluded. In the context of India increasingly moving towards financial digitization (for instance, through platforms like India Stack that enable higher levels of data interoperability) [38], these developments are also especially important. However, the potential for alternative data also comes with trade-offs regarding transparency, bias, and the ethics of using people's information.

### 7.5.3 Possible Bias and Fairness Issues

Although the increased use of AI and other data sources improves access, it comes with real risks of algorithmic bias and discriminatory impact. Moreover, as studies explain, an algorithm that is non-mainstream but is trained on biased or incomplete data sets will mimic current societal prejudice [39]. Hence, if historical lending data had a harmful disparity in lending to women, minorities, or rural borrowers, the AI systems may learn those patterns and recreate this in future credit decisions. The Consumer Financial Protection Bureau [40] highlights the need for explainability in automated decision-making (ADM) systems, as black-box algorithms can undermine both accountability and efforts to protect consumers. This opacity stops regulators from detecting discriminatory results and makes it hard for borrowers to understand adverse credit decisions or challenge them. In addition, alternative data around mobile usage, social media activity, or high-frequency transactional data offer proxy variables that stand in for race, gender, or socio-economic status, leading to indirect discrimination. These unanticipated effects contradict the very principles of fair lending and should demand robust governance frameworks regarding the design and implementation of credit scoring models [41].

### 7.5.4 Regulation and Ethics

Regulatory bodies have started to create ethical and legal frameworks for credit systems powered by AI in order to address these challenges. Specifically, Article 22 of the European Union's General Data Protection Regulation (GDPR) establishes an individual's right not to be subjected to a decision based solely on automated processing, including profiling. It also requires human oversight and explainability as well as non-discrimination for decision-making systems [42, 43]. India is also heading towards a more regulated AI ecosystem with the introduction of consent, purpose limitation, and accountability of data fiduciary in the recently enacted Digital Personal Data Protection Act (DPDPA) of 2023 [34]. It also includes provisions that apply to automated credit decisions and aims to strike a balance between innovation and your data rights. Along with existing RBI guidelines on digital lending, such legislation would be the first visible step towards responsible AI governance in the financial sector. Ultimately, predictive analytics and AI-based credit scoring have expanded access to economic opportunity. However, these innovations must be balanced with sufficient regulation, ethical guidelines, and public accountability structures. This is the only way that they can reach their potential without compromising equity or destroying trust in the financial system.

## 7.6 DISCUSSION

Based on available evidence [44–46], AI models have the potential to improve lending's inclusivity and efficiency. But it is impossible to overlook the dangers of algorithmic opacity, data exploitation, and social discrimination.

The following are important trade-offs:

a. *Explainability versus Accuracy*: More intricate models could be less clear.
b. *Privacy versus Inclusion*: Using alternative data presents moral dilemmas.

Newer approaches like Explainable AI (XAI) and tools for model interpretability (such SHAP and LIME) are becoming more popular [40]. Financial firms must create governance frameworks that meet public trust and regulatory requirements.

## 7.7 CONCLUSION AND FUTURE DIRECTIONS

Credit is being reimagined through AI and predictive analytics, not just optimized along existing practices – and that is a good thing. These systems show promise, but they need transparent algorithms, bias audits, and regulatory oversight to mitigate harm.

Future scope for research includes:

a. Creating a strong framework for XAI for Financial Use,
b. Constructing ML algorithms with fairness in mind,
c. Examining long-term effects of AI lending on borrower welfare.

While lending solutions must continue to evolve, the evolution of credit scoring also needs to meet this balancing act to truly transform lending practices.

## REFERENCES


1. Hemachandran K, Rodriguez RV, editors. *Artificial intelligence for business: An implementation guide containing practical and industry-specific case studies.* CRC Press; 2023.
2. Malik MY, Jafar SH, Dixit A. Efficiency analysis and macroeconomic determinants of non-tax revenues: Evidence from Special Category States of India. *Indian Econ J.* 2025. https://doi.org/10.1177/00194662251330385
3. Jagtiani J, Lemieux C. The roles of alternative data and machine learning in fintech lending: Evidence from the LendingClub consumer platform. *Financ Manag.* 2019;48(4):1009–29.
4. Jafar SH, Oyedele OM, Nawaah D, Bolanle AS. Exploring leadership challenges for adoption of digital innovation and sustainability. In: *Innovation ecosystems and sustainable technologies.* Emerald Publishing Limited; 2025. p. 253–69.
5. Nawaah D, Asare PY, Quarshie MA. Climate finance and natural capital: Linking global initiatives with local impact. In: *Climate neutrality through smart eco-innovation and environmental sustainability.* Springer Nature; 2025. p. 317–32.
6. Bazarbash M. Fintech in financial inclusion: Machine learning applications in credit risk [IMF Working Paper No. 19/109]. 2019. https://www.imf.org/en/Publications/WP/Issues/2019/05/24/Fintech-in-Financial-Inclusion-Machine-Learning-Applications-in-Credit-Risk-46953
7. Quarshie MA, Akhtar S, Nawaah D. Barriers to breakthroughs: The crucial role of support services in advancing accounting practices, financial literacy and performance in disability-led SMEs. *Qual Quant.* 2025;59:1–23.
8. Addy WA, Ajayi-Nifise AO, Bello BG, Tula ST, Odeyemi O, Falaiye T. AI in credit scoring: A comprehensive review of models and predictive analytics. *Glob J Eng Technol Adv.* 2024;18(2):118–29.
9. Locatelli R, Pepe G, Salis F. *Artificial intelligence and credit risk.* Springer Books; 2022.
10. Mahmud MR, Hoque MR, Ahammad T, Hasib MNH, Hasan MM. Advanced AI-driven credit risk assessment for Buy Now, Pay Later (BNPL) and e-commerce financing: Leveraging machine learning, alternative data, and predictive analytics for enhanced financial scoring. *J Bus Manag Stud.* 2024;6(2):180–9.
11. Susana DMP. Optimizing credit scoring models in face of global economic uncertainty: A comprehensive risk analysis in banking loans [Master's thesis]. Universidade NOVA de Lisboa, Portugal; 2024.
12. Frost J, Gambacorta L, Huang Y, Shin HS, Zbinden P. BigTech and the changing structure of financial intermediation [BIS Working Paper No. 779]. 2019. https://www.bis.org/publ/work779.htm
13. Best J. Redefining poverty as risk and vulnerability: Shifting strategies of liberal economic governance. *Third World Q.* 2013;34(1):109–29.
14. Bank for International Settlements. *The use of artificial intelligence and machine learning by financial institutions.* BIS; 2021.
15. Holzmann R, Jørgensen S. Social risk management: A new conceptual framework for social protection, and beyond. *Int Tax Public Finance.* 2001;8:529–56.
16. Quarshie MA, Djimatey R, Akhtar S, Nawaah D. Maximizing financial efficiency through technological synergy: Unleashing ICT for enhanced cash management in SMEs. *J Int Counc Small Bus.* 2025:1–31.
17. Stiglitz JE. Participation and development: Perspectives from the comprehensive development paradigm. *Rev Dev Econ.* 2002;6(2):163–82.
18. Van Greuning H, Bratanovic SB. *Analyzing banking risk: A framework for assessing corporate governance and risk management.* World Bank Publications; 2020.

19. Wilson TA. Supporting social enterprises to support vulnerable consumers: The example of community development finance institutions and financial exclusion. *J Consum Policy.* 2012;35:197–213.
20. Baesens B, Van Gestel T, Stepanova M, Suykens J, Vanthienen J. Benchmarking state-of-the-art classification algorithms for credit scoring. *J Oper Res Soc.* 2003;54(6):627–35. https://doi.org/10.1057/palgrave.jors.2601545
21. Lessmann S, Baesens B, Seow HV, Thomas LC. Benchmarking state-of-the-art classification algorithms for credit scoring. *Eur J Oper Res.* 2015;247(1):124–36. https://doi.org/10.1016/j.ejor.2015.05.030
22. Hurley M, Adebayo J. Credit scoring in the era of big data. *Yale J Law Technol.* 2017;18(1):148–216. https://yjolt.org/credit-scoring-era-big-data
23. Crook J. Credit scoring and its applications. *J Oper Res Soc.* 2002;52:997–1006.
24. Domingos P. A few useful things to know about machine learning. *Commun ACM.* 2012;55(10):78–87. https://doi.org/10.1145/2347736.2347755
25. Basel Committee on Banking Supervision. *International convergence of capital measurement and capital standards.* Bank for International Settlements; 2006. https://www.bis.org/publ/bcbs128.htm
26. Kahneman D, Tversky A. Prospect theory: An analysis of decision under risk. *Econometrica.* 1979;47(2):263–91. https://doi.org/10.2307/1914185
27. Laxmanan S. Awareness of Credit Score Mechanism in India: A Study with reference to Credit Information Bureau India Limited (CIBIL). 2020.
28. CASHe. SLQ-based lending and financial inclusion. 2023. https://www.cashe.co.in/
29. Shi, S, Tse, R, Luo, W. et al. Machine learning-driven credit risk: A systemic review. *Neural Comput Applic.* 2022;34(17):14327–39. https://doi.org/10.1007/s00521-022-07472-2
30. Ghosh S. *India Stack and digital public infrastructure: Building a new credit architecture.* NITI Aayog Discussion Paper; 2021. https://www.niti.gov.in/
31. Binns R, Veale M, Van Kleek M, Shadbolt N. "It's reducing a human being to a percentage": Perceptions of justice in algorithmic decisions. In: *Proc CHI Conf Hum Factors Comput Syst.* 2018;1–14. https://doi.org/10.1145/3173574.3173951
32. European Commission. General Data Protection Regulation (GDPR). 2016. https://gdpr.eu/
33. European Commission. General Data Protection Regulation (GDPR). 2016. https://eur-lex.europa.eu/legal-content/EN/TXT/?uri=CELEX:32016R0679
34. MeitY. Digital Personal Data Protection Act, 2023. Government of India; 2023. https://www.meity.gov.in/
35. Adeoye OB, Addy WA, Ajayi-Nifise AO, Odeyemi O, Okoye CC, Ofodile OC. Leveraging AI and data analytics for enhancing financial inclusion in developing economies. *Finance Account Res J.* 2024;6(3):288–303.
36. Omokhoa HE, Odionu CS, Azubuike C, Sule AK. AI-powered fintech innovations for credit scoring, debt recovery, and financial access in microfinance and SMEs. *Gulf J Adv Bus Res.* 2024;2(6):411–22.
37. Ribeiro MT, Singh S, Guestrin C. "Why should I trust you?": Explaining the predictions of any classifier. In: *Proc 22nd ACM SIGKDD Int Conf Knowl Discov Data Min.* 2016;1135–44. https://doi.org/10.1145/2939672.2939778
38. Upstart. Upstart Q4 2022 Financial Results. 2022. https://www.upstart.com/
39. Konina A. Banks as delegated regulators of technology. *Alta Law Rev.* 2021;59:753.
40. Consumer Financial Protection Bureau. CFPB issues circular on adverse action notice requirements. 2021. https://www.consumerfinance.gov/about-us/newsroom/
41. Consumer Financial Protection Bureau. CFPB warns that Black-box credit models may violate the law. 2021. https://www.consumerfinance.gov/about-us/newsroom/
42. Hemachandran K, Rodriguez RV, editors. *The business of the metaverse: How to maintain the human element within this new business reality.* CRC Press; 2023.

43. Frost J, Gambacorta L, Huang Y, Shin HS, Zbinden P. BigTech and the changing structure of financial intermediation. *Econ Policy*. 2019;34(100):761–99. https://doi.org/10.1093/epolic/eiaa003
44. Galindo J, Tamayo P. Credit risk assessment using statistical and machine learning: Basic methodology and risk modeling applications. *Comput Econ*. 2000;15:107–43.
45. Moscato V, Picariello A, Sperlí G. A benchmark of machine learning approaches for credit score prediction. *Expert Syst Appl*. 2021;165:113986.
46. Bhatore S, Mohan L, Reddy YR. Machine learning techniques for credit risk evaluation: A systematic literature review. *J Bank Financ Technol*. 2020;4(1):111–38.

# 8 AI-Driven Fraud Detection and Prevention Strategies

*Dzisenu Dziedzorm and Kotagiri Sai Deepak*

## 8.1 INTRODUCTION

### 8.1.1 The Growing Threat of Financial Fraud in the Digital Era

With increasing digital transactions, internet banking, and e-commerce platforms, the risk of financial fraud has significantly increased [1]. While technological innovations eased up access to financial services, they also provided room for criminals to exploit the flaws of identity authentication, payment systems, and financial regulations. The transition to cashless economies and digital banking has led to a significant surge in fraud cases; financial crimes have grown alongside rising financial technology adoption across Europe [2]. Identity theft, payment fraud, and digital banking scams are on the rise, and fraud-related losses in the European financial system amounted to €1.5 billion in a year according to the European Banking Authority [3, 4]. Traditional fraud detection methods based on human supervision and static heuristic-based mechanisms struggle to adapt to the evolving tactics of fraudsters [5, 6]. Artificial intelligence (AI)-powered anti-fraud solutions are analysing enormous transaction records and noting anomalies, such as a sudden spike in activity, to immediately signal suspicious activity [7]. To combat this growing threat, the European Union (EU) has amended laws and encouraged the adoption of AI-driven fraud-detection technologies. Already, banks across Europe are starting to implement and adopt AI algorithms that can learn from past fraudulent activity, predict future fraud trends, and detect cyberthreats at a much faster rate than human analysts [8]. The role that AI plays in fraud prevention has become essential; it is central to financial security in the digital economy [9, 10].

### 8.1.2 Key Drivers of AI Adoption in Fraud Prevention

Recently, rising sophistication in financial fraud has mandated the implementation of advanced AI-driven strategies for fraud detection [11–13]. There are various factors that have triggered quickening the adoption of AI in fraud prevention in Europe:

a. *Cyber Threats Evolving at a Boundless Speed*: Cybercriminals are deploying AI-powered deepfakes, cloned identities, and automated fraud models to evade conventional security measures [14]. In addition, AI also helps

DOI: 10.1201/9781003611646-8

in advancing predictive monitoring, adaptive risk assessments (which can ensure that security is not compromised by new threats) and features on fraud detection systems, etc.

b. *Regulatory Compliance and EU Directives*: The EU has passed strict legislation surrounding financial fraud, such as the Revised Payment Services Directive (PSD2) and the General Data Protection Regulation (GDPR), which requires financial institutions to implement more robust fraud detection capabilities. Real-time transactional data analysis by AI models assists banks in compliance of these regulations along with maintaining robust security practices [15].
c. *Growing Digital Payment and Cryptocurrency Payment*: Cryptocurrency, utilizing blockchain-based financial services, and DeFi are bringing in new risks of fraud such as money laundering, phishing, and illicit financial flows [16–18]. Fraud detection using AI helps financial companies monitor suspicious blockchain transactions that can help in better enforcement of anti-money laundering (AML) norms.
d. *Need for Real-Time Fraud Detection*: Traditional fraud detection usually involves a postmortem investigation; fraud is detected only after losses occurred [19]. AI-based fraud detection is carried out in real time and can detect fraud attempts before they can be executed, reducing monetary losses and improving consumer trust [20].

As AI is becoming popular in fraud detection, AI-based financial security will pave a way for Digital Banking Security and E-commerce Security for the new age [21].

## 8.2 THEORETICAL FRAMEWORK

The utilization of AI for financial fraud detection has theoretical foundations and models that have been proven to be effective. Through the lens of established theories from computational and behavioural finance, this section critically assesses the use of AI approaches in practical financial security.

### 8.2.1 A Theoretical View on AI Methods in Fraud Detection

Various methods of machine learning (ML) and deep learning are used in AI-driven fraud detection that are aligned with theoretical paradigms such as Computational Learning Theory and the Fraud Triangle Theory. These models depict the conditions that give rise to fraud as well as how AI systems learn to recognize a particular pattern of fraud [22]. Based on the Outlier Detection Theory, AI systems apply unsupervised learning methods, which allow for the detection of unusual financial behaviour. Such algorithms scan data in large transaction databases and leave one identifiable pattern in deviation from the user behaviour, and they could even solve the problem of fraud transactions ahead of time. ML based on AI-powered risk-scoring models provides probabilistic risk scores for transactions using the Bayesian Decision Theory. Using historical patterns of fraud layered on real time behavioural analysis, these algorithms predict the likelihood of fraud, enabling financial institutions to better allocate their investigative resources. Deep learning, including models such as Convolutional Neural Networks (CNNs), Recurrent Neural Networks (RNNs), is based on the science of Artificial Neural Network Theory [23] and has achieved exceptional performance managing huge volumes of financial data. So far, traditional statistical fraud detection approaches are substituted with these models, as they are capable of better accuracy in pattern recognition and anomaly [24]. Natural language processing approaches leverage the Computational Linguistics Framework [25] to analyse text-based financial transactions by detecting deceitful communication patterns in financial statements, phishing emails, and e-mails. This method enhances early fraud detection [26] because it enables the detection of fraudulent intention even before transactions.

### 8.2.2 AI-Powered Identity Verification and Behavioural Analytics

In fact, the use of behavioural analytics is consistent with the Prospect Theory and the Behavioural Biometrics Framework. These theories describe how AI can be used for detecting abnormal behaviour in a user interaction and cognitive bias for engaging in a fraudulent activity:

a. *Behavioural Monitoring Using AI:* Inspired by ideas derived from Human-Computer Interaction (HCI) research, behavioural analytics, after collecting usage data from financial systems, uses AI to monitor user activities within it [27]. These algorithms identify abnormal behaviour that may indicate fraud, such as frequent logins, unusual money movement, or contradictory geolocation data.
b. *AI-Enabled Authentication:* Financial institutions are relying more and more on biometrics as a tool for Authentication driven by the Biometric Security Model [28]. These models use voice authentication, keystroke dynamics, and facial recognition to validate identities and block unauthorized entries.

As Zhang et al. [25] noted, the increased use of AI-created deepfake faces for facilitating financial fraud highlights the pressing need for AI-based biometric security. As a result, current examples of this technology being used on a mass scale include organized crime syndicates across Europe using AI-generated deep-fakes for realistic identity creation to allow or facilitate illegal financial transactions, as noted in a 2023 Europol report [29]. In response to the enactment of legislation such as the European AI Act (2023), many institutions, especially in the financial sector, have laid down AI-based biometric authentication systems aimed to prevent illegal access or a transaction at the account level. This framework provides a theory with implications of a multidisciplinary approach to AI-based authorities in order to enhance financial security through a combination of computational, linguistic, and behaviour model [30].

## 8.3 ETHICAL ISSUES AND AI TECHNIQUES IN FRAUD DETECTION

### 8.3.1 AI-Driven Fraud Detection Strategies

With criminal groups making increasing use of sophisticated digital tools, automating fraud and using AI to perpetrate fraud at scale without detection [31, 32], schemes around financial fraud have become increasingly complex. Financial fraud detection becomes more and more easier with real-time analytics of massive transaction datasets with anomalies via AI-powered strategies that allow financial institutions to take pre-emptive action to prevention by conducting operation itself even before fraud actually occurs to save financial losses. Unlike these traditional fraud detection systems that rely on static rule-based algorithms, AI-based fraud detection systems learn to evolve new patterns of fraud as they emerge [33, 34]. Pattern recognition, anomaly detection, and behavioural analysis AI and ML systems make it easier for financial institutions to distinguish between real and dubious transactions, which serves as the foundation of AI-driven fraud detection measures [35, 36]. These systems learn continuously from previous cases of fraud, enhancing the accuracy of detection over time. In fact, one of the most powerful benefits of AI for fraud detection is the ability to analyse vast amounts of structured and unstructured financial data (from transaction logs and customer behaviour to communication records and regulatory filing) allowing institutions to replace gut instinct security decisions with risk-based solutions. As many digital fraud cases occurred in the European financial sector, the financial regulators and many financial institutions are asking on activity-based solutions where AI-powered fraud detection capabilities have been deployed [37–39]. European banks have sped up the adoption of AI, especially after the Wirecard scandal in Germany in 2020, where a fintech firm claimed €1.9 billion in non-existent assets. The Wirecard Scandal highlighted the shortcomings of existing financial oversight mechanisms and systems and made a clear case for AI spearheaded fraud detection tools instead of human audits. For a larger mass of money deception, European financial institutions have now adopted AI-based fraud detection systems. The European Central Bank (ECB) had ordered banks to have more robust fraud detection, including ML algorithms for detecting high-risk transactions in real time [40]. Using advanced AI strategies, financial organizations can reduce the risk of fraud while complying with ever-changing requirements from regulators.

### 8.3.2 AI in Transaction Monitoring and Anomaly Detection

Real-time transaction monitoring is perhaps the most valuable way to make use of AI in the fraud prevention and detection field [41–44]. With thousands of millions of transaction deals in a day, the financial institutions cannot practically review every single transaction to find a hint of fraud activity through human analysis. Fraud detection models powered by AI will analyse the patterns of the frequency and number of transactions that the user executes, the usage behaviour by the user establishing a sort of profile and, nowadays, also the geolocation data of the user [45–48]. AI models learn from new patterns of transactions and, therefore, can identify fraud that they have never seen before, whereas static, rule-based systems cannot. In the case of an AI system, if somebody does a transfer involving big amounts of money to offshore accounts, or any other financial movements, in any high-risk jurisdiction, the AI will immediately flag the activity for further investigation.

There are numerous cases of high-profile fraud in Europe that have been successfully mitigated with AI-based transaction monitoring and hence neither party has suffered financial losses. Amongst them, the most notorious was the identification of bogus claims for the COVID-19 relief fund in the United Kingdom in 2021 [38]. The UK government step forward with help loans for those impacted by the pandemic. Yet nearly £5 billion was claimed fraudulently through false business identities and forged financial documents [49, 50]. Fraud detection systems powered by AI and used by the UK's financial crime task force used algorithms to flag suspicious applications for the funds by identifying inconsistencies across company records, tax records, and transaction data [50]. Prior to the disbursal of payments, these AI models flagged fraudulent applications, resulting in billions in taxpayer dollars saved.

In 2022, a multinational bank in France detected a case involving its monitoring solution reporting many unauthorized cross-border transactions related to a money laundering syndicate [50] highlighting again the significance of AI-enabled transaction monitoring. Using their AI-powered anomaly detection models, the financial institution discovered the history of multiple, lower-value transactions structured below detection thresholds, allowing them to notify regulators and stop the subsequent unauthorized funds transfer.

A variety of ML and AI techniques will secure the global financial transaction process as financial fraud tactics become more advanced, and as such, the real-time alert anomaly detection systems will provide a better defence against this growing malaise [51–53]. Unsupervised ML algorithms will be used to detect fraud patterns without requiring labelled data. It is anticipated that these algorithms will improve the accuracy of actual fraud detection and minimize false positives [54, 55]. Hence, legitimate transactions that are incorrectly flagged as inappropriate and that can cause serious harm to a financial institution through customer relationship damage and associated metrics.

## 8.4 FUTURE TRENDS AND POLICY IMPLICATIONS

### 8.4.1 The Future Scope of AI in Fraud Detection and Prevention

AI-enabled fraud detection is set up for massive dislocation as banks, governments, and tech continue to pump capitalism into next-gen AI [56]. In a European context, where financial fraud is still a significant issue, there are several trends that will shape the future of AI-based fraud prevention [57, 58]. One of the most favoured waits is the combination of Blockchain with A. In all, blockchain with its decentralized and immutable character makes it much harder for fraudsters to modify financial records, or create synthetic identities [59], therefore the ability of AI-based platforms to analyse the blockchain to enable real-time detection of collated transactions, and then trigger alerts whenever anomalies are detected, seems to be a viable solution for banks searching for this kind of decentralized confirmation mechanism. Another emerging trend is employing AI-based facial recognition and biometric verification for fraud prevention [30, 59]. As identity theft and synthetic identity fraud are growing, AI-based facial recognition systems are being used for user authentication during high-value purchases, credit application processing and account onboarding. As all of those still in the states struggle to pick up the pieces from people hijacking passwords with dark web data, European banks are already pouring funds into AI-powered, biometrically based authentication tools that guarantee that even if a criminal has the credentials of a customer, they cannot invade the privacy of a live, actual customer. This would help in getting a step further in predictive fraud analysis, where institutions would be able to predict not only when, but also where fraud could take place. Instead of responding to the fraud in hindsight, AI-based predictive models consider historical fraud patterns, trends in user behaviour, and other external risk factors to predict fraud proactively. This proactive approach towards fraud prevention trends will create a more sustainable environment for financial institutions to reduce fraud losses and improve financial stability.

### 8.4.2 Policy Recommendations to Prevent Fraud in an AI-Governed Context

With a focus on the EU's AI Act, European regulators are drafting policies to regulate the application of ML for fraud prevention and are mandating AI models be accountable, fair, and interpretable. Policymakers have primary levers they can wield to support AI-inhibited fraud prevention including:

a. *Bias Audit:* Models of AI used for fraud detection should be audited for bias to ensure that specific population groups are not over-targeted.
b. *Having Cooperation on Detection AI within Jurisdictions:* Financial fraud crimes usually occur and are committed by perpetrator that affect citizens of many countries at once which caused them to need international cooperation.
c. *Governance*: European financial regulators should create common AI-based fraud detection policies that allow EU financial institutions to exchange fraud intelligence in real-time while permitting vast lapses of security.
d. *Bolstering Consumer Protection and Transparency:* The fraud detection models used by financial institutions for protecting consumer interests should be explainable and auditable [58]. Customers should be able to dispute false fraud flags and ask for clarity on AI-driven financial security determinations.

Through these policy efforts, regulators can help position AI as a tool that fights fraud rather than introducing new ethical and legal challenges.

## 8.5 CONCLUSION

Today, AI-powered fraud detection and prevention measures are an indispensable staple of secure financial ecosystems. As cybercriminals hone ever more sophisticated fraud, non-automated fraud detection simply will not work anymore. Financial institutions are rethinking how to prevent fraud before it happens with AI-based real-time transaction monitoring, anomaly detection, and biometric verification. AI adoption to prevent fraud in Europe, already accelerated by major fraud cases such as the Wirecard scandal in Germany, COVID-19 relief fund frauds in the United Kingdom, and cross-border money laundering in France, has been further triggered by the pandemic. As financial institutions ramp up investments in security powered by AI, ethical AI governance, regulatory compliance, and transparency against AI-powered fraud detection will all be critical in shaping a defraudable digital economy.

## REFERENCES


1. Udeh EO, Amajuoyi P, Adeusi KB, Scott AO. The role of big data in detecting and preventing financial fraud in digital transactions. *World J Adv Res Rev.* 2024;22(2):1746–60.
2. Sigetova K, Uzikova L, Dotsenko T, Boyko A. Recent trends in the financial crime of the world. *Financ Credit Act Probl Theory Pract.* 2022;5(46):258–70.
3. Malik MY, Jafar SH, Dixit A. Efficiency analysis and macroeconomic determinants of non-tax revenues. *Indian Econ J.* 2025. https://doi.org/10.1177/00194662251330385.
4. Reznik O, Samsin R, Nikolenko L, Butyrska I, Kozakova I. Examining Ukraine's approaches and obstacles in addressing cyber-financial fraud amid armed conflict. *J Inf Syst Eng Manag.* 2025;10(10s):330–46. https://doi.org/10.52783/jisem.v10i10s.1382.
5. Quarshie MA, Akhtar S, Nawaah D. Barriers to breakthroughs: The crucial role of support services in advancing accounting practices, financial literacy and performance in disability-led SMEs. *Qual Quant.* 2025;59:1–23.
6. Xia P, Zhu X, Charles V, Zhao X, Peng M. A novel heuristic-based selective ensemble prediction method for digital financial fraud risk. *IEEE Trans Eng Manag.* 2024; 71:8002–8018.
7. Aziz LAR, Andriansyah Y. The role of AI in modern banking: An exploration of AI-driven approaches. *Rev Contemp Bus Anal.* 2023;6(1):110–32.
8. Bansal U, Bharatwal S, Bagiyam DS, Kismawadi ER. Fraud detection in the era of AI. In: *AI-driven decentralized finance.* IGI Global; 2024. p. 139–60.
9. Nawaah D, Asare PY, Quarshie MA. Climate finance and natural capital: Linking global initiatives with local impact. In: *Climate neutrality through smart eco-innovation and environmental sustainability.* Springer Nature; 2025. p. 317–32.
10. Bello OA, Olufemi K. Artificial intelligence in fraud prevention: Exploring techniques and applications—Challenges and opportunities. *Comput Sci IT Res J.* 2024; 5(6):1505–20.
11. El Abiad Z, Abraham R, ElChaarani H, Skaf Y, Binsaddig RO, Jafar SH. The impact of CEO characteristics on the financial performance of family businesses listed in the Euronext Exchange. *J Risk Financ Manag.* 2024;17(3):129.
12. Salim M, Khan PA, Jalil NA, Johl SK, Jafar SH, Irfan F, Khan M. Fusion of blockchain and sustainable development goals: A bibliometric analysis for future trends. *KnE Soc Sci.* 2023:633–54.
13. Singh A, Shanker N. Redefining cybercrimes in light of artificial intelligence: Emerging threats and challenges. *Int J Innov Sci Eng Manag.* 2024;3:192–201.

14. Agarwal U, Rishiwal V, Tanwar S, Yadav M. Blockchain and crypto forensics: Investigating crypto frauds. *Int J Netw Manag.* 2024;34(2):e2255.
15. Hemachandran K, Rodriguez RV, editors. *The business of the metaverse: How to maintain the human element within this new business reality.* CRC Press; 2023.
16. Quarshie MA, Djimatey R, Akhtar S, Nawaah D. Maximizing financial efficiency through technological synergy: Unleashing ICT for enhanced cash management in SMEs. *J Int Counc Small Bus.* 2025:1–31.
17. Hilal W, Gadsden SA, Yawney J. Financial fraud: A review of anomaly detection techniques and recent advances. *Expert Syst Appl.* 2022;193:116429.
18. Khurana R. Fraud detection in ecommerce payment systems: The role of predictive AI in real-time transaction security and risk management. *Int J Appl Mach Learn Comput Intell.* 2020;10(6):1–32.
19. Valiant LG. A theory of the learnable. *Commun ACM.* 1984;27(11):1134–42. https://doi.org/10.1145/1968.1972.
20. Hemachandran K, Rodriguez RV, editors. *Artificial intelligence for business: An implementation guide containing practical and industry-specific case studies.* CRC Press; 2023.
21. Hodge V, Austin J. A survey of outlier detection methodologies. *Artif Intell Rev.* 2004; 22:85–126.
22. McCulloch WS, Pitts W. A logical calculus of the ideas immanent in nervous activity. *Bull Math Biophys.* 1943;5(4):115–33. https://doi.org/10.1007/BF02478259.
23. Stephanidis C, Salvendy G, Antona M, Chen JY, Dong J, Duffy VG, et al. Seven HCI grand challenges. *Int J Hum Comput Interact.* 2019;35(14):1229–66.
24. Jafar SH, Oyedele OM, Nawaah D, Bolanle AS. Exploring leadership challenges for adoption of digital innovation and sustainability. In: *Innovation ecosystems and sustainable technologies.* Emerald Publishing Limited; 2025. p. 253–69.
25. Zhang CJ, Gill AQ, Liu B, Anwar MJ. AI-based identity fraud detection: A systematic review. *arXiv Prepr.* 2025. https://doi.org/10.48550/arXiv.2501.09239.
26. Shirish A, Komal S. A sociolegal inquiry on deepfakes. *Calif West Int Law J.* 2024; 54(2):6.
27. Jafar SH, Dhandhukia V, Kumar GB. Application of artificial intelligence in banking: A review. In: *Machine learning for business analytics.* Productivity Press; 2022. p. 145–51.
28. Hemachandran K, George PM, Rodriguez RV, Kulkarni RM, Roy S. Performance analysis of k-nearest-neighbour classification algorithms. In: *Smart intelligent computing.* IOS Press; 2021. p. 9–13.
29. Sharma R, Mehta K, Sharma P. Role of artificial intelligence and machine learning in fraud detection. In: *Risks and challenges of AI-driven finance.* IGI Global; 2024. p. 90–120.
30. Mishra AK, Tyagi AK, Richa, Patra SR. Introduction to machine learning in banking and finance. In: *Blockchain technology and AI.* Springer; 2024. p. 239–90.
31. Sultanova A. *Il livello di sviluppo e implementazione del framework ESG in tutta Europa: Uno studio comparativo* [Master's thesis]. Univ Studi di Pavia; 2023. https://hdl.handle.net/20.500.14239/29287.
32. Ahmadi S. Advancing fraud detection in banking: Real-time applications of explainable AI (XAI). *J Electr Syst.* 2022;18(4):141–50.
33. Burugulla JKR. The future of digital financial security: Integrating AI, cloud, and big data. *MSW Manag J.* 2024;34(2):711–30.
34. Jafar SH, Akhtar S, Johl SK. AI in insurance. In: *Artificial intelligence for business.* Productivity Press; 2023. p. 164–73.
35. Murrar F. Fraud schemes during COVID-19: A comparison from FATF countries. *J Financ Crime.* 2022;29(2):533–40.

36. Baechler S. Document fraud: Will your identity be secure in the 21st century? *Eur J Crim Policy Res.* 2020;26(3):379–98.
37. Asher J. *Fraud markers, de-Banking, and financial crime.* Taylor & Francis; 2025.
38. Vorobyev I, Krivitskaya A. Reducing false positives in bank anti-fraud systems. *Comput Secur.* 2022;120:102786.
39. Atkinson RD. “It is going to kill us!” and other myths about AI. *IUP J Comput Sci.* 2018;12(4):7–56.
40. Hemachandran K, Rodriguez RV, Toshniwal R, Junaid M, Shaw L. Performance analysis of classification algorithms. In: *Intelligent sustainable systems.* Singapore: Springer; 2021. p. 191–202.
41. Jafar SH, Hemachandran K, ElChaarani H, Moturi S, Gupta N, editors. *Artificial intelligence for capital markets.* CRC Press; 2023.
42. Jafar SH, Kashid AU, Ghosh S, Srividhya S, Sharma D, Bodhankar A. Performance optimization of ATM networks. In: *2024 15th Int Conf Comput Commun Netw Technol.* IEEE; 2024. p. 1–5.
43. Kanjula MR, Sravya J. AI-driven security in banking. In: *Int ethical hacking conf.* Springer Nature; 2024. p. 225–32.
44. Paul E, Callistus O, Somtobe O, Esther T, Somto K, Clement O, Ejimofor I. Cybersecurity strategies for safeguarding data. *Int J Soft Comput.* 2023;14(3):1–16.
45. Seizov O, Wulf AJ. AI and transparency: A blueprint for EU regulation. *Eur Bus Law Rev.* 2020;31(4):611–640.
46. Abdiyeva-Aliyeva G, Hematyar M, Bakan S. Development of system for detection and prevention of cyber attacks using AI methods. In: *2021 2nd Global Conference for Advancement in Technology (GCAT).* IEEE; 2021. p. 1–5.
47. Ortynskyi V, Chornous Y, Pavliuk N. Cooperation in financial fraud investigation. *Balt J Econ Stud.* 2018;4(4):252–7.
48. Ahmad W, Vashist A, Sinha N, Prasad M, Shrivastava V, Muzamal JH. Transparency in fraud detection: XAI + federated learning. In: *ICSEDE Conf.* Springer; 2024. p. 139–56.
49. Olutimehin AT. Advancing cloud security in digital finance. In: *Cryptographic solutions and privacy challenges.* SCIENCEDOMAIN International; 2025.
50. Esoimeme E, Kamara P, Kwanue R. Reducing cross-border financial crime risks in AfCFTA. *Int J Curr Sci.* 2023;13(3):1–28.
51. Hemachandran K, Rodriguez RV. *Artificial intelligence for business.* CRC Press; 2023.
52. Jafar SH. Financial applications of Gaussian processes and Bayesian optimization. In: *Bayesian reasoning.* CRC; 2022. p. 111–22.
53. Ashfaq T, Khalid R, Yahaya AS, Aslam S, Azar AT, Alsafari S, Hameed IA. A machine learning and blockchain-based efficient fraud detection mechanism. *Sensors.* 2022;22(19):7162.
54. Baesens B, Van Gestel T, Stepanova M, Suykens J, Vanthienen J. Benchmarking state-of-the-art classification algorithms for credit scoring. *J Oper Res Soc.* 2003;54(6):627–35. https://doi.org/10.1057/palgrave.jors.2601545.
55. Lessmann S, Baesens B, Seow HV, Thomas LC. Benchmarking state-of-the-art classification algorithms for credit scoring. *Eur J Oper Res.* 2015;247(1):124–36. https://doi.org/10.1016/j.ejor.2015.05.030.
56. Hurley M, Adebayo J. Credit scoring in the era of big data. *Yale J Law Technol.* 2017;18(1):148–216. https://yjolt.org/credit-scoring-era-big-data.
57. Crook J. Credit scoring and its applications. *J Oper Res Soc.* 2002;52:997–1006.
58. Domingos P. A few useful things to know about machine learning. *Commun ACM.* 2012;55(10):78–87. https://doi.org/10.1145/2347736.2347755.
59. Basel Committee on Banking Supervision. *International convergence of capital measurement and capital standards.* Bank for International Settlements; 2006. https://www.bis.org/publ/bcbs128.htm.

# 9 AI in Sustainable Finance and ESG Analysis
## *A Practical Guide*

*Michael Ayikwei Quarshie, Cornelius Adorm-Takyi, Reginald Djimatey, and Dominic Achari*

## 9.1 INTRODUCTION

Sustainability has necessitated modifying contemporary business models to align with the changing dynamics of digital environments and the responsible use of emerging technologies to enhance current and future societal well-being. The Sustainable Development Goals (SDGs) articulate a practical context for global issues geared towards achieving a sustainable future. Stakeholders have argued that quite a significant funding, projected between US$ 5–7 trillion, is needed to achieve the SDG Agenda by 2030. Taking this into consideration, the importance of addressing challenges connected to sustainability is brought to bear. The calls for sustainable finance reflect the growing relevance of environmental, social, and governance (ESG) issues that must guide the decisions of institutions regarding their operations [1–3]. ESG has been duly acknowledged over the years for its strategic contribution to addressing sustainable development goals. Financial institutions over the years have observed with keen interest the influence of environmental concerns, especially the physical effect of climate concerns and the growing need to have a low-carbon society [4]. Social issues are also gaining ground owing to their implication on employees' welfare and labour practices, client loyalty and community engagement, as these sustainable practices must lead to addressing social standards. Governance is essential in an institution's relationship with its stakeholders. As such, governance in financial institutions must guarantee stability and trust, as effective governance resolves issues of malpractices and scandals and promotes ethical conduct [5]. The necessity of ESG considerations in the financial sector cannot be overemphasised. Financial institutions that adopt ESG principles comply with regulatory requirements from governments and international bodies that advocate for sustainability considerations.

ESG is vital for an institution's risk management strategy; thus, by incorporating ESG criteria, financial institutions can better mitigate environmental risks, social unrest, or governance scandals [6, 7]. Institutions that consider sustainability principles enhance their intangible assets, as evidenced by the growth of ESG funds' total assets from $41 trillion in 2022 to $50 trillion in 2024 [8–10]. Despite financial institutions' efforts to promote sustainability, their attempt to implement ESG concerns is


DOI: 10.1201/9781003611646-9

impeded by both internal and external hindrances. A critical concern emanates from data collection and quality issues. Thus, inconsistencies arise from unreliable and unstandardised ESG data, which makes it quite challenging to accurately compare the ESG performance of different investment portfolios [11]. Also, another hurdle is regulatory compliance and incorporating ESG concerns into the decision-making process and existing financial models. Ayaz and Zahid [3] intimated that globally, there is an acknowledgement of ESG's long-term benefit; however, financial institutions encounter short-term trade-offs that require them to balance the trade-offs and commit to sustainable goals strategically. In light of these prevailing challenges, implementing ESG concerns calls for a more comprehensive effort and concerted approach that is backed by a very strong commitment to sustainable business practices. Financial technology (Fintech) is vital in ameliorating these challenges via artificial intelligence (AI) integration in financial institutions' processes. AI deployment in the financial sector has rapidly altered its activities in contemporary times and has shaped the way financial institutions react to risk [12, 13]. AI's analysis of financial institutions' information is key in dealing with ESG concerns, and more importantly, this has come at a time when ESG concerns are crucial, thus, leveraging AI to achieve sustainable goals has become imperative.

## 9.2 AI APPLICATIONS IN ESG ANALYSIS AND SUSTAINABLE FINANCE

AI is being utilised to enhance ESG elements across various sectors. From a data collection and analysis perspective, AI, via natural language processing (NLP), is employed to extract ESG data, while deep learning is applied to analyse large ESG datasets to ascertain trends and insights and predictive models employed to estimate future ESG metrics [14]. Also, NLP is applied to review complaints arising from human rights violations and to improve lending practices by assessing borrowers' creditworthiness from a risk assessment viewpoint [15, 16]. Regarding investment and compliance-related issues, quantitative algorithms are applied to optimise ESG investment portfolios. In contrast, machine learning is used to monitor regulations to flag relevant new requirements and gather ESG data for compliance. From an environmental application perspective, AI is used to collect satellite and sensor data to evaluate environmental and physical risk exposure and quantify GHG emissions [9].

AI applications further enable financial institutions to evaluate enterprises' ESG performance, pricing fluctuations, and investments in carbon offset projects efficiently. AI through NLP and machine learning can detect biases from employee engagement surveys. AI algorithms are further employed to measure employee sentiments regarding internal ESG efforts as well as to track vendor ESG performance over time, analyse customer information to ascertain preferences and behaviours related to ESG products and analyse community feedback to inform sustainability initiatives [17]. Kotsantonis and Serafeim [16] espoused that the ESG governance framework assesses how an institution monitors its internal controls, compliance, and adherence to corporate policies. For example, AI is deployed to trace the environmental effect of products within the supply chain, ensuring transparency and the institution's supply chain disclosure practices. AI, through textual analysis, can identify and measure the most relevant ESG incidents and commitments and also examine real-time corporate information to assess concerns about child labour, working conditions, and corruption scandals [7, 18, 19].

## 9.3 CASE STUDIES AND INDUSTRY APPLICATIONS

AI's deployment in industries has gained some prominence, and its pertinent role in ESG issues has paved the way to innovatively deal with sustainability practices [20–24]. For instance, applications of AI can be observed in the Bank of America and Citibank operations as these banks utilise AI in risk management principles and finance, including AI integration in ESG strategies while optimising efficiencies in business practices [10, 15]. Similarly, HDFC Bank and HSBC have applied AI for customer operations and loan automation and track companies that benefit from improved ESG risk [25–28]. JP Morgan Chase, via AI, has integrated double materiality into its ESG process and Morgan Stanley and NatWest, for example, use AI for sustainable investing and enhancing SMEs' ESG data [11, 29]. These initiatives demonstrate clearly how AI can effectively support the innovation mechanisms that are economically viable and conform to sustainability principles in the financial sector. AI has also seen some applications in projects in the areas of forest restoration, soil and air quality, and waste management in recent times [30–32]. AI is further deployed in air quality data processing for pollution sources, pattern analysis, automating waste sorting processes, optimising recycling methods, and mitigating traffic and industrial emission management strategies [6, 33].

## 9.4 OPPORTUNITIES, CHALLENGES, AND FUTURE TRENDS

AI has grown to become an important pillar in ESG, considering the role it plays in ensuring institutions align their objectives with sustainable standards. The importance of AI in ESG considerations emanates from its potential to drive creativity and innovation and optimise resource use that promotes environmental consciousness [34–37]. Although AI integration has become an integral part of most institutions, especially financial institutions, implementing ESG is impeded by some hindrances, including ethical issues, regulatory inconsistencies, and challenges in aligning AI with sustainable goals [38–41]. The issue of reliable and quality data has emerged as a challenge as financial institutions strive to provide accurate information to easily compare ESG performance among different investments. Integrating ESG criteria into existing financial models has become one of the major challenges of financial institutions as they focus primarily on financial issues rather than ESG risks and opportunities [42, 43]. Changing this model often requires technical adjustments and a major shift within the institution to cultivate an appreciation of ESG issues. The ESG environment calls for the urgent need for institutions to ensure compliance and demonstrate ethical behaviour in business conduct [44], as they may have to forgo some opportunities to achieve sustainability goals despite the associated challenges. Transforming an institution to embrace the ESG framework entails some investment in corporate strategy [45]. The strategy should include prioritising finance sources and leveraging AI analytical power geared towards improved ESG practices in line with international standards [37].

## 9.5 CONCLUSIONS

Including AI in sustainable finance offers a convincing path to realise a more robust and environmentally friendly financial system. Financial institutions may augment their significant contributions to achieving sustainable development and guarantee that their activities complement their main goals through the use of AI models. Although the use of AI in corporate operations can bring about positive change and enhance the performance of an organisation, it also requires extra actions to actively solve issues around data protection and ethics. Through collaboration, involvement of stakeholders, and adherence to ethical standards, institutions can advance their path more sustainably. Financial institutions must be recognised as part of the solution to achieve sustainable goals if they are to make use of the transforming possibilities of AI within the framework of ESG. The extent to which AI applications can reconcile technological advancement with ethical responsibility will determine its influence on sustainable finance. The changing financial sector offers results that provide vital support and direction for stakeholders, thus providing a framework for the suitable use of AI in sustainable finance policies.

## REFERENCES

1. Burnaev E, Mironov E, Shpilman A, Mironenko M, Katalevsky D. Practical AI cases for addressing ESG challenges. *Sustainability.* 2023;15:12731.
2. Musleh Al-Sartawi AMA, Hussainey K, Razzaque A. The role of artificial intelligence in sustainable finance. *J Sustain Financ Invest.* 2022;11:1–6.
3. Ayaz G, Zahid M. Trends, shifts, and prospects of sustainable finance research: A bibliometric analysis. *Sustain Account Manag Policy J.* 2024;15(5):1094–117.
4. Elouidani R, Outouzzalt A. *Artificial intelligence for sustainable finance: A bibliometric analysis.* Cham: Springer Nature Switzerland; 2022.
5. Quarshie MA, Akhtar S, Nawaah D. Barriers to breakthroughs: The crucial role of support services in advancing accounting practices, financial literacy and performance in disability-led SMEs. *Qual Quant.* 2025;59:1–23.
6. Ditlev-Simonsen CD. *A guide to sustainable corporate responsibility: From theory to action.* Switzerland: Palgrave Macmillan; 2022.
7. Jafar SH, Akhtar S, Johl SK. AI in insurance. In: *Artificial intelligence for business.* New York: Productivity Press; 2023. p. 164–73.
8. Quarshie MA, Djimatey R, Akhtar S, Nawaah D. Maximizing financial efficiency through technological synergy: Unleashing ICT for enhanced cash management in SMEs. *J Int Counc Small Bus.* 2025:1–31.
9. Adedoyin TO, Omotayo BA, Wilhelmina AA, Chinwe CO, Onyeka CO, Chinonye EU. Promoting sustainability in finance with AI: A review of current practices and future potential. *World J Adv Res Rev.* 2024;21(3):590–607.
10. Croce M. *Sustainable finance and ESG investing: A guide for investment professionals.* London: Routledge; 2023.
11. Jain R, Jain P, Jain R. ESG and financial performance: Evidence from global markets. *Int J Financ Econ.* 2023;28(2):1331–46.

12. Duppati G, Rao NV, Locke S, Narayan A. ESG disclosures and financial performance: Evidence from emerging markets. *Sustainability.* 2023;15(1):448.
13. Fatemi A, Fooladi I, Tehranian H. Valuation effects of corporate social responsibility. *J Bank Finance.* 2015;59:182–92.
14. Drempetic S, Klein C, Zwergel B. The influence of firm size on ESG scores: Corporate sustainability ratings under review. *J Bus Ethics.* 2020;167(2):333–60.
15. Husted BW, Allen DB. Corporate social strategy and competitive advantage. *Strategic Manag J.* 2007;28(2):123–44.
16. Kotsantonis S, Serafeim G. Four things no one will tell you about ESG data. *J Appl Corp Finance.* 2019;31(4):50–8.
17. Boffo R, Marshall C. *ESG investing: Practices, progress and challenges.* Paris: OECD; 2020.
18. Peloza J. The challenge of measuring financial impacts from investments in corporate social performance. *J Manage.* 2009;35(6):1518–41.
19. Berg F, Koelbel JF, Rigobon R. Aggregate confusion: The divergence of ESG ratings. *Rev Finance.* 2022;26(6):1315–41.
20. Murray A, Sinclair D. Ethical AI in sustainable investing: A comparative study. *J Ethics Comput Technol.* 2024;3(1):77–94.
21. Chen L, Zhang Z, Zhou Y. AI-based sustainability metrics in portfolio management. *Financ Innov.* 2023;9(2):55.
22. Hassan MK, Mollah S. Islamic finance and ESG: Intersections and prospects. *J Islamic Financ Account.* 2022;9(1):23–37.
23. Khan M, Serafeim G, Yoon A. Corporate sustainability: First evidence on materiality. *Account Rev.* 2016;91(6):1697–724.
24. Broadstock DC, Chan K, Cheng LT, Wang X. The role of ESG performance during times of financial crisis: Evidence from COVID-19 in China. *Financ Res Lett.* 2021; 38:101716.
25. Arjaliès DL, Mundy J. The use of management control systems to manage CSR strategy: A levers of control perspective. *Manage Account Res.* 2013;24(4):284–300.
26. Aboud A, Di Stasio F, Ullah S. The economic consequences of ESG disclosure: A contextual analysis. *Bus Strategy Environ.* 2022;31(1):1–15.
27. Chatterji AK, Levine DI, Toffel MW. How well do social ratings actually measure corporate social responsibility? *J Econ Manage Strategy.* 2009;18(1):125–69.
28. Alshahmy S, Sahiner M. Enhancing the issuance and monitoring of sustainable finance instruments through AI. In *Artificial intelligence, finance, and sustainability: Economic, ecological, and ethical implications* (pp. 217–241). Cham: Springer Nature Switzerland; 2024. https://doi.org/10.1007/978-3-031-66205-8_9.
29. Jain R, Jain P, Jain R. ESG risk and return: An emerging markets perspective. *J Emerging Market Finance.* 2022;21(3):344–60.
30. Khan M. Corporate sustainability performance and firm value: The mediating role of reputation. *Sustainability.* 2020;12(5):1843.
31. Lo K, Khemka A. AI-driven climate risk analysis in sustainable investment decisions. *J Climate Finance.* 2023;1(1):18–33.
32. Haider S, Mir B, Iqbal R. Big data and ESG investing: The rise of smart sustainable portfolios. *Data Sci Sustain.* 2022;4(2):99–115.
33. Heinkel R, Kraus A, Zechner J. The effect of green investment on corporate behavior. *J Financ Quant Anal.* 2001;36(4):431–49.
34. Khan M, Nadeem M. ESG disclosure and cost of equity capital: Evidence from emerging markets. *Emerg Markets Rev.* 2021;46:100729.
35. Oikonomou I, Brooks C, Pavelin S. The impact of corporate social performance on financial risk and utility: A longitudinal analysis. *Financ Manage.* 2012;41(2):483–515.

36. Orlitzky M, Schmidt FL, Rynes SL. Corporate social and financial performance: A meta-analysis. *Organiz Stud.* 2003;24(3):403–41.
37. OECD. *Business and finance outlook 2020: Sustainable and resilient finance.* Paris: OECD Publishing; 2020.
38. Scholtens B. Finance as a driver of corporate social responsibility. *J Bus Ethics.* 2006;68(1):19–33.
39. Buchholz RA, Rosenthal SB. Toward a contemporary conceptual framework for stakeholder theory. *J Bus Ethics.* 2005;58(1):137–48.
40. Freeman RE, Reed DL. Stockholders and stakeholders: A new perspective on corporate governance. *Calif Manage Rev.* 1983;25(3):88–106.
41. Sharfman MP, Fernando CS. Environmental risk management and the cost of capital. *Strategic Manage J.* 2008;29(6):569–92.
42. Shen H, Wu Y, Sun Q. Environmental, social, and governance investing: The China case. *China Econ Rev.* 2021;66:101597.
43. Unep FI. *Rethinking impact to finance the SDGs.* Geneva: United Nations Environment Programme Finance Initiative; 2018.
44. Tingbani I, Saidu S, Majid A. Board diversity and corporate social responsibility: Evidence from the UK. *Bus Strategy Environ.* 2020;29(8):3197–211.
45. United Nations. *Transforming our world: The 2030 agenda for sustainable development.* New York: United Nations; 2015.

# 10 An African Perspective on Artificial Intelligence and Climate Finance

*Wilson E. Herbert and Maureen N. Nwala*

## 10.1 INTRODUCTION

As nations attempt to address climate change, it is important to also draw from African perspectives on the incorporation of artificial intelligence (AI) in climate finance [1–3]. Leveraging AI can offer creative ways to address Africa's specific needs, from maximizing resource distribution to improving data interpretation for efficient decision-making. With AI technologies, Africa can discover new avenues for sustainable growth and climate finance mechanisms that will work significantly more effectively and be better able to trigger big environmental results. By interacting with AI, you strengthen local communities, and you make Africa incontournable in the worldwide challenge against climate change. Africa has been labelled as the 'last frontier' of the world for economic growth; but in the ongoing global climate narrative this poses a paradoxical challenge. The African continent makes up less than 4% of global greenhouse gas emissions [4], but it disproportionately suffers from the impact of climate change [4]. The rising temperatures, erratic weather patterns, and diminishing natural resources turn the economic and social ecosystem fragile, particularly in areas that are already struggling with food insecurity, poverty, and inequality. In the face of these daunting challenges, how does Africa secure its future? The answer is possibly in leveraging state-of-the-art technology, specifically AI, to transform climate finance and deliver sustainable investment solutions that address Africa's specific vulnerabilities.

Climate finance is the intentional mobilization and flow of funds to combat and adapt to climate change [5]. It requires investments from public and private sectors in projects like reducing emissions, advancing renewable energy and promoting sustainable development. International proclamations, like those in the context of the Paris Agreement or the UNFCCC, reinforce that it is developing countries need funds and technology support not more gesture and broken promises from developed countries. Yet, climate financing is particularly underfunded in high-risk, low-income African countries. Climate threats have deep roots in Africa due to its reliance on natural resources and climate sensitive sectors such as agriculture, fisheries, and energy. The region is experiencing extreme weather events, from drought in the Sahel to flooding in East Africa, while tides are rising along coastlines, all of which can pose existential threat to the livelihood and national economies. Widespread droughts in the Horn of Africa, for example, have wiped out crops and livestock, leaving millions hungry and


DOI: 10.1201/9781003611646-10

impoverished. Higher sea levels also threaten coastal urban areas such as Lagos, where flooding can impact transport, businesses, and people. These challenges require bold answers to the composition process that exchange long-standing finance solutions.

Climate change exacts a huge human cost in Africa. The ripple effects of climate change are displacing some communities, deepening food insecurity for others, and fuelling conflict over limited resources. Thus, worsening the social injustices that already make environmental degradation worse. Resource scarcity, for example, impacts women and children even more in rural areas, having to walk long distances to be able to gain access to water and having lower chances to a prosperous economic life. Ecologically, the Congo Basin (an essential carbon sink) is imperilled by deforestation and climate variability [6]. These challenges are the reason for specific investments in sustainable development: investments that fall under climate finance. By providing the opportunity for data-driven investments, AI can help fill the gaps in climate finance by enabling strategic, efficient, and effective investments to close Africa's financing gap [7, 8]. Innovation in Predictive analytics improves climate risk assessments and policymakers can better prioritize projects that support resilience. Similarly, AI-enabled platforms can improve transparency in green financing and ensure that capital is directed to the intended recipients and applied as desired. AI tools, furthermore, can optimize resource allocation by detecting critical climate issues and connecting them with specific solutions. Incorporating human-centric AI solutions will enable Africa to take a step towards being a nation that leverages climate finance, providing the key to international investments into the continent whilst also promoting local innovations that can be sustainable. By letting us know the weather forecasts accurately and by giving the accurate market details, AI-powered applications have had a significant role in the productivity enhancement of smallholder farmers. Working towards investment and policy alignment, this adaptation to changing conditions.

### 10.1.1 Background and Rationale

Climate financing refers to a funding required for implementing projects and programmes aimed at addressing climate change. From being a simple trend or buzzword, it has matured into what might be considered one of the defining features of public interventions in the climate space, with automation technology playing the primary role. Yet, the function of technology in climate finance has been poorly documented. It outlines the historical allocation of climate finance in Africa, evaluates the compulsory and elective measures that have been put in place to assist countries in taking effective climate actions and finally discusses the use and purpose of AI and blockchain in climate finance. The global need for climate finance will increase dramatically over the next couple of decades (new estimated global climate finance requirements are \$2–\$9 trillion per annum by 2030 and \$266 trillion in cumulative by 2050 to avoid global climate change and damage [9]). From 2020 to 2030, the total climate-related financing needs of African countries is estimated at USD 2.8 trillion, with around USD 500 billion needed by 2030 to fulfil their climate commitments [10]. Climate impacts will escalate, and with it the demand for climate finance. Estimates of climate finance indicate a large gap in financing for 2030 and 2050 where current flows are far under the necessary figures. Total climate finance required is based on estimates by organizations like Climate Policy Initiative (CPI). The figures also include both mitigation efforts and adaptation measures to manage climate change impacts.

Africa faces significant mitigation and adaptation costs, ranging from 5% to 17% of GDP, with the cost of adaptation estimated at USD 3.6 billion annually between 2006 and 2015 and USD 4.3 billion between 2016 and 2025 [11]. Mobilizing finance for Africa is a major barrier to securing support for adaptation and resilience. The key challenges include the availability of financial resources, technology transfer, and capacity development. Effective governance, institutional arrangements, and robust financial systems, especially regarding climate finance, are crucial to addressing these issues. The allocation of climate finance should involve discussions about who gets to spend the money, on what projects, and through which systems and types of funds. The remainder of this chapter is an overview of the mode of analysis and the types of challenges that this chapter is concerned with. Section 10.1 sets out a preliminary description of the basic context of the links between AI and climate finance. Section 10.2 explores the role that AI could play in climate finance and examines the key mechanisms and technologies that will be necessary for this role to be delivered. In Section 10.3, we explore AI as a powerful enabler of sustainable investment throughout Africa. It is a very important domain which has the potential to lead to economic development and at the same time tackle environment issues. AI in Climate Finance is an immense opportunity but also a challenge for Africa. Section 10.4 focuses on how to overcome barriers to adopt AI in climate finance across Africa. Section 10.5 identifies opportunities for improving AI-based climate finance in Africa. Concluding the chapter in Section 10.6 by emphasizing some best insights came out throughout the chapter.

## 10.2 THE POTENTIAL OF AI IN CLIMATE FINANCE

Climate finance can be significantly improved with AI-powered data analytics, machine learning, and predictive modelling to analyse, assess, mitigate, and manage climate-related risks and opportunities [12]. The analytical power of AI allows financial institutions to comprehend climate risk exposure, environmental coverage, and data-based investment decisions from large datasets. AI-based predictive models can mimic climate change effects by region, sector and asset level, allowing investors to forecast and measurement portfolio risk. Consequently, such predictive modelling is critical to shape financial instruments that promote climate resilience, agriculture, infrastructure, and energy sectors in Africa where climate impacts could be sudden and extreme. By deep learning and sophisticated analytics of climate data, AI can help deliver a more precise comprehension of the impacts of climate on financial systems, making it feasible to build portfolios that meet sustainable and low-carbon objectives.

### 10.2.1 THE ROLE OF AI IN CLIMATE FINANCE: KEY MECHANISMS AND TECHNOLOGIES

AI, particularly through techniques such as machine learning and predictive analytics, is transforming the face of climate finance, helping develop accurate models for predicting environmental developments and their economic impacts. A paraphrase: These technologies analyse complex climate data like satellite imagery, historical weather patterns, and emissions data, spotting trends, and predicting future conditions with much greater accuracy than traditional methods. The data can help investors through machine learning algorithms that provide new insights into how climate-related risks: both physical, like extreme weather conditions, and transition, such as changing agricultural productivity, may affect the value and return of assets. Using these predictions, algorithms analyse real-time data to forecast drought risk of specific areas, allowing investors to modify their portfolios to achieve financial goals alongside sustainability targets [13]. In this context, AI-driven climate risk assessments can provide useful information to policymakers by making it easier to create adaptation and resilience policies that are backed by data and calculations of projected economic and social impacts. Due to the often sudden and severe nature of climate impacts in Africa [14, 15], such insights are particularly important, with predictive models helping governments to allocate resources [13]. Predictive models can also guide investment decisions. Predictive analytics helps governments and local governments to predict and be prepared for extreme climate event such as flooding or drought through early warning and adaptation systems. Thus, AI can boost predictive abilities for climate finance, enabling enhanced risk management and thereby also resilient economies and communities throughout the continent while also aligning financial interests with sustainable development priorities [16, 17].

### 10.2.2 Big Data and Climate Data Analysis

Overcoming gaps in technology, expertise, and skills is essential for using big data to drive sustainable development in Africa. Data-driven insights through AI can spot the regions that are most susceptible to climate-related problems and allow for focused investments in adaptation and mitigation projects. For example, in agriculture, the utility of AI lies in analysing soil characteristics, rainfall records, and crop health parameters to encourage the climate-smart practices [18]. This allows investors to finance climate-resilient projects and contribute to food security. And with it, big data can be utilized to find renewable energy investment opportunities, through mapping areas that are most suited for solar or wind farms, projects that can complement Africa's energy requirements while still meeting its sustainable development goals. Not only risk assessment, big data analysis can be also utilized to track the environmental progress of investments to see if they are contributing to environmental, social, and governance (ESG) objectives. Such data on carbon emissions, resource consumption, and biodiversity loss can be incorporated into investment models, enabling financial institutions to revise strategies in response to changing conditions [19]. The dynamic nature of the approach allows investors to stay aligned with international climate commitments and to track how well their portfolios are delivering on real-world outcomes. Big Data caters to the need for an evidence-based foundation to measure investment impact, thus improving the possibility for transparency and accountability for climate finance flows in Africa which has regulatory frameworks that have not yet matured enough. Deep integration of this big data into AI comes therefore to increase the accuracy, transparency, and sustainability of climate finance, and become an indispensable tool for any investors seeking to build climate-resilient economies and ecosystems across the continent.

### 10.2.3 Blockchain and Smart Contracts in Climate Finance

Blockchain has the potential to revolutionize climate finance, especially through the tracking and verification of sustainable investments [20]. While accountability and transparency are imperative in climate finance, blockchain can produce unalterable ledgers of cash streams and carbon offset trades and track the lifecycle of an investment. Through this technology, the money spent on climate projects can be securely recorded, guaranteeing the planned management of financing and reducing the risk of greenwashing [21]. Blockchain responds to one of the critical needs for sustainable finance in Africa: to have a solid framework for tracking investments in renewable energy, sustainable agriculture and other conservation projects. Blockchain is a critical enabler of transparency that will build investor confidence in Africa climate financing. Blockchain allows institutional investors and development banks a clear, real-time view of project impacts, including emissions reductions and community benefits. Moreover, carbon credits based on blockchain enables countries and companies in Africa to securely tap into the international carbon markets, backed by irrefutable and permanent evidence of emission reductions. This will ensure that African projects meet global standards and creates trust for global partners. Thus, blockchain tech provides the assets for climate finance expansion in Africa to track, verify, and demonstrate the continent business by destination of sustainable investments. In the end, this facilitates increased local and international participation in the green economy in Africa.

## 10.3 APPLICATIONS OF AI IN SUSTAINABLE INVESTMENTS: A FOCUS ON AFRICA

### 10.3.1 AI-Enhanced Investment Analysis for Green Bonds

The issuance and monitoring of green bonds in Africa suits the AI-enhanced investment analysis, providing an efficient mechanism for sustainable financing of projects. Green bonds are a debt instrument that can be used only to financing green projects but should face a tight assessment under the sustainability purpose. For example, AI can simplify this manual process by searching a variety of external datasets like ESG datasets to provide opportunities or projects that fall within the green bond definition. This information and data can be more easily and faster analysed using the AI-driven analyses regarding the opportunities for renewables generation, biodiversity impact, resource efficiency, etc., providing information to the bond issuers regarding the environmental and financial soundness of those projects. In Africa, where green bond markets are still developing, AI can reduce the project selection time and save costs, facilitating local governments and institutions to issue issuable bonds that can meet international standards to attract overseas investment. AI can also enhance predictive powers to help African governments and institutions manage portfolios of green bonds better and predict risks. Through machine learning models, these potential challenges (climate disruptions, regulatory disruptions, and economic disruptions that could impair project feasibility) can be forecasted [22, 23]. Such information allows bond issuers to create risk hedging plans, given the sustainability of their projects and the repayment of the planned financial returns to investors in the long run. Using predictive analytics using AI, the reliability and materiality of green investments can be improved, which in turn builds investor confidence in markets that are so nascent such as the green bond markets across Africa. AI enables sustainable funding solutions that help accelerate Africa's climate action agenda while building a resilient low-carbon economy by enhancing efficiency and credibility of issuance and monitoring of green bonds.

### 10.3.2 Assessing ESG Metrics with AI

ESG metrics are gaining attention for decision-making regarding sustainable investment opportunities, especially in Africa which has many climate and development challenges requiring innovative solutions. AI can improve identification of ESG factors by analysing large and complex datasets that are not accessible to traditional methods [24]. Numerous African companies exist within geo-spatial contexts where data is variably or incompletely collected, and where investors must nonetheless make informed decisions concerning sustainability performance. Companies leverage AI to manage ESG data by sourcing, processing, and validating data from financial reports, environmental audits, social media, and regulatory filings. Equally the social aspect of ESG is paramount for investments in Africa, as many companies exist across multiple challenging but emerging communities. Measurement of social metrics, including labour, community engagement, and socioeconomic impact of corporate activities are facilitated by AI. Through sentiment analysis data analysis from social media posts and local news the AI identifies the company's image, whether positive or negative, assessing risks or highlighting positive impacts. If a mining company operated in a more rural Africa, for example, concerns over labour rights or displacement of communities may arise. These issues are monitored in real-time by AI tools, which issue early warnings to investors and enable companies to take corrective measures. But this granularity means that social factors are included in investment decisions, effectively correcting the neglect of social factors in so-called ESG assessments, which can be backed by proprietary data to identify performing companies.

## 10.4 CHALLENGES OF IMPLEMENTING AI IN CLIMATE FINANCE IN AFRICA

### 10.4.1 Data Scarcity and Quality

The lack of reliable climate and financial data presents a major obstacle to harnessing AI in climate finance across Africa. Accurate, high-resolution data is essential for training algorithms on masses of information to create actionable decision support, which in turn, is a prerequisite to effective AI systems. Most African countries have weak climate data collection systems with few meteorological stations, irregular data reporting, and little historical data. Areas vulnerable to drought or flooding frequently do not have adequate hydrological or climatic data to project these future risks. This constraint prevents AI models from correctly forecasting climate patterns and whether certain activities may help or harm the environment, making them less useful in guiding sustainable investing. Addressing these data challenges will require an investment in the infrastructure to collect and manage such data, but more should be done to create standardization across sectors and data-sharing frameworks. Bridging these gaps is a key to unleashing the full potential of AI, in propelling climate finance in Africa.

### 10.4.2 Infrastructure and Resource Constraints

Insufficient computer infrastructure and access to advanced technologies play a considerable role in hindering the deployment of AI in climate finance across Africa. AI-based remedies mostly need high-performance computing (HPC) systems for analysing large datasets for complicated machine learning functions. Yet, the majority of African nations do not have the necessary data centres and cloud computing and hardware infrastructure to meet these needs. Such high expenses involved in establishing those facilities are something most of those developing economies cannot afford and are thus forced to rely on external platforms that do not necessarily have African interests at hand. If a country does not have a sufficient processing capacity or does not have access to any global AI platforms, regional climate risks may be misjudged for investment planning or delayed. The lack of technical capacity in AI and data science remains a major hindrance in African nations. However, there is a shortage of trained professionals in most of Africa who can develop, implement, and maintain AI. The region has massive potential in AI, but needs focused training programmes, international partnerships and impactful government initiatives to be able to mobilize the socioeconomic transformative potential of AI. Closing this knowledge gap is key in enabling Africa to less dependence on imported tools and develop AI-powered low-carbon adaptation-suited solutions to its climatic and economic problems.

### 10.4.3 Regulatory and Ethical Considerations

The ability of AI to enhance financial inclusion in climate finance also presents individuals from lower income socioeconomic groups the opportunity to access sustainable funding. AI tools could leverage atypical data sources such as mobile phone payment data and social media usage to assess credit scores to deploy financial services more broadly across communities that are not currently served. For instance, AI-driven microfinance platforms could provide incentives to target funding towards grassroots climate solutions in Africa, from community-driven reforestation to off-grid renewable energy systems, integrating vulnerable communities into green economy efforts and improving the climate resilience of smallholder farmers all at once. This poses major regulatory hurdles to the integration of AI in climate finance in Africa, given the absence of widespread governance policies and frameworks. Despite the rapid pace of AI development, the absence of AI-specific legislation puts many African countries in a regulatory void in which strategic integration of AI technologies into climate finance is limited. Such absence of prescriptive guidelines for the design, deployment and monitoring of AI systems will either dampen the deployment of these technologies by financial institutions and investors or result in legal battleground over claims of IP ownership or regulatory compliance for nascent carbon markets. Harmonized regional policies would help to mitigate risks and build trust through common standards of AI-driven climate finance solutions. In addition, it is necessary to tackle ethical issues related to data privacy and possible bias in AI models. Many African countries lack rigid data protection laws which raises fears that this data could be abused or that access may be granted to unauthorized personnel.

### 10.4.4 Financial Inclusion: Balancing Accessibility and Innovation

AI can also improve access to climate finance for impoverished communities and thus advance financial inclusion. For instance, AI tools are already leveraging unconventional data sources, such as mobile payment records and social media activity, to assess creditworthiness and promote financial inclusion within under-banked populations. AI-powered microfinance platforms can open up financing opportunities for grassroots climate projects, such as community-driven reforestation or off-grid renewable energy systems in Africa and help integrate vulnerable populations in the green economy and a more sustainable future for smallholder farmers. To overcome these gaps, concerted efforts need to be undertaken to ensure that AI-enabled climate finance is inclusive and equitable. In conclusion, economic and technology policymakers must work closely with technology developers to ensure systems are designed to serve the needs of under-represented groups. These could be regulatory incentives towards AI-based microloans, digital literacy programmes, and infrastructure investments. If done inclusively rather than through exclusionary practices, AI can be that turning point for equitable climate finance in Africa, enabling sustainable practices around climate solutions and sustainable climate adaptive practices whilst improving the livelihoods of marginalized communities.

## 10.5 OPPORTUNITIES FOR STRENGTHENING AI-DRIVEN CLIMATE FINANCE IN AFRICA

### 10.5.1 Building AI Capacity through Partnerships and Training

Africa now stands a crossroads in a tech revolution poised to change the climate finance landscape. Despite the challenges, there are also exemplary chances of unlocking the continent's latent wealth. Africa has the untapped potential and, through well thought-out partnerships and focused training programmes, can fill in the climate finance gaps and be a laboratory for sustainable innovation for the rest of the world. Yet the real question is who leads and how are the stakeholders able to lead this transformation. With global tech firms, NGOs and local governments being able to drive AI capability across Africa. By partnering with some of the best AI developers, African universities can be laboratories for the transfer of knowledge, allowing the next generations of African engineers and data scientists to develop context-specific AI tools. Initiatives such as the AI research centre that Google is establishing in Ghana, are examples of multinational corporations playing a role in developing a workforce to build AI that will match the continent's specific climate needs. NGOs, for their part, can play a complementary role, by offering on-ground training in digital literacy and digital applications of AI, to ensure that remote communities can take part of the benefits of AI-enabled climate finance solutions.

### 10.5.2 Improving Data Infrastructure and Quality

It is essential to have good data to enable effective climate finance. The reality is that no amount of sophisticated AI systems will work without a strong data infrastructure to underpin them. Strong data ecosystems could present never-before-seen opportunities for climate resilience and sustainable investment. So, the critical question is: how does Africa turn this data dearth into a climate finance goldmine? Systematic public-private partnerships (PPPs) targeting the attributes of data between climate and finance can help close Africa's climate and finance data gaps through improved data collection, storage, and sharing mechanisms. Governments can, together with private entities, build centralized platforms to collect real-time environmental data related to rainfall, deforestation, and carbon emissions. High-resolution datasets equipped with satellite technology and IoT-enabled sensors can empower algorithms to predict climate risks and optimal investments. Such platforms may also include open-access elements allowing researchers, policymakers and investors to make evidence-based decisions towards sustainability objectives. Building transnational collaboration on data collection and reporting practices should also be a priority for policy frameworks, especially in relation to ESG indicators [25]. African nations should enlist regional institutions such as the African Union, as well as other global actors, to coordinate regulations that unify data quality and accessibility to be utilized for AI across the continent. Furthermore, it is important for public authorities to procure AI-enabled green solutions for their projects so they can spur a local market offering businesses a space to bloom. Africa at the forefront of AI-enabled climate finance opportunities: through innovation incentives, regulatory clarity, and cross-border alignment.

## 10.6 CONCLUSION

Africa's climate finance challenges are a good use case for the power of AI, and the continent is uniquely positioned to benefit from its potential. AI can enhance sustainable investments from the improved evaluation of ESG factors to the facilitation of green bond issuances across Africa. These innovations support accelerated access to funding, establish clear protocols for transparency/auditing and align Africa's climate finance priorities with the SDGs for long-term investments and programming. However, the merging of AI in climate finance faces challenges like unavailability of data, lack of infrastructure, and regulatory compliance issues. Nonetheless, there are significant opportunities to address these barriers through PPPs, focused policy reforms, and building capacity. This allows stakeholders to access new avenues of green investments from an inclusive and impact-driven perspective while driving an AI-enabled ecosystem tailored to the African use case. Here in this chapter, had shown that AI is not just a digitization tool but a strategy for sustainable growth of Africa climate finance ecosystem which suggests the need to act as quickly and decisively as possible to join forces for collaborative action.

## REFERENCES


1. Chen L, Chen Z, Zhang Y, et al. Artificial intelligence-based solutions for climate change: A review. *Environ Chem Lett.* 2023;21:2525–57. https://doi.org/10.1007/s10311-023-01617-y
2. Leal Filho W, Wall T, Mucova SAR, Nagy GJ, Balogun AL, Luetz JM, et al. Deploying artificial intelligence for climate change adaptation. *Technol Forecast Soc Change.* 2022;180:121662.
3. Quarshie MA, Djimatey R, Akhtar S, Nawaah D. Maximizing financial efficiency through technological synergy: Unleashing ICT for enhanced cash management in SMEs. *J Int Counc Small Bus.* 2025;1–31.
4. Resnick D, Diao X, Tadesse G, editors. Sustaining Africa's agrifood system transformation: The role of public policies. In: *ReSAKSS 2020 annual trends and outlook report.* Washington, DC, and Kigali: International Food Policy Research Institute (IFPRI) and AKADEMIYA; 2020.
5. Nawaah D, Akhtar S, Jafar SH, Azmi SN. Balancing the books and values: The interplay of ethics in tertiary accounting education. *Cogent Educ.* 2024;11(1):2432108.
6. Beekmann M, Gallois S, Rondinini C. Uncertain future for Congo Basin biodiversity: A systematic review of climate change impacts. *Biol Conserv.* 2024;297:110978.
7. Abir SI, Sarwer MH, Hasan M, Sultana N, Dolon MSA, Arefeen SS, et al. Accelerating BRICS economic growth: AI-driven data analytics for informed policy and decision making. *J Econ Finance Account Stud.* 2024;6(6):102–15.
8. Jafar SH, Oyedele OM, Nawaah D, Bolanle AS. Exploring leadership challenges for adoption of digital innovation and sustainability. In: *Innovation ecosystems and sustainable technologies.* Cham, Switzerland: Emerald Publishing Limited; 2025. p. 253–69.
9. Newell P. Towards a more transformative approach to climate finance. *Clim Policy.* 2025;25(2):257–68.
10. Abdelrazik MK, Abdelaziz SE, Hassan MF, Hatem TM. Climate action: Prospects of solar energy in Africa. *Energy Rep.* 2022;8:11363–77.
11. Khimulu RM. Assessment of the nexus of energy, climate change, urbanization and industrialization for Africa's transformation [Master's thesis]. 2017.
12. Quarshie MA, Akhtar S, Nawaah D. Barriers to breakthroughs: The crucial role of support services in advancing accounting practices, financial literacy and performance in disability-led SMEs. *Qual Quant.* 2025:1–23.
13. Oyounalsoud MS, Yilmaz AG, Abdallah M, Abdeljaber A. Drought prediction using artificial intelligence models based on climate data and soil moisture. *Sci Rep.* 2024;14:19700. https://doi.org/10.1038/s41598-024-70406-6
14. Jain H, Dhupper R, Shrivastava A, Kumar D, Kumari M. AI-enabled strategies for climate change adaptation: Protecting communities, infrastructure, and businesses from the impacts of climate change. *Comput Urban Sci.* 2023;3:25. https://doi.org/10.1007/s43762-023-00100-2
15. World Meteorological Organization (WMO). *State of the climate in Africa 2019.* Geneva: World Meteorological Organization; 2020. Report No.: 1253. Available from: https://library.wmo.int/idurl/4/57196

16. Ibomoiye DM, Yanxia S, Ileber E. Artificial intelligence and sustainable development in Africa: A comprehensive review. *Mach Learn Appl.* 2024;18.
17. United Nations Framework Convention on Climate Change (UNFCCC). Artificial intelligence and applied machine learning for climate action: Advancing mitigation and adaptation in developing countries. Draft Technical Paper TEC/2024/29/6; 2024.
18. Javaid M, Haleem A, Singh RP, Suman R. Artificial intelligence applications for Industry 4.0: A literature-based study. *J Ind Integr Manag.* 2022;7:83–111. https://doi.org/10.1142/S2424862221300040
19. Bickley SJ, Macintyre A, Torgler B. Artificial intelligence and big data in sustainable entrepreneurship. *J Econ Surv.* 2024;39(1):103–145.
20. Loukoianova E, Natalucci MF, Wang DY, Kanada S. Fintech applications for boosting climate finance. *Int Monet Fund.* 2024;2024(008).
21. Antwi B, Adelakun B, Eziefule A. Transforming financial reporting with AI: Enhancing accuracy and timeliness. *Int J Adv Econ.* 2024;6(6):205–23. https://doi.org/10.51594/ijae.v6i6.1229
22. Hamdan A, Ibekwe K, Etukudoh E, Umoh A, Ilojianya V. AI and machine learning in climate change research: A review of predictive models and environmental impact. *World J Adv Res Rev.* 2024;21:1999–2008.
23. Rane N, Rane J, Paramesha M. Artificial intelligence and business intelligence to enhance Environmental, Social, and Governance (ESG) strategies: Internet of things, machine learning, and big data analytics in financial services and investment sectors. In: *Trustworthy artificial intelligence in industry and society.* Mumbai, India: Deep Science Publishing; 2024. Chapter 3.
24. Nawaah D, Asare PY, Quarshie MA. Climate finance and natural capital: Linking global initiatives with local impact. In: *Climate neutrality through smart eco-innovation and environmental sustainability.* Cham: Springer Nature Switzerland. 2025. p. 317–332.
25. Malik MY, Jafar SH, Dixit A. Efficiency analysis and macroeconomic determinants of non-tax revenues: Evidence from special category states of India. *The Indian Economic Journal.* 2025:00194662251330385.

# 11 AI in Sustainable Risk Management and Compliance

*Michael Ayikwei Quarshie and Reginald Djimatey*

## 11.1 INTRODUCTION

As globalisation, new emerging technologies, shifting market dynamics, and natural catastrophes continue to remain risk factors that impact an entity's operational environment, businesses improve their chances of survival, ensure the well-being of society and the environment through sustainable risk management (SRM) and compliance [1, 2]. SRM seeks to manage risks from an environmental, social, and governance (ESG) perspective in stakeholders' value creation and ensures society's long-term success. SRM and compliance emphasise long-term resilience, ethical responsibility, and regulatory alignment to achieve sustainability goals, unlike traditional risk management strategies, which mainly concentrate on financial and operational risks [3, 4]. Artificial intelligence (AI) is a transforming agent which drives efficiency, accuracy, and creativity in many spheres, including risk management and regulatory compliance [5, 6]. Most business entities depend more on AI-driven technologies, including predictive analytics, machine learning, and natural language processing, to improve their decision-making and efficiently manage risks [7, 8]. By processing vast volumes of structured and unstructured data, AI helps companies promptly identify possible financial risks and detect fraud.

According to Milana and Ashta [9], AI is altering conventional risk management strategies as financial markets become more data-driven, driven by fast technology developments and legislative changes. Its application in SRM and compliance has become increasingly crucial as global regulatory systems tighten and businesses are under increasing scrutiny over governance and sustainability criteria. AI-powered compliance solutions are essential in this change, as they automate regulatory reporting, identify irregularities, and guarantee conformity to sustainability requirements. AI application lowers human errors and improves predicted accuracy in intricate financial systems through stress testing, scenario analysis, and automated risk assessment [10–12]. The conventional approach largely depends on historical data, manual monitoring, and rule-based frameworks, which might be ineffective in adjusting to regulatory changes. The growing speed and volume of financial transactions, the complexity of regulatory systems, economic crimes, and the emergence of advanced cyber threats significantly hinder the traditional risk management approach. Again,

DOI: 10.1201/9781003611646-11

the over-reliance on static models hinders real-time evaluation and decision-making, resulting in a delayed reaction to significant vulnerabilities [13, 14]. Given these challenges, this chapter investigates how AI could change compliance and SRM.

## 11.2 EVOLUTION OF AI-driven RISK MANAGEMENT FRAMEWORKS

Fundamentally, the evolution of AI-driven risk management techniques has altered the discourse around SRM and compliance, thus from a reactive, rule-based perspective to a more proactive, data-driven system [15–17]. Historically, risk management has focused on studying historical data and human knowledge, often constrained by inefficiencies, biases, and the difficulty of processing vast, complicated information in real time [18]. AI, especially machine learning and deep learning has made risk identification, assessment, and mitigation possible, enabling companies to precisely foresee more developing risks [19, 20]. Generally, AI-driven algorithms evaluate structured and unstructured data, exposing hidden risk patterns through anomaly detection, natural language processing, and predictive analytics while complying with regulatory standards [21]. Incorporating AI in risk management as a proactive strategy helps institutions enhance decision-making, reduce operational risks, and uphold sustainability obligations.

Beyond financial and legal compliance, the development of AI risk management systems has expanded their importance in sustainable risk governance to include ethical and environmental considerations. For instance, companies have addressed sustainability concerns remarkably by incorporating AI into supply chain due diligence, corporate governance evaluations, and climate risk modelling [22]. Reinforcement learning and generative adversarial networks, among other advanced AI models, replicate various risk situations, optimise risk-reducing measures, and enhance regulatory reporting systems. Fan, Yan, and Wen [23] argue that by addressing problems of algorithmic bias and regulatory supervision problems, explainable AI has become increasingly important in improving openness and responsibility in AI-driven risk analyses. Financial institutions that use AI for SRM and compliance benefit from integrating technology, regulatory control, and corporate responsibility, thereby establishing a strong framework that links financial success with long-term sustainability goals.

## 11.3 MODELS SUPPORTING AI ADOPTION IN FINANCIAL RISK MANAGEMENT

Various theoretical models and frameworks have highlighted AI's efficiency, integration, and transformative potential, underscoring its application in financial risk management [24, 25]. For instance, the Efficient Market Hypothesis (EMH) provides a required basis and makes it quite challenging for investors to outperform the market consistently. EMH postulates that financial markets represent all information currently accessible within the market [26]. However, the application of AI challenges this presumption by employing big data analytics and machine learning models to identify inefficiencies, abnormalities, and hidden patterns [27]. Also, predictive analytics and high-frequency trading algorithms are employed in managing risk to enhance portfolio diversification techniques, lower exposure to volatility, and increase decision-making [28]. Incorporating behavioural finance into the Adaptive Market Hypothesis (AMH) further enhances the EMH. Further, it suggests that, through continuous learning from data, AI can adapt to evolving market conditions [29].

This aligns with SRM and compliance, where AI continually adjusts risk models based on changing environmental and economic factors, thereby enhancing resilience to market shocks and regulatory unpredictability. Apart from the ideas of market efficiency, the Technology Acceptance Model (TAM) explains the factors affecting AI's acceptance in financial risk control [30]. TAM states that regulatory authorities and financial institutions' adoption of AI-driven risk management solutions depends on their apparent value and simplicity of use [31]. From the institutional theory perspective, financial institutions respond to normative, coercive, and mimetic influences using AI-driven risk management. Competitive market dynamics, regulatory requirements, and changing sustainability criteria drive businesses to integrate AI models to guarantee adherence to international financial rules, including the EU Taxonomy for Sustainable Finance, Sustainable Finance Disclosure Regulation (SFDR) and Basel III [32–34].

## 11.4 AI PRACTICAL APPLICATIONS IN SUSTAINABLE RISK MANAGEMENT

AI applications have revolutionised credit risk assessment through fraud detection and accurate credit scoring algorithms, unlike the conventional credit rating techniques that mainly rely on past financial data and fixed standards [35]. AI-driven models explore massive datasets to produce more complete credit ratings, especially those utilising machine learning and deep learning [36]. Using AI-powered fraud detection systems, anomalies, and suspicious behaviours are detected at early stages, thus lowering financial institutions' credit fraud risk. These changes, to a greater extent, increase financial inclusion and help reduce risk. Using AI in market risk analysis has improved financial organisations' ability to project investment risks and respond quickly to changes in the market. To detect possible hazards and opportunities, AI-driven predictive analytics combine comprehensive structured and unstructured financial data, including real-time market feeds, economic indicators, and sentiment analysis from news and social media [37].

The inclusion of AI into financial risk management has drastically changed how entities recognise, evaluate, and reduce risks. Leading global banks, including HSBC and JPMorgan Chase, have applied AI-driven technologies to enhance market risk analysis, credit risk assessment, and fraud detection [38–40]. Using natural language processing, JPMorgan's AI-based COiN (Contract Intelligence) system analyses intricate financial records, reducing risk assessment time from hours to minutes [41]. HSBC uses AI-based anomaly detection algorithms to solve financial crimes, enabling real-time fraud prevention and guaranteeing regulatory compliance [42]. Growing needs for openness in sustainability practices from regulatory authorities and investors have made AI more important in evaluating ESG concerns. BlackRock is a shining example of how analytics driven by AI evaluate ESG risks in worldwide investment portfolios [43]. Using machine learning and natural language processing, BlackRock's Aladdin platform evaluates financial disclosures, climate data, and sustainability reports, thereby spotting ESG risks that can compromise long-term investment performance [44]. Through AI application, the Morgan Stanley Capital International (MSCI) platform enhanced ESG grading systems and improved data accuracy and prediction capacity on social and environmental hazards [45].

## 11.5 CHALLENGES AND FUTURE DIRECTIONS

AI-driven risk management is greatly challenged by fairness and bias in algorithmic decision-making. In credit scoring, fraud detection, and ESG evaluations, machine learning models, especially those related to credit scoring, depend on past data that could fundamentally show social and economic inequalities [46, 47]. Enforcing ethical AI practices depends mostly on regulatory frameworks. Implementing AI for SRM is impeded to some extent by data privacy and security concerns. Dependency on large databases, mainly obtained from business disclosures, climate reports, and financial activities, increases vulnerability to cyber-attacks, data breaches, and unauthorised access [48]. Compliance with worldwide data protection legislation requires that AI models integrate robust encryption, anonymisation techniques, and safe data-sharing protocols. Strong governance regulations are ethically required for AI-driven surveillance and automated decision-making to balance risk mitigation with individual privacy rights. Enhancing AI-driven security protocols via blockchain-based data integrity solutions will help to safeguard financial and sustainability-related risk management systems, given the growing complexity of cyber threats [49]. Regulatory compliance and the building of stakeholder confidence in AI's decisions depend on openness and explainability in the processes [50, 51]. The future of AI for sustainable finance will depend mainly on improving model interpretability and developing technologies such as quantum computing. The integration of real-time risk assessments, ESG standards and green fintech solutions might help transform sustainable investments in the future.

## 11.6 CONCLUSIONS

Including AI in SRM and compliance marks a significant development in the approach many stakeholders use to negotiate unpredictability in the world environment. AI models have enhanced the efficiency of managing and analysing an entity's operational, credit, and market risks to address uncertainty in the global landscape. AI's capacity to examine a considerable amount of data in real time helps a forward-looking strategy meant to identify and mitigate risks. Successful use of AI in risk management and compliance calls for stronger economic, social, and governance systems, openness in algorithmic decision-making, and continuous changes to ethical and legal requirements. Recent advancements in AI systems enhance the precision of forecasts, mitigate systematic risks, and simplify intricate decision-making processes that traditional methods may have overlooked over the years. A more sustainable approach to AI warrants carefully integrating technological advancements to ensure that AI-driven risk management systems align with ethical standards and contribute to global sustainability objectives.

## REFERENCES


1. Adeniran IA, Abhulimen AO, Obiki-Osafiele AN, Osundare OS, Agu EE, Efunniyi CP. Strategic risk management in financial institutions: Ensuring robust regulatory compliance. *Finance Acc Res J.* 2024;6(8):1582–96.
2. Jafar SH, Kashid AU, Ghosh S, Srividhya S, Sharma D, Bodhankar A. An enhanced performance optimization of ATM networks for cross-border money transfers. In: *2024 15th International Conference on Computing Communication and Networking Technologies (ICCCNT).* IEEE; 2024. p. 1–5.
3. Leal Filho W, Tripathi SK, Andrade Guerra JBSOD, Giné-Garriga R, Orlovic Lovren V, Willats J. Using the sustainable development goals towards a better understanding of sustainability challenges. *Int J Sustain Dev World Ecol.* 2019;26(2):179–90.
4. Jafar SH, Oyedele OM, Nawaah D, Bolanle AS. Exploring leadership challenges for adoption of digital innovation and sustainability. In: *Innovation ecosystems and sustainable technologies.* Emerald Publishing Limited; 2025. p. 253–69.
5. Aziz LAR, Andriansyah Y. Artificial intelligence's role in modern banking: Exploring AI-driven approaches for enhanced fraud prevention, risk management, and regulatory compliance. *Rev Contemp Bus Anal.* 2023;6(1):110–32.
6. Quarshie MA, Akhtar S, Nawaah D. Barriers to breakthroughs: The crucial role of support services in advancing accounting practices, financial literacy and performance in disability-led SMEs. *Qual Quant.* 2025;59:1–23.
7. Emeihe EV, Nwankwo EI, Ajegbile MD, Olaboye JA, Maha CC. The impact of artificial intelligence on regulatory compliance in the oil and gas industry. *Int J Life Sci Res Arch.* 2024;7(1):028–39.
8. Salim M, Khan PA, Jalil NA, Johl SK, Jafar SH, Irfan F, et al. Fusion of blockchain and sustainable development goals: A bibliometric analysis for future trends. *KnE Soc Sci.* 2023:633–54.
9. Milana C, Ashta A. Artificial intelligence techniques in finance and financial markets: A literature survey. *Strateg Change.* 2021;30(3):189–209.
10. Xi W. Regulatory changes and compliance challenges. In: *Strategic financial management: A managerial approach.* Emerald Publishing Limited; 2024. p. 119–34.
11. Hemachandran K, Rodriguez RV, editors. *Artificial intelligence for business: An implementation guide containing practical and industry-specific case studies.* CRC Press; 2023.
12. Nawaah D, Asare PY, Quarshie MA. Climate finance and natural capital: Linking global initiatives with local impact. In: *Climate neutrality through smart eco-innovation and environmental sustainability.* Springer Nature Switzerland; 2025. p. 317–32.
13. Xu J, Yang T, Zhuang S, Li H, Lu W. AI-based financial transaction monitoring and fraud prevention with behaviour prediction. *Appl Comput Eng.* 2024;77:218–24.
14. Malik MY, Jafar SH, Dixit A. Efficiency analysis and macroeconomic determinants of non-tax revenues: Evidence from special category States of India. *Indian Econ J.* 2025:00194662251330385.
15. Agzayal Y, Bouhorma M. AI-driven cyber risk management framework. In: *Proc Int Conf Smart City Appl.* Springer Nature Switzerland; 2023. p. 571–84.
16. Ikudabo AO, Kumar P. AI-driven risk assessment and management in banking: Balancing innovation and security. *Int J Res Publ Rev.* 2024;5(10):3573–88.

17. Jafar SH, Akhtar S, Johl SK. AI in insurance. In: *Artificial intelligence for business.* Productivity Press; 2023. p. 164–73.
18. Oko-Odion C, Angela O. Risk management frameworks for financial institutions in a rapidly changing economic landscape. *Int J Sci Res Arch.* 2025;14(1):1182–204.
19. Zekos GI. AI risk management. In: *Economics and law of artificial intelligence: Finance, economic impacts, risk management and governance.* 2021. p. 233–88.
20. Hemachandran K, Rodriguez RV, editors. *The business of the metaverse: How to maintain the human element within this new business reality.* CRC Press; 2023.
21. Pancholi K, Shukla P. Harnessing AI for sustainability: Innovations, policies, and investment paradigms. In: *Diversity, AI, and sustainability for financial growth.* IGI Global Scientific Publishing; 2025. p. 97–124.
22. Annesi N, Battaglia M, Ceglia I, Mercuri F. Navigating paradoxes: Building a sustainable strategy for an integrated ESG corporate governance. *Manag Decis.* 2025;63(2):531–59.
23. Fan Z, Yan Z, Wen S. Deep learning and artificial intelligence in sustainability: A review of SDGs, renewable energy, and environmental health. *Sustainability.* 2023; 15(18):13493.
24. Kanti PS, Sadia R, Suchismita D. Artificial intelligence adoption in supply chain risk management: Scale development and validation. *Ho Chi Minh City Open Univ J Sci Econ Bus Adm.* 2022;12(2):15–32.
25. Faqihi A, Miah SJ. Artificial intelligence-driven talent management system: Exploring the risks and options for constructing a theoretical foundation. *J Risk Financ Manag.* 2023;16(1):31.
26. Ghazani MM, Jafari MA. Cryptocurrencies, gold, and WTI crude oil market efficiency: A dynamic analysis based on the adaptive market hypothesis. *Financ Innov.* 2021; 7(1):29.
27. Seo K, Yang J. Exploring the efficient market hypothesis for accurate stock movement prediction via feature-axis transformer. In: *Proc 39th ACM/SIGAPP Symp Appl Comput.* 2024. p. 892–901.
28. Peng KL, Wu CH, Lin PM, Kou IE. Investor sentiment in the tourism stock market. *J Behav Exp Financ.* 2023;37:100732.
29. Chu J, Zhang Y, Chan S. The adaptive market hypothesis in the high-frequency cryptocurrency market. *Int Rev Financ Anal.* 2019;64:221–31.
30. Kalayou MH, Endehabtu BF, Tilahun B. The applicability of the modified technology acceptance model (TAM) on the sustainable adoption of eHealth systems in resource-limited settings. *J Multidiscip Healthc.* 2020;13:1827–37.
31. Salim A. Accelerating sustainability environment: Understanding electric vehicles (EVs) adoption with expanded technology acceptance model (TAM). *Int J Adv Sci Eng Inf Technol.* 2024;14(2):629–36.
32. King P, Tarbert H. Basel III: An overview. *Bank Financ Serv Policy Rep.* 2011;30(5):1–18.
33. Cremasco C, Boni L. Is the European Union (EU) Sustainable Finance Disclosure Regulation (SFDR) effectively shaping sustainability objectives? An analysis of investment funds' behaviour. *J Sustain Financ Invest.* 2024;14(4):1018–36.
34. Waykar YA, Yambal S. AI and the evolution of green finance: Transforming Banking for a greener world. In: *Convergence of AI, education, and business for sustainability.* IGI Global Scientific Publishing; 2025. p. 285–306.
35. Shkalenko AV, Nazarenko AV. Integrating AI and IoT into corporate social responsibility strategies for financial risk management and sustainable development. *Risks.* 2024;12(6):87.
36. Žigienė G, Rybakovas E, Alzbutas R. Artificial intelligence-based commercial risk management framework for SMEs. *Sustainability.* 2019;11(16):4501.
37. Ganesh AD, Kalpana P. Future of artificial intelligence and its influence on supply chain risk management–A systematic review. *Comput Ind Eng.* 2022;169:108206.

38. Karnam C. AI revolution in finance: Transforming banking, investment, and risk management. *Int J Comput Eng Technol.* 2024;15(4):406–15.
39. Saxena A, Verma S, Mahajan J. Transforming banking: The next frontier. In: *Generative AI in banking financial services and insurance: A guide to use cases, approaches, and insights.* Apress; 2024. p. 85–121.
40. Quarshie MA, Djimatey R, Akhtar S, Nawaah D. Maximizing financial efficiency through technological synergy: Unleashing ICT for enhanced cash management in SMEs. *J Int Counc Small Bus.* 2025;16:1–31.
41. Praveen RVS. *Banking in the cloud: Leveraging AI for financial transformation.* Addition Publishing House; 2024.
42. Lau T, Leimer B. The era of connectedness: How AI will help deliver the next generation of banking experiences. In: *Generative AI in banking financial services and insurance: A guide to use cases, approaches, and insights.* Apress; 2024. p. 65–83.
43. Gupta P, Arora S. Artificial intelligence: A path to future Banking in India. *Int J Adv Res.* 2024;12(4):219–26.
44. Narayan RK, Soni D. FinTechs and digital transformation in banking: India Perspective. *Asian J Econ Bank.* 2023;7(2):275–90.
45. Sinha A, Dutt A. Adoption of artificial intelligence in Indian banking sector. *Int J Comput Sci Mob Comput.* 2023;12(3):58–65.
46. Sharma R, Bansal A. Fintech and financial inclusion: The role of AI and big data in the Indian context. *J Econ Financ Res.* 2024;10(1):91–102.
47. Tripathi SK, Sharma S. Leveraging AI for inclusive finance: A study of rural banking models in India. *Int J Soc Sci Econ Res.* 2024;9(2):213–27.
48. Venkatesh V, Davis FD. A theoretical extension of the technology acceptance model: Four longitudinal field studies. *Manage Sci.* 2000;46(2):186–204.
49. Bawack RE, Wamba SF, Carillo KD. Artificial intelligence in practice: Implications for AI adoption in organizations. *Bus Process Manag J.* 2021;27(6):1573–93.
50. Gomber P, Koch JA, Siering M. Digital finance and fintech: Current research and future research directions. *J Bus Econ.* 2017;87(5):537–80.
51. Kumar A, Shah S, Patel S. Artificial intelligence and machine learning in banking: A review of recent developments. *Int J Inf Technol.* 2023;15(3):667–77.

# 12 Exploring the Influence of Gold Prices on Forex Rates, Equity Index, and Crude Oil Amid Disruptions

## *A Comparative Analysis of Machine Learning and Deep Learning Approaches*

*Mulukalapally Susruth, Mahesh Admankar, and Ch. Purnachander*

## 12.1 INTRODUCTION

Gold is not only valuable for its elegance and periodical role as a monetary standard but also stands as a key metric of economic health. During periods of political turbulence, economic slumps, or other forms of global turmoil, the eyes of both investors and economic analysts often turn to the changing prices of gold for guidance [1]. Whether faced with geopolitical conflict or shocks from a global crisis, the shifts in gold prices tend to have extensive effects on forex rates, stock market indices, and the crude oil [2]. By reviewing past instances and recent developments, we aim to find the high interdependencies that occur in global financial markets. The correlation between gold and the value of currency, particularly the U.S. dollars, is intriguing; in general, the rupee's strength declines in proportion to other currencies when gold prices rise. This situation occurs as investors regard gold as a more secure investment compared to any currency [3]. Consequently, they tend to invest more in gold when they predict a decline in currency values, leading to an increase in gold's price. Additionally, since transactions involving gold are primarily conducted in dollars, a fall in the dollar's value makes purchasing gold more affordable for investors using different currencies, potentially boosting demand and further elevating the prices of gold [4]. During the period of economic turmoil like the 2008 financial crisis, gold has seen a significant increase in value as investors required safe investment place


DOI: 10.1201/9781003611646-12

[5]. This shift from the dollar to gold leads to the dollar's depreciation in the forex markets. Similarly, amid the COVID-19 pandemic, gold prices surged to groundbreaking levels as investors turned to it seeking stability and finally impacting global forex rates in the process [6].

In general, the relationship between gold prices and stock market indices like the S&P 500 and Nifty shows the opposite direction [7]. During periods of sound stock market performance, investors often prefer stocks that offer dividends, rather than gold, which do not provide such returns. This preference generally results in a decrease in gold prices. However, during periods of stock market risk, gold becomes a more attractive choice for investors looking for a safer investment, leading to elevation in its prices [8]. The price of crude oil and gold are closely related. Due to their mutual susceptibility to changes in the value of the US dollar, gold and oil prices frequently fluctuate [9]. Since both gold and oil are priced in dollars, a weak dollar usually leads to higher prices for both commodities. Furthermore, gold is frequently used as a hedge against inflation, and rising oil prices frequently exacerbate inflationary pressures [1]. During the times of geopolitical conflict that breaks oil supply, like the Gulf War, oil price and gold price tend to increase. This spike is due to the resulting uncertainty in the oil markets, which makes investors turn to gold as a safer investment choice, thus elevating its price. In contrast, when oil prices decline because of reduced demand or an oversupply situation, it may result in deflationary trends, diminishing gold's allure as a hedge against inflation and possibly decreasing its price [10]. Understanding the intricate relationships between gold prices, forex rates, equity index, and crude oil provides a critical understanding of the global economy's state and trajectory. Due to its status as a "safe haven" asset, variations in the price of gold can be used as a gauge of shifts in investor sentiment and overall economic trends. Monitoring gold allows analysts and investors to assess market risk levels and make decisions that are better informed.

## 12.2 LITERATURE REVIEW

It appears most studies focused on forecasting the prices of gold, crude oil, foreign exchange rates, and stocks. Little attention has been paid in the literature to the effects of gold prices on currency rates, crude oil prices, and equity indexes using machine learning and deep learning in the face of various disturbances. These studies typically employ a combination of machine learning, deep learning, and statistical prediction techniques. Research indicates that the global prices of crude oil and gold, the USD-INR exchange rate, and the Indian stock market are all connected [11]. The data indicates that both the benchmark stock index and the value of the Indian Rupee have declined as a result of the declining prices of gold and crude oil. A study on economic uncertainty looks at how important the crude oil-gold connection is in influencing the financial and economic landscape of the world [12]. Five Southeast Asian countries' currency rates and crude oil prices were compared in a study [13]. The results demonstrate that, with the exception of Indonesia, both short-term and long-term persistence are highly significant for the oil price and the currency rate. To investigate the relationship between the volatility and returns of the gold and crude oil markets, a study [14] suggested a novel approach that takes into consideration both the quantile and time-varying Granger causality. A static quantile causation approach between these two strategic commodities is often deemed inappropriate by the results, especially when the sample period is lengthy. The Karachi Stock Exchange, Pakistan's top stock exchange, and COVID-19 indexes were correlated in a study [15] to determine the best machine learning model for forecasting KSE trends throughout the pandemic. During the COVID-19 epidemic, one study [16] examined the short-term and long-term relationships between the commodity prices of crude oil, gold, the USD-INR reference rate, and the stock market index. The long-term relationships between the variables were measured using Johansen's cointegration test. A study [17] looked into how global supply networks and energy prices were affected by the conflict in Ukraine in 2022 and the economic sanctions that followed on Russian exports. To examine how these events affected the foreign exchange market, this study used DS-ARDL and time-varying Granger Causality.

## 12.3 METHODOLOGY

This study relies on secondary data on gold prices, crude oil prices, equity indices, and forex rates from January 2011 to December 2023. The Gold Council of India provided the statistics on gold prices, and the Reserve Bank of India provided the exchange rates (rupee per dollar). The Gold Council of India provides the data on gold prices. The Reserve Bank of India was also consulted for the rupee-to-dollar exchange rates. In this analysis, the NIFTY and National Stock Exchange stock indices were used. Furthermore, the Money Control website and the Ministry of Petroleum, which is situated in the Government of India, are the sources of the crude oil price data. A specific time frame of January 2010 to October 2023 was selected to evaluate the effect of prices of gold on the crude oil, equity index, and forex rate during the disruptions selected as part of the study. The data was gathered specifically from January 2011 to December 2023 in order to analyse the impact of gold prices on the equity index, FX rate, and crude oil during the demonetization in November 2016, the 2020 COVID-19 epidemic, and the Russia-Ukraine war in February 2022. An increased uncertainty and volatility in the economies of the select countries was witnessed due to these unprecedented events. The chosen data enables examining the ongoing and immediate aftermath effects of the chosen disruptions. To study how the price of gold impacts the crude oil prices, stock market index, forex rate, under the given disruptions, Artificial Neural Networks (ANN), Support Vector Machines (SVMs), and Multiple Linear Regression (MLR) are employed. By using Python 3.12 and IBM SPSS (version 25), the data analysis was carried out in this study.

## 12.4 RESULTS AND DISCUSSION

Table 12.1 details the data on the price of gold daily along with the forex rate, crude oil prices, Nifty from the year 2011 to 2023. Since the Forex rate comprises of lower standard deviation, this reflects that forex rate is associated with relatively lower volatility among the given four variables. Since the index of NIFTY comprises the maximum standard deviation, we can conclude that it's associated with utmost volatility among all the given four variables. Since the price of gold is observed to be significantly maximum value along with high value of mean, this reveals that the price of gold is the costliest among the given four variables. The price of crude oil is observed with minimal value and minimal value of mean. This shows that the price of crude oil is low cost among given all four variables.

**TABLE 12.1**
**Descriptive Statistics of Gold Price, Forex Rate, Crude Oil, and Nifty**

| | Parameters | Gold Price | Forex Rate | Nifty | Crude Oil |
|---|---|---|---|---|---|
| Overall period | Mean | 100,431.9 | 66.37505 | 10,345.34 | 5,035.958 |
| | Median | 87,342.07 | 66.80300 | 9,311.950 | 5,047.180 |
| | Maximum | 167,324.4 | 85.19400 | 20,192.35 | 10,177.35 |
| | Minimum | 60,364.04 | 44.01000 | 4,544.200 | 698.2272 |
| | Std. Dev. | 28,403.71 | 9.733627 | 4,286.269 | 1,602.256 |
| | Skewness | 0.833813 | −0.382485 | 0.680878 | 0.263207 |
| | Kurtosis | 2.248117 | 2.664192 | 2.326725 | 2.713231 |
| | Jarque-Bera | 429.5822 | 89.59888 | 296.2478 | 46.13131 |
| Demonetization | **Statistic** | **Gold Price** | **Forex Rate** | **Nifty** | **Crude Oil** |
| | Mean | 81,035.90 | 67.56 | 8,458.45 | 3,535.37 |
| | Median | 81,489.90 | 67.77 | 8,399.17 | 3,637.59 |
| | Maximum | 85,190.03 | 68.80 | 9,153.70 | 3,794.80 |
| | Minimum | 76,485.69 | 65.78 | 7,929.10 | 2,767.38 |
| | Std. Dev. | 2,160.27 | 0.68 | 345.23 | 255.24 |
| | Skewness | −0.45 | −0.38 | 0.28 | −1.36 |
| | Kurtosis | −0.58 | −0.76 | −1.34 | 0.71 |
| | Jarque-Bera | 4.18 | 4.16 | 7.56 | 28.46 |
| COVID-19 | **Statistic** | **Gold Price** | **Forex Rate** | **Nifty** | **Crude Oil** |
| | Mean | 134,933.97 | 74.24 | 12,531.73 | 3,613.15 |
| | Median | 134,814.58 | 73.94 | 12,263.55 | 3,354.28 |
| | Maximum | 154,870.88 | 77.57 | 15,869.25 | 5,715.52 |
| | Minimum | 116,424.63 | 72.30 | 7,610.25 | 698.23 |
| | Std. Dev. | 6,317.31 | 1.21 | 2,233.06 | 1,088.40 |
| | Skewness | 0.16 | 0.53 | −0.18 | −0.17 |
| | Kurtosis | 0.17 | −0.60 | −1.24 | −0.45 |
| | Jarque-Bera | 1.65 | 19.17 | 21.53 | 4.06 |
| Russia-Ukraine conflict | **Statistic** | **Gold Price** | **Forex Rate** | **Nifty** | **Crude Oil** |
| | Mean | 150,054.51 | 80.70 | 17,808.14 | 7,472.75 |
| | Median | 149,715.48 | 81.82 | 17,777.63 | 7,232.97 |
| | Maximum | 167,324.36 | 83.30 | 20,192.35 | 10,177.35 |
| | Minimum | 132,663.45 | 74.62 | 15,293.50 | 5,875.30 |
| | Std. Dev. | 9,505.44 | 2.32 | 1,116.70 | 1,034.83 |
| | Skewness | −0.03 | −0.93 | 0.03 | 0.65 |
| | Kurtosis | −1.33 | −0.49 | −0.55 | −0.46 |
| | Jarque-Bera | 28.41 | 59.22 | 4.81 | 30.04 |

*Source:* Authors construct.

In terms of the skewness, the NIFTY index and the Forex rate are observed to have negative skewness. From this, it may be concluded that both the NIFTY index and the Forex rate have higher proportion of values above the mean in comparison to below the mean. Since the price of gold and the price of crude oil are observed to be associated with the positive skewness, it can be concluded that they are associated with higher proportion of values below their mean in comparison to above the mean values. Similarly, the price of crude oil is associated with the highest kurtosis. From this, it may be concluded that crude oil is associated with maximum peaking observation of distribution among all the given four variables. Further, the index of NIFTY is associated with smaller kurtosis. From this, it may be concluded that the NIFTY index is associated with a distribution that is flat among all four variables given. At a very low probability level, the Jarque-Bera test rejects the null hypothesis of normality for each of the four variables, indicating that none of them has a normal distribution. Because of their negative correlation, the forex rate and the price of gold typically fluctuate in opposing directions. The NIFTY index and the price of crude oil have a positive correlation, meaning they often move in the same direction.

The descriptive data for the main financial variables—the price of gold, the forex rate, the NIFTY, and crude oil—across various time periods and economic events are shown in Table 12.1. It includes overall metrics such as mean, median, standard deviation, skewness, and kurtosis, offering a baseline understanding of these variables. The table also captures their statistical behaviour during the demonetization period, illustrating asset price fluctuations and distributional shifts. Additionally, it highlights changes in central tendency and variability during the COVID-19 pandemic and reflects the impact of geopolitical uncertainty on market indicators during the Russia-Ukraine conflict.

The standard deviations of gold prices and FX rates during the demonetization period show much less volatility than those of the Nifty and crude oil. The skewness and kurtosis values indicate that none of the distributions perfectly fit a normal distribution, with each showing unique characteristics in terms of tail length and peak height. The Jarque-Bera test results further support the deviations from normality, especially notable in the crude oil data, suggesting that more complex models than those assuming normal distribution may be necessary for accurate predictions or analyses. The statistics reflect the financial markets' response to the COVID-19 pandemic, characterized by volatility and shifts in investor behaviour. Gold's high mean and median values underscore its role as a safe-haven asset during crises. The crude oil price fluctuations reveal the worldwide major shifts in demand for the same along with the influence of the geopolitical aspects. Index of the NIFTY with its performance reflects a significant recovery along with a promising resilience in the stock market of India, even with its fluctuations. The impact of the World economy dynamics and the changes in the monetary policy may be witnessed in the performance of the forex rate. Since the median and mean values are in proximity, a distribution which is symmetric is observed for the prices of the gold. A negative kurtosis and a smaller skewness indicate a normal distribution which is a little flat than the Curve Gaussian. Deviation from normality is observed in the Jarque-Bera test. Since negative skewness is observed in the forex rate, this indicates that there is a skewed distribution along with values which are lower in nature. Since the median is higher than the mean, this may be concluded. Not a very peak or flat distribution is being witnessed since the kurtosis is close to zero. Further, there is high deviation from normality since the Jarque-Bera test values are observed as high. The mean and median of Nifty are again closely aligned, showing a symmetric distribution. The skewness and kurtosis values are near zero, suggesting a distribution that closely resembles a normal distribution, albeit slightly flatter. The Jarque-Bera value is low, indicating minor deviations from normality. Crude oil shows a positive skewness, indicating a tail with higher values. The distribution is slightly peaky but mostly normal as indicated by the kurtosis value. The Jarque-Bera test value suggests some deviations from a normal distribution.

### 12.4.1 Regression Analysis

*H0: There is no influence of gold price on forex rate, equity index, and crude oil amid the overall period.*

An MLR model that forecasts the price of gold over the long term based on three independent variables—the price of crude oil, the NIFTY index, and the exchange rate—is presented in Table 12.2. With a high *R*-squared value of 0.772877, the model can account for roughly 77.29% of the volatility in the price of gold. Each independent variable has a positive and statistically significant coefficient at the 5% level of significance. It is also feasible that the null hypothesis was rejected and that the price of gold influences the stock market, currency exchange rates, and crude oil prices because all independent variables have a considerable impact on the price of gold.

*H0: There is no influence of gold price on forex rate, equity index, and crude oil amid the demonetization period.*

Table 12.3 displays the results of an MLR model that predicts the price of gold by considering three independent variables: The currency rate, the NIFTY, and the price of crude oil. The model explains roughly 46.10% of the fluctuation in the

**TABLE 12.2**
**Results of Multi-Linear Regression with Dependent Variable—Gold Price**

| Variable | Coefficient | Std. Error | *t*-Statistic | Prob. |
|---|---|---|---|---|
| C | −4,578.559 | 2,955.242 | −1.549301 | 0.1214 |
| Forex rate | 783.1109 | 55.88122 | 14.01385 | 0.0000 |
| NIFTY | 3.880063 | 0.133412 | 29.08324 | 0.0000 |
| Crude oil | 2.559759 | 0.174819 | 14.64235 | 0.0000 |
| *R*-squared | 0.772877 | Mean dependent variable | | 100,431.9 |
| Adjusted *R*-squared | 0.772655 | S.D. dependent variable | | 28,403.71 |
| S.E. of regression | 13,543.08 | Akaike info criterion | | 21.86644 |
| Sum squared resid. | 5.64E+11 | Schwarz criterion | | 21.87427 |
| Log likelihood | −33,681.25 | Hannan-Quinn criterion | | 21.86925 |
| *F*-statistic | 3,490.237 | Durbin-Watson statistic | | 0.008014 |

*Source:* Field data.

**TABLE 12.3**
**Results of Multi-Linear Regression with Dependent Variable—Gold Price**

| Variable | Coefficient | Std. Error | *t*-Statistic | Prob. |
|---|---|---|---|---|
| C | −59,610.58 | 35,389.61 | −1.684409 | 0.0959 |
| Forex rate | 1,619.453 | 448.5284 | 3.610591 | 0.0005 |
| NIFTY | 5.928282 | 0.898073 | 6.601116 | 0.0000 |
| Crude oil | −5.348078 | 0.807699 | −6.621379 | 0.0000 |
| *R*-squared | 0.461028 | Mean dependent variable | | 81,035.90 |
| Adjusted *R*-squared | 0.441310 | S.D. dependent variable | | 2,160.271 |
| S.E. of regression | 1,614.707 | Akaike info criterion | | 17.65709 |
| Sum squared resid | 2.14E+08 | Schwarz criterion | | 17.77125 |
| Log likelihood | −755.2549 | Hannan-Quinn criterion | | 17.70303 |
| *F*-statistic | 23.38052 | Durbin-Watson statistic | | 0.312328 |

*Source:* Field data.

price of gold, according to its moderate *R*-squared value of 0.461028. At a significance level of 5%, every independent variable's coefficient is statistically significant. It also implies that the null hypothesis was rejected and that the price of gold affects the stock market, currency rate, and crude oil because all of the independent variables have a significant impact on the price of gold.

*H0: There is no influence of gold price on forex rate, equity index, and crude oil amid the COVID-19 period.*

The results of an MLR model that analyses three independent variables—the price of crude oil, the NIFTY, and the forex rate—to predict the price of gold are displayed in Table 12.4. As seen by its low *R*-squared value of 0.049069, the model can only

**TABLE 12.4**
**Results of Multi-Linear Regression with Dependent Variable—Gold Price**

| Variable | Coefficient | Std. Error | *t*-Statistic | Prob. |
|---|---|---|---|---|
| C | 284,992.6 | 40,466.14 | 7.042743 | 0.0000 |
| Forex rate | −1,891.827 | 500.8400 | −3.777308 | 0.0002 |
| NIFTY | −0.728104 | 0.535455 | −1.359785 | 0.1749 |
| Crude oil | −0.134689 | 0.906406 | −0.148596 | 0.8820 |
| *R*-squared | 0.049069 | Mean dependent variable | | 134,934.0 |
| Adjusted *R*-squared | 0.039716 | S.D. dependent variable | | 6,317.315 |
| S.E. of regression | 6,190.595 | Akaike info criterion | | 20.31231 |
| Sum squared resid | 1.17E+10 | Schwarz criterion | | 20.36064 |
| Log likelihood | −3,134.252 | Hannan-Quinn criterion | | 20.33163 |
| *F*-statistic | 5.246134 | Durbin-Watson statistic | | 0.067549 |

*Source:* Field data.

**TABLE 12.5**
**Results of Multi-Linear Regression with Dependent Variable—Gold Price**

| Variable | Coefficient | Std. Error | *t*-Statistic | Prob. |
|---|---|---|---|---|
| C | 128,889.0 | 21,634.88 | 5.957465 | 0.0000 |
| Forex rate | −54.64615 | 251.7596 | −0.217057 | 0.8283 |
| NIFTY | 2.871359 | 0.471456 | 6.090406 | 0.0000 |
| Crude oil | −3.420184 | 0.542218 | −6.307765 | 0.0000 |
| *R*-squared | 0.395519 | Mean dependent variable | | 150,054.5 |
| Adjusted *R*-squared | 0.390747 | S.D. dependent variable | | 9,505.439 |
| S.E. of regression | 7,419.440 | Akaike info criterion | | 20.67196 |
| Sum squared resid | 2.09E+10 | Schwarz criterion | | 20.71311 |
| Log likelihood | −3,965.016 | Hannan-Quinn criterion | | 20.68828 |
| *F*-statistic | 82.87943 | Durbin-Watson statistic | | 0.052420 |

*Source:* Field data.

account for 4.91% of the variance in the price of gold. Only the coefficient for the exchange rate is statistically significant at the 5% level. At 5% significance, there is no statistically significant relationship between the NIFTY index coefficients and the price of crude oil. Additionally, it suggests that the price of gold influences FX rates but not the NIFTY or crude oil, proving that the null hypothesis has been rejected.

*H0: There is no influence of gold price on forex rate, equity index, and crude oil amid the Russia-Ukraine conflict.*

Table 12.5 displays the findings of an MLR model that forecasts the price of gold by taking into account three independent variables: The NIFTY, the currency rate, and the price of crude oil. The model explains roughly 39.55% of the fluctuation in the price of gold, according to its moderate *R*-squared value of 0.395519. Only the crude oil and NIFTY coefficients are statistically significant at the 5% level. At the 5% significance level, the Forex rate coefficients show little statistical significance. The null hypothesis has been rejected, according to this finding, which suggests that the price of gold significantly affects the NIFTY and crude oil but not the FX rate.

### 12.4.2 Support Vector Machine (Features Average Importance)

A SVM model that forecasts gold prices based on a number of external events or variables throughout a range of time periods—including the entire period, demonetization, the COVID-19 pandemic, and the Russian-Ukrainian invasion—is used to determine feature importances, as shown in Table 12.6. The Forex rate has an important score of 9.26, making it a highly significant predictor of gold prices over the general timeframe considered. During demonetization, the Forex rate's importance drops to 0.00, indicating it had no predictive value for gold prices in this specific period. The importance becomes negative (−2.26) during COVID-19, suggesting an inverse relationship or a decrease in predictive power. It regains some predictive power with a score of 1.23, suggesting a moderate impact on gold prices. From a low

**TABLE 12.6**
**Variables Average Importance by Using SVM**

| Variables | Overall Period | Demonization | COVID-19 | Russia-Ukraine Conflict |
|---|---|---|---|---|
| Forex rate | 9.26 | 0.00 | −2.26 | 1.23 |
| Nifty | 8.45 | 1.01 | 3.54 | 5.10 |
| Crude oil | 8.6 | −1.03 | −2.73 | 5.22 |
| $R^2$ | 0.90 | 0.85 | 0.54 | 0.57 |

*Source:* Field data.

of 1.01 during demonetization to a high of 5.10 during the Russian-Ukrainian invasion, Table 12.6 also demonstrates different levels of importance throughout time, suggesting that its significance varies greatly with local and global events. Like the Forex rate and Nifty, the impact of crude oil on gold prices varies. It peaked at 5.22 during the Russian-Ukrainian invasion, suggesting a robust relationship between gold and crude oil prices at times of geopolitical unrest. With an $R^2$ value of 0.90, the model performs exceptionally well, explaining 90% of the variation in gold prices during the whole study period. During demonetization, the model's explanatory power drops slightly to an $R^2$ of 0.85, still indicating strong performance. The $R^2$ value significantly drops to 0.54, suggesting the model's predictive power was much weaker during the pandemic, possibly due to the unprecedented nature of the event and its effects on the global economy. A similar $R^2$ value of 0.57 during this period indicates a slight improvement from the COVID-19 period but still represents a relatively low explanatory power, which could be due to the complex and evolving nature of geopolitical events and their impact on gold prices.

### 12.4.3 ANN Modelling

The neural network model for IBM's SPSS was used to carry out the ANN investigation, as seen in Figure 12.1. Both linear and nonlinear interactions may be captured by the ANN method, which does not require a normal distribution. One input, one or more hidden layers, and one output level are among the numerous hierarchical levels that make up a typical ANN. Although the output layer only contained one outcome, the input layer of this study covered three distinct pertinent criteria, including the exchange rate, Nifty, and crude oil. Ten-fold cross-validation was employed, with 90% of the data used for network testing and 10% for training in order to reduce overfitting issues. Figure 12.1 illustrates the ANN model architecture used for the overall period, featuring two hidden layers. This setup captures complex relationships among forex rate, NIFTY, and crude oil in predicting gold price trends.

Root mean square error (RMSE) and additional performance indicators for ANN models across the whole time frame are displayed in Table 12.7.

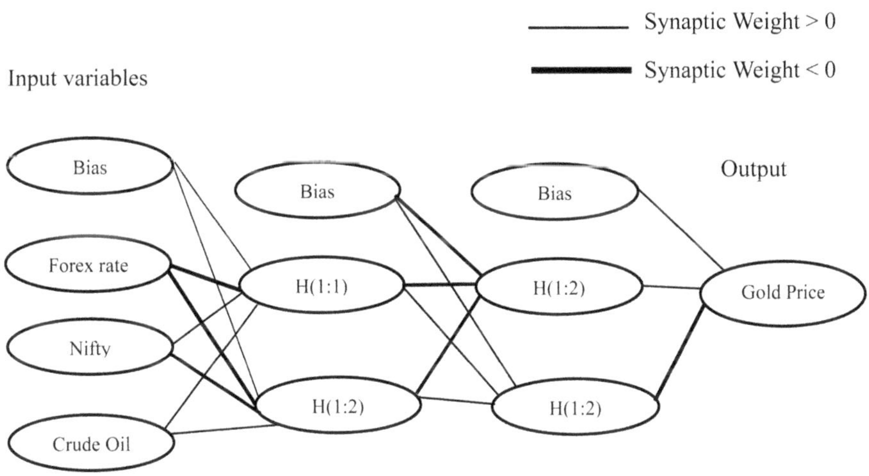


**FIGURE 12.1** The ANN model with two hidden layers for the overall period. (Authors construct.)

**TABLE 12.7**
**RMSE Values during Training and Testing Phases for Overall Period**

| Network | ANN Model ($R^2$ = 94%) | | | | | |
|---|---|---|---|---|---|---|
| | Training | | | Testing | | |
| | Samples | SSE | RMSE | Samples | SEE | RMSE |
| 1 | 2,773 | 88.05 | 0.178 | 308 | 9.74 | 0.178 |
| 2 | 2,779 | 88.07 | 0.178 | 302 | 9.49 | 0.177 |
| 3 | 2,754 | 97.32 | 0.188 | 327 | 11.58 | 0.188 |
| 4 | 2,742 | 82.77 | 0.174 | 339 | 11.81 | 0.187 |
| 5 | 2,786 | 90.08 | 0.180 | 295 | 10.26 | 0.186 |
| 6 | 2,734 | 98.36 | 0.190 | 347 | 12.22 | 0.188 |
| 7 | 2,776 | 84.18 | 0.174 | 305 | 9.58 | 0.177 |
| 8 | 2,760 | 90.93 | 0.182 | 321 | 10.72 | 0.183 |
| 9 | 2,735 | 95.65 | 0.187 | 346 | 11.64 | 0.183 |
| 10 | 2,771 | 98.69 | 0.189 | 310 | 10.95 | 0.188 |
| Average | | 91.41 | 0.182 | | 10.79 | 0.1835 |
| Standard Deviation | | 5.82 | 0.006 | | 1.00 | 0.005 |

*Notes:*

1. SSE = Sum of squares error, RMSE = root mean square error.
2. In the ANN model, forex rate, Nifty, and crude oil price taken as the input neurons; while gold price taken as the output neuron.
3. $R^2$ = 1—RMSE/S2, where S2 is the variance of the desired output for the test data.

**TABLE 12.8**
**Sensitivity Analysis for Overall Period**

| Variable | 1 | 2 | 3 | 4 | 5 | 6 | 7 | 8 | 9 | 10 | I | NI |
|---|---|---|---|---|---|---|---|---|---|---|---|---|
| Exchange rate | 0.426 | 0.498 | 0.563 | 0.545 | 0.547 | 0.563 | 0.517 | 0.556 | 0.568 | 0.574 | 0.545 | 100 |
| NIFTY | 0.364 | 0.328 | 0.312 | 0.344 | 0.310 | 0.311 | 0.360 | 0.294 | 0.305 | 0.302 | 0.344 | 63 |
| Oil rate | 0.210 | 0.174 | 0.125 | 0.111 | 0.143 | 0.126 | 0.123 | 0.149 | 0.127 | 0.124 | 0.111 | 20.4 |

*Note:* I—Importance and NI—Normalized Importance.
*Source:* Field data.

Table 12.8 shows sensitivity analysis for the ANN model across the overall period, identifying the relative impact of each input variable.

Figure 12.2 depicts the ANN model with two hidden layers applied to the demonetization period. It highlights how the model adapts to sudden economic policy changes and their effect on gold pricing.

Table 12.9 contains RMSE performance data for different ANN networks during the demonetization period.

Table 12.10 presents sensitivity analysis results from ANN for the demonetization period, highlighting variable influence.

The results of a sensitivity analysis that ordered factors based on their normalized relative importance to the dependent variable are shown in Table 12.10. By

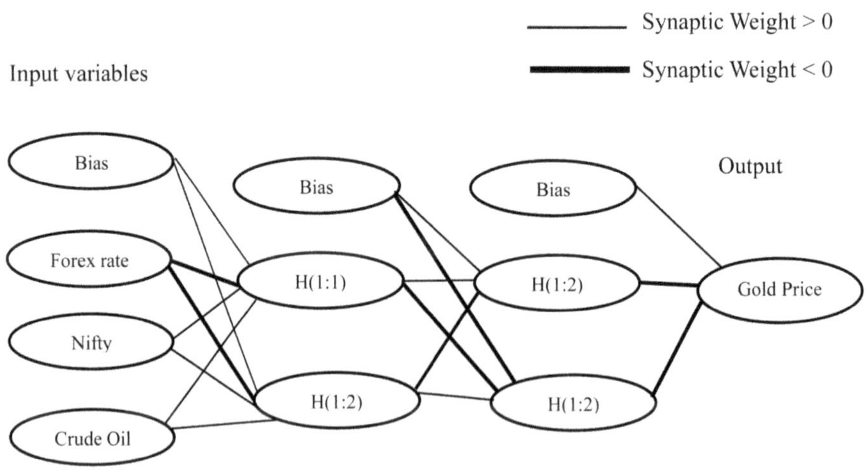


**FIGURE 12.2** The ANN model with two hidden layers for the demonetization period. (Authors construct.)

**TABLE 12.9**
**RMSE Values during Training and Testing Phases for the Demonetization Period**

| Network | ANN Model ($R^2$ = 76%) | | | | | |
|---|---|---|---|---|---|---|
| | Training | | | Testing | | |
| | Samples | SSE | RMSE | Samples | SEE | RMSE |
| 1 | 75 | 11.08 | 0.384 | 11 | 2.69 | 0.495 |
| 2 | 81 | 14.82 | 0.428 | 5 | 0.76 | 0.390 |
| 3 | 79 | 12.01 | 0.390 | 7 | 0.25 | 0.189 |
| 4 | 74 | 11.67 | 0.397 | 12 | 2.48 | 0.455 |
| 5 | 79 | 20.11 | 0.505 | 7 | 0.51 | 0.270 |
| 6 | 77 | 16.62 | 0.465 | 9 | 0.94 | 0.323 |
| 7 | 76 | 10.26 | 0.367 | 10 | 1.28 | 0.358 |
| 8 | 76 | 13.15 | 0.416 | 10 | 1.42 | 0.377 |
| 9 | 77 | 17.85 | 0.481 | 9 | 0.99 | 0.332 |
| 10 | 76 | 9.60 | 0.355 | 10 | 0.83 | 0.288 |
| Average | | 13.72 | 0.419 | | 1.22 | 0.348 |
| Standard Deviation | | 3.51 | 0.050 | | 0.80 | 0.089 |

*Source:* Field data.

*Notes:*

1. SSE = Sum of squares error, RMSE = root mean square error.
2. In the ANN model, forex rate, Nifty, and crude oil price taken as the input neurons; while gold price taken as the output neuron.
3. $R^2$ = 1—RMSE/S2, where S2 is the variance of the desired output for the test data.

demonstrating how changes in the values of independent variables impact the predictions produced by the network structure, this analysis brought attention to the importance of each predictor. Notably, the NIFTY index was shown to be the most reliable indicator of gold prices, with the currency rate and crude oil prices coming in second and third, respectively. Figure 12.3 shows the ANN

**TABLE 12.10**
**Sensitivity Analysis for the Demonetization Period**

| Variable | 1 | 2 | 3 | 4 | 5 | 6 | 7 | 8 | 9 | 10 | I | NI |
|---|---|---|---|---|---|---|---|---|---|---|---|---|
| Forex rate | 0.249 | 0.236 | 0.271 | 0.280 | 0.082 | 0.266 | 0.267 | 0.226 | 0.068 | 0.129 | 0.129 | 55.2 |
| NIFTY | 0.451 | 0.448 | 0.415 | 0.492 | 0.465 | 0.436 | 0.379 | 0.448 | 0.515 | 0.465 | 0.465 | 100 |
| Oil rate | 0.300 | 0.316 | 0.314 | 0.228 | 0.453 | 0.298 | 0.354 | 0.326 | 0.416 | 0.400 | 0.400 | 66.6 |

*Note:* I—Importance and NI—Normalized Importance.
*Source:* Field data.

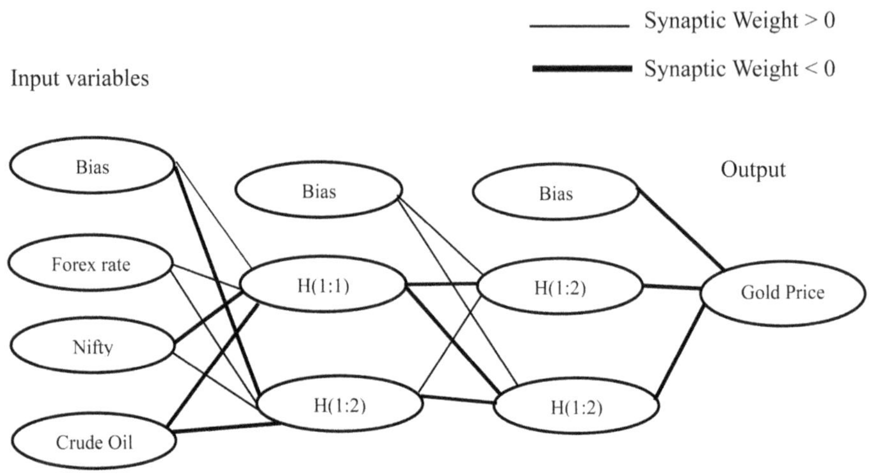


**FIGURE 12.3** The ANN model with two hidden layers for the COVID-19 period. (Authors construct.)

structure used during the COVID-19 period. This configuration reflects the model's attempt to learn from volatile market data caused by pandemic-induced disruptions.

Table 12.11 evaluates ANN model accuracy during the COVID-19 period using RMSE and training/testing error statistics.

**TABLE 12.11**
**RMSE Values during Training and Testing Phases for the COVID-19 Period**

| Network | ANN Model ($R^2$ = 66%) | | | | | |
|---|---|---|---|---|---|---|
| | Training | | | Testing | | |
| | Samples | SSE | RMSE | Samples | SEE | RMSE |
| 1 | 273 | 64.46 | 0.486 | 36 | 5.06 | 0.375 |
| 2 | 281 | 57.17 | 0.451 | 28 | 4.76 | 0.412 |
| 3 | 281 | 54.95 | 0.442 | 28 | 4.42 | 0.397 |
| 4 | 275 | 45.48 | 0.407 | 34 | 7.46 | 0.468 |
| 5 | 269 | 63.10 | 0.484 | 40 | 8.48 | 0.460 |
| 6 | 279 | 50.12 | 0.424 | 30 | 4.69 | 0.395 |
| 7 | 270 | 46.91 | 0.417 | 39 | 6.89 | 0.420 |
| 8 | 278 | 50.73 | 0.427 | 31 | 6.32 | 0.452 |
| 9 | 274 | 48.16 | 0.419 | 35 | 6.01 | 0.414 |
| 10 | 280 | 77.56 | 0.526 | 29 | 4.17 | 0.379 |
| Average | | 55.86 | 0.45 | | 5.83 | 0.42 |
| Standard Deviation | | 10.03 | 0.04 | | 1.45 | 0.03 |

*Source:* Field data.

**TABLE 12.12**
**Sensitivity Analysis for COVID-19**

| Variable | 1 | 2 | 3 | 4 | 5 | 6 | 7 | 8 | 9 | 10 | I | NI |
|---|---|---|---|---|---|---|---|---|---|---|---|---|
| Forex rate | 0.381 | 0.483 | 0.107 | 0.021 | 0.394 | 0.215 | 0.154 | 0.102 | 0.159 | 0.358 | 0.021 | 3.9% |
| NIFTY | 0.318 | 0.225 | 0.452 | 0.542 | 0.268 | 0.389 | 0.472 | 0.456 | 0.423 | 0.276 | 0.542 | 100% |
| Oil rate | 0.301 | 0.291 | 0.441 | 0.437 | 0.338 | 0.396 | 0.374 | 0.442 | 0.418 | 0.366 | 0.437 | 80.5% |

*Note:* I—Importance and NI—Normalized Importance.

Table 12.12 shows the sensitivity of Gold Price to input variables during COVID-19 as derived from the ANN model. Table 12.12 presents the results of the sensitivity analysis, which systematically ranks the variables according to their normalized importance to the dependent variable. It captures the effect of fluctuations in independent variables on the network's output and clarifies the role of each predictor. The Nifty index was identified as the foremost predictor of gold prices, succeeded by the forex rate and crude oil prices.

Figure 12.4 presents the ANN model for the Russia-Ukraine conflict period, emphasizing how the network structure interprets the economic impact of geopolitical tensions on the gold price.

Table 12.13 reports RMSE and training metrics for ANN models during the Russia-Ukraine conflict period.

Table 12.14 displays ANN-based sensitivity analysis during the conflict period, showing normalized importance of each variable.

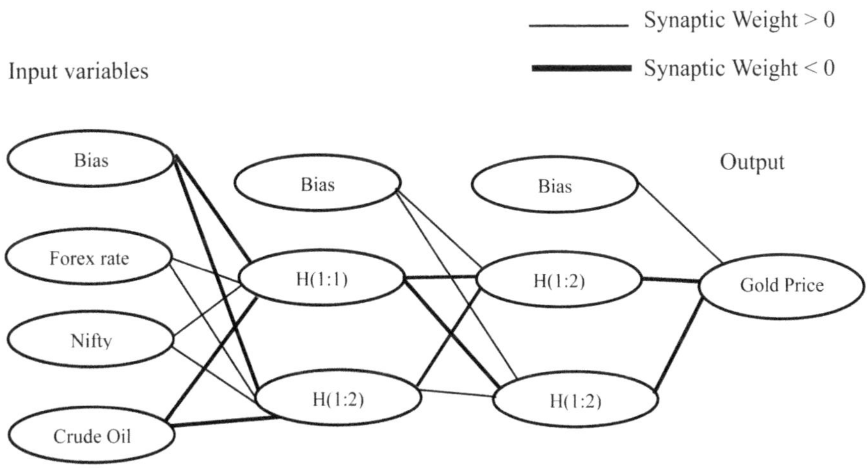


**FIGURE 12.4** The ANN model with two hidden layers for the Russia-Ukraine conflict period. (Authors construct.)

**TABLE 12.13**
**RMSE Values during Training and Testing Phases for the Russia-Ukraine Conflict Period**

| Network | ANN Model ($R^2$ = 84%) | | | | | |
|---|---|---|---|---|---|---|
| | Training | | | Testing | | |
| | Samples | SSE | RMSE | Samples | SEE | RMSE |
| 1 | 346 | 48.3 | 0.374 | 38 | 6.7 | 0.42 |
| 2 | 345 | 41.79 | 0.348 | 39 | 3.03 | 0.279 |
| 3 | 339 | 40.97 | 0.348 | 45 | 4.87 | 0.329 |
| 4 | 335 | 44.9 | 0.366 | 49 | 6.2 | 0.356 |
| 5 | 348 | 54.89 | 0.397 | 36 | 4.5 | 0.354 |
| 6 | 341 | 57.71 | 0.411 | 43 | 5.08 | 0.344 |
| 7 | 347 | 51.07 | 0.384 | 37 | 6.84 | 0.43 |
| 8 | 337 | 43.89 | 0.361 | 47 | 2.88 | 0.25 |
| 9 | 346 | 43.87 | 0.356 | 38 | 4.66 | 0.35 |
| 10 | 343 | 69.91 | 0.451 | 41 | 2.42 | 0.24 |
| Average | | 49.70 | 0.40 | | 4.70 | 0.30 |
| Standard Deviation | | 9.02 | 0.03 | | 1.58 | 0.06 |

*Notes:*

1. SSE = Sum of squares error, RMSE = root mean square error.
2. In the ANN model, forex rate, Nifty, and crude oil price taken as the input neurons; while gold price taken as the output neuron.
3. $R^2$ = 1—RMSE/S2, where S2 is the variance of the desired output for the test data.

**TABLE 12.14**
**Sensitivity Analysis for Russia-Ukraine Conflict Period**

| Variable | 1 | 2 | 3 | 4 | 5 | 6 | 7 | 8 | 9 | 10 | I | NI |
|---|---|---|---|---|---|---|---|---|---|---|---|---|
| Forex rate | 0.305 | 0.306 | 0.313 | 0.316 | 0.302 | 0.311 | 0.277 | 0.271 | 0.270 | 0.292 | 0.313 | 76.27 |
| NIFTY | 0.284 | 0.322 | 0.307 | 0.299 | 0.329 | 0.315 | 0.269 | 0.354 | 0.327 | 0.345 | 0.307 | 81.11 |
| Crude oil | 0.411 | 0.372 | 0.380 | 0.385 | 0.369 | 0.373 | 0.455 | 0.374 | 0.403 | 0.363 | 0.380 | 100.00 |

*Note:* I—Importance and NI—Normalized Importance.

## 12.5 FINDINGS OF THE STUDY

Table 12.15 compares model performance ($R^2$) across MLR, SVM, and ANN methods for all four time periods. It highlights the most effective modelling approach per scenario.

**TABLE 12.15**
**Model Performance Comparison ($R^2$)**

| Methods | Overall Period | Demonetization Period | COVID-19 Period | Russia-Ukraine Conflict Period |
|---|---|---|---|---|
| MLR | 0.77 | 0.46 | 0.04 | 0.39 |
| SVM | 0.90 | 0.71 | 0.54 | 0.57 |
| ANN | 0.94 | 0.76 | 0.66 | 0.84 |

### 12.5.1 Model Performance

- *Artificial Neural Networks (ANN)*: The ANN models consistently show the highest $R^2$ values across all periods, indicating their superior capability in predicting gold prices under both stable and volatile conditions.
- *Support Vector Machines (SVMs)*: SVM generally works better than MLR, especially in unstable periods, although its performance is closer to MLR in more stable conditions.
- *Multiple Linear Regression (MLR)*: When it comes to handling the complexities of volatile market situations, MLR is limited, particularly during the COVID-19 pandemic and the Russian-Ukrainian conflict.

### 12.5.2 Overall Influence

- Across the overall period, gold prices have significant interactions with forex rates, equity indices, and crude oil prices. With the greatest $R^2$ value of 0.94, the ANN model is the most effective model for capturing these connections.
- During the demonetization period, MLR indicates a moderate $R^2$ value of 0.46, with all independent variables significantly influencing gold prices.
- In the COVID-19 period, the influence of gold prices on forex rates is significant, but not on equity indices and crude oil prices, as evidenced by a low $R^2$ value of 0.04.
- The Russia-Ukraine conflict period exhibits moderate $R^2$ values across all models, with significant influence of gold prices on equity indices and crude oil prices, but not on forex rates.

### 12.5.3 Predictor Importance

- The forex rate is an important predictor of the prices of gold given the sensitivity analysis from the ANN model during the overall period. After the forex rate, index of NIFTY and the prices of crude oil are the next important predictors of the gold prices.
- During the demonetization period, the NIFTY index emerged as the most significant predictor, followed by the forex rate and crude oil prices.

- The COVID-19 period identified the NIFTY index as the foremost predictor, succeeded by crude oil prices and the forex rate.
- In the Russia-Ukraine conflict period, crude oil prices were the most important predictor, followed by the NIFTY index and the forex rate.

## 12.6 CONCLUSION

This study emphasizes the role of deep learning and machine learning methods in understanding and examining the financial markets. Particularly, the study contributes to examining the impact oil the economic turmoil on the prices of gold with appropriate predictions. The proven high-quality performance of the ANN model in all the given periods asserts the effectiveness of the model not only in capturing the linear interactions among the economic variables but also the nonlinear ones. According to the study's results, gold is regarded as a safe haven in difficult economic times. This finding is significant not only for the scientific community but, more significantly, for investors and decision-makers. With the additional knowledge and insight this study offers on the connections and interdependencies between the prices of crude oil, gold, currency, and equity indexes, stakeholders should be able to make well-rounded decisions, especially during times of extreme economic turbulence.

## REFERENCES

1. Wang Y, Lee CC, Thi TBN. Time and place where gold acts as an inflation hedge: An application of long-run and short-run threshold model. *Econ Model.* 2011;28(3):806–19.
2. Apergis N, Christina B. The impact of geopolitical events on gold prices. *Res Int Bus Finance.* 2019;47:124–34.
3. Sharma N, Mahendru M. Impact of macro-economic variables on stock prices in India. *Glob J Manag Bus Res.* 2010;10(7):19–26.
4. Ciner C, Gurdgiev C, Lucey BM. Hedges and safe havens: An examination of stocks, bonds, gold, oil and exchange rates. *Int Rev Financ Anal.* 2013;29:202–11.
5. Baur DG, McDermott TK. Is gold a safe haven? International evidence. *J Bank Finance.* 2010;34(8):1886–98.
6. Cheema MA, Faff RW, Szulczuk KR. The 2008 global financial crisis and COVID-19 pandemic: How safe are the safe haven assets? *Int Rev Financ Anal.* 2022;83:102316. https://doi.org/10.1016/j.irfa.2022.102316
7. Blose LE. Gold prices, cost of carry, and expected inflation. *J Econ Finance.* 2010;34(3):329–39.
8. Hillier D, Draper P, Faff R. Do precious metals shine? An investment perspective. *Financ Anal J.* 2006;62(2):98–106.
9. Zhang YJ, Wei YM. The crude oil market and the gold market: Evidence for cointegration. *Appl Energy.* 2010;87(10):3269–77.
10. Reboredo JC. Is gold a hedge or safe haven against oil price movements? *Resour Policy.* 2013;38(2):130–7.
11. Jain A, Biswal P. Dynamic linkages among oil price, gold price, exchange rate, and stock market in India. *Resour Policy.* 2016;49:179–85.
12. Pandit S, Luo X. A novel prediction model to evaluate the dynamic interrelationship between gold and crude oil. *Int J Data Sci Anal.* 2025;20:1161–82. https://doi.org/10.1007/s41060-024-00519-8

13. Yeoh Y, Phoong SW, Lau C. Dynamic correlation between crude oil price and exchange rate: The case of ASEAN-5. *EDUCATUM J Sci Math Technol.* 2022;9:24–34.
14. Raggad B, Bouri E. Gold and crude oil: A time-varying causality across various market conditions. *Resour Policy.* 2023;86:104273.
15. Munir T, Al Mamlook R, Rahman AR, Alrashidi A, Yaseen A. COVID-19's influence on Karachi stock exchange: A comparative machine learning algorithms study for forecasting. *Heliyon.* 2024;10:e33190.
16. Sarma N. Linkage between crude oil, gold, INR-USD reference rate and sensex amidst Covid-19 pandemic: A cointegration and causality analysis. *Asian Finance Rev.* 2024;2:37–46.
17. Sokhanvar A. Impacts of ongoing global geopolitical and economic turbulences on exchange rates: A case study of the Australian dollar. *Ekon Cas.* 2023;71:405–27.

# 13 Intelligent Robo-advisors and Personalized Financial Planning

*Cornelius Adorm-Takyi and Fredrick Appiah Asare*

## 13.1 INTRODUCTION

### 13.1.1 The Rise of AI in Wealth Management

The financial services industry is experiencing a radical transformation, with a fundamental cause being the advances in artificial intelligence (AI), big data and algorithmic automation witnessed in the last few decades [1, 2]. Intelligent robo-advisors are changing the game of financial planning, a process that was previously aided only through human financial advisors. Previously, human advisors would prescribe investments based on one's risk profile, income, and other long-run financial objectives. However, these services were expensive, not widely accessible, and prone to human bias [3, 4]. With technology-based portfolio management solutions that provide a cost-effective, rapid scalability, and technological advantage to ensure the portfolio investment is done in a precision, AI robo-advisors have turned this whole equation on its head. Robo-advisors are automated financial planning and portfolio management services that are delivered through digital platforms and use AI without any human component [5]. By combining advanced machine learning (ML) and real-time data analysis with established behavioural finance theory, these systems create personalized investment portfolios tailored to each investor's unique financial profile, risk tolerance, and other investment goals. This kind of automation allows for delivering personalized financial services at just a minute fraction of the cost as compared to the traditional advisory models. The 2014 European Paradox Robo-advisors have taken off in Europe, where regulatory frameworks like MiFID II (Markets in Financial Instruments Directive) have produced a climate of transparency and accountability for automated financial services. International wealth management firms and several fintech startups have been able to capitalize on these regulatory benefits to providing AI-powered tools to its clients, giving an ever-increasing number of investors access to more customized, goal-oriented investment solutions.

### 13.1.2 Key Drivers of AI-powered Financial Planning

There are several reasons why the shift towards AI robo-advisors and personalized financial planning is speeding up:


DOI: 10.1201/9781003611646-13

a. *Cost-Effective Investment Options*: Traditional financial advisors come with high costs, making wealth management inaccessible to smaller investors. Robo-advisors, however, provide cheap alternatives that open top-notch financial planning to a larger demographic.
b. *Technological Advances in AI and Data Analytics*: AI-powered robo-advisors use highly technical data analytics, real-time and long-term predictive modelling for market trends, asset behaviour, and even investor behaviour. As a result, it allows them to provide much more precise, data-oriented financial recommendations that were only available to high-net-worth clients.
c. *More Regulatory Push Around Transparency and Digital Financial Services*: In Europe, financial regulations like MiFID II and GDPR (General Data Protection Regulation) have pushed the adoption of AI-based investment platforms, creating a higher degree of transparency and consumer protection in the market and ultimately spurring greater confidence in the technology (e.g., MiFID II).
d. *Behavioural Finance and Personalized Wealth Management*: By applying behavioural finance, an AI system measures an individual's spending, saving, and other financial behaviours. By having access to an investor's risk tolerance, goals, and asset classes that they would like to avoid, robo-advisors are able to create these highly personalized investment strategies.
e. The age of AI will drive technology-focused innovation in wealth management. As the world's financial systems incorporate more and more automation, AI-based financial planning will be the bedrock of modern wealth management ahead. This is highly relevant to current innovations that are opening investment opportunities for all, giving individuals around the world more agency over their financial future, requiring little reliance on the human element.

## 13.2 THEORETICAL FRAMEWORK

### 13.2.1 Understanding Robo-Advisors and Personalized Finance

Robo-advisors are a great evolution in wealth management industry leveraging AI, ML, and automation to provide personalized financial advisory services [6, 7]. These AI-based platforms are responsible for using algorithms to manage a portfolio of investments, which incorporates statistical optimization techniques, risk assessment models, and predictive analytics. Robo-advisors do not have human emotions, and this affect their decision-making process as it is done by an algorithm that takes into account only data to generate investment recommendations as compared to traditional financial advisors [8]. Robo-advisory systems democratize access to high-quality financial planning tools for a wider audience through low-cost, scalable, and objective portfolio management. Robo-advisors can be viewed as segmented into three generations using technology, operating model, and complexity of interaction as the segmentation dimensions:

a. *First-Generation Robo-Advisors*: The first models were driven by rule-based algorithms implementing pre-established asset allocation strategies. The emphasis was on basic automated portfolio recommendations with little personalization [9]. Although they were affordable, they also could not adapt and be personalized in real-time to match the ever-changing market.
b. *Second-Generation AI Robo-Advisors*: Robo-advisory frameworks that integrated ML opened the floodgates. These models applied adaptive learning algorithms where they observed not just the market state, but also the actions of other investors and were able to re-optimize the portfolio to remain optimal even as conditions and behaviours changed. With the availability of ML, robo-advisors enabled customers to offer a comparatively sophisticated and customized investment strategies by enhancing customer satisfaction [10].
c. *Third-Generation Hybrid Robo-Advisors*: The latest generation of robo-advisory technology merges the two to create the best of both worlds: AI-driven automation to reduce human errors paired with human supervision to reduce algorithmic errors. Such hybrid systems offer an ideal compromise between the best that automated decision-making can provide and the need for human prudence with respect to financial matters by allowing human advisors to examine complex or high-risk decisions. This partly addresses the ethical and trust issues surrounding fully automatic systems, as it is a more balanced and, therefore, more human-centred approach to individualized financial planning.

### 13.2.2 Theoretical Models Supporting AI-Driven Financial Planning

The development and use of AI in wealth management is based on various classical and recent financial theories. These models provide a conceptual basis that supplements the functional roles of robo-advisory systems and extends our understanding of their impact on investment behaviours.

#### 13.2.2.1 Modern Portfolio Theory (MPT) in Robo-Advisory Systems

One of the bedrocks of investment management is Modern Portfolio Theory (MPT), which was developed by Harry Markowitz in 1952. MPT states that investors can create an optimal portfolio by maximizing the risk-adjusted return using the least risk for the most return by making an ideal trade-off between risk and return, thus allowing for the best overall diversification of the portfolio among different asset classes. Robo-advisors process data using AI and ML to assess the risk-adjusted portfolios and use MPT-based optimization algorithms to determine the optimal asset allocation and to balance the exposure to the market with the growth potential of the asset [11]. Robo-advisors are further enhanced by AI, which allows them to constantly rebalance portfolios with moving markets and individual risk profiles, so that assets are allocated more effectively than this human discretion alone. In addition, MPT has been practically applied in robo-advisory systems with the aid of big data analytical techniques. This permits robo-advisors to compute an enormous amount of financial information and update their portfolio composition in real-time, a necessity in the volatile markets of today. The real-world applicability of MPT becomes stronger with portfolio management adjusted based on such high-level data by AI.

#### 13.2.2.2 Behavioural Finance and AI-Driven Investor Profiling

The traditional argument in finance is that financial markets reflect rational decisions made by market participants as investors are assumed to behave rationally while taking their decisions [12, 13], but behavioural finance challenges this view and focuses on the irrational choices investors make and how these decisions are affected by their cognitive biases and emotional responses. AI-powered robo-advisors are well placed to tackle these biases as they can weave in insights from behavioural finance within their profiling and recommendation algorithms. Robo-advisors leverage data on historical financial behaviour, transaction patterns, and real-time decision-making information to detect recurring psychological errors of individual investors, including excessive confidence, loss aversion, and herd behaviour, that lead to poor investment decisions. This behavioural data can be used by AI-driven systems to build smarter, disciplined investment strategies, preventing impulsive financial choices and ensuring recommendations align with an investor's long-term goals and risk tolerance. Robo-advisory services play an important role in establishing investor trust with automated recommendations due to the need within the applied research branch and individual behavioural finance studies to adapt automated recommendations to any investor preference and economic discipline.

### 13.2.3 Real-life Financial Planning Trends in Europe

AI driven wealth management is maturing across Europe, and there seems to be a perfect storm of regulatory environment, technological advancements and shifting investor demand fuelling the trend. There has been significant growth in this space across countries like Germany and the United Kingdom with a 60% user growth of robo-advisory services being recorded in 2023. The increase has been massive and as the investment landscape continues to evolve, robo-advisors are specially equipped to deliver cheap, passive investment solutions that are quickly aligning with their larger audiences. These platforms are particularly attractive to retail investors seeking low-cost alternatives to traditional wealth management services due to their algorithm-driven models of investment [14]. This change has been especially facilitated by some European financial regulations. Various regulations like MiFID II and GDPR have created an environment conducive to AI adoption in financial services by promoting transparency, consumer protection, and data security. This, in turn, has prompted financial institutions to adopt AI tools, providing investors with customized, highly transparent, and fact-based financial planning solutions [15, 16]. In addition, the rise of passive investing, particularly via low-cost Exchange Traded Funds (ETFs), has been a perfect match for robo-adviser portfolios, which often emphasize automated, inexpensive, investment fads. These points reflect an overall transitioning of Europe towards digital financial services, as experts believe that the future of personalized wealth management will involve robo-advisors.

## 13.3 ANALYTICAL FRAMEWORK FOR AI-DRIVEN FINANCIAL ADVISORY SYSTEMS

### 13.3.1 AI-Enhanced Investment Strategies and Portfolio Optimization

Robo-advisory services revolutionized the investment management industry with data-driven, bottom-up, and scalable wealth-building strategies, primarily driven by AI [17]. In contrast, conventional financial advisor typically relies on the subjective analysis and human judgement, AI-powered robo-advisors utilized advanced statistical models, ML and predictive analytics to optimize the construction and management of investment portfolios. Such systems work in real-time and take factors such as the financial goals of the investor, their risk factor and the market conditions into consideration for derivatives of well-customized and fluid investment schemes. Continuous portfolio optimization is one of the defining features of AI-driven robo-advisors. In contrast to the quarterly or yearly investment review of traditional advisory models, AI algorithms conduct continuous market analyses, dynamically altering portfolios to reflect daily changes in market conditions, interest rates, and geopolitical events [18, 19]. So, during cases of expected downfalls in the economy, robo-advisors can automatically shift assets into a defensive position such as government bonds or gold, which means decreased exposure to shaky equities. And this adaptability to portfolio management is why AI platforms are uniquely positioned to be successful in more complicated and rapid trading environments.

### 13.3.2 Algorithmic Portfolio Construction and Advanced Risk Management Techniques

Using advanced techniques, AI-powered robo-advisory systems are able to build tailored portfolios to drive the highest risk-adjusted returns. Among these methods are:

a. *Mean-Variance Optimization (MVO)*: Based on ideas from MPT, MVO constitutes the backbone of most robo-advisor portfolio construction. Based on the portfolio return/standard deviation relation, MVO calculates the optimal asset allocation to maximize the expected return subject to a given level of risk (or standard deviation), which means, as the underlying premise behind MVO is diversification, portfolios are designed to match the risk-return preferences of the investor.
b. *Monte Carlo Simulations*: Using stochastic modelling, robo-advisors run thousands of simulations to project how a portfolio would perform over various potential market and economic conditions. Such method improves choices with probabilistic insights on what potential risks and what potential returns to balance in a portfolio to optimize performance across market environments.
c. *Factor-based Investing*: AI-led robo-advisors integrate factor-based investing methodologies that analyse fundamental drivers of the market including but not limited to momentum, volatility, and macroeconomic indicators.

Such data along with behaviour can help in building portfolio construction which robo-advisors are missing to do and this drives away investment strategies from long-term growth with minimum downside risk.

The trend towards automated passive investing via ETFs has really taken off in the European space. Presently, several robo-advisory platforms emphasize investing in low-cost index funds rather than actively managed portfolios, essentially taking advantage of AI for managing diversified portfolios with minimal human intervention. As investors increasingly gravitate towards cheaper, more transparent ways to allocate their capital, it makes sense that passive investing strategies, which typically provide a similar rate of return at a much lower fee, would flourish.

### 13.3.3 The Role of AI in Personalized Financial Planning and Holistic Wealth Management

Apart from portfolio management, robo-advisors powered by AI are also revolutionizing the personal financial planning market with advanced solutions for all types of financial goals like retirement planning, tax optimization, and debt management:

a. *Retirement Planning*: Based on income, expenses, inflation, and life expectancy, AI-based platforms can simulate scenarios for retirement. The metrics of such systems tell you how much you need to save today and how much you need to accumulate and how much to consume. Instead, AI-powered retirement plans are more flexible and agile than the conventional, one-size-fits-all retirement planning because the algorithm will continue to be calibrated based on changing market conditions and based on changes in personal circumstances or objectives.
b. *Debt and Credit Optimization*: AI models further analyse the borrower's credit profile, the expenditure patterns, and the total loans outstanding to provide an individual recommendation on debt management and credit improvement to reduce the applicable interest. Providing personalized financial advice that helps individuals make better decisions on how to pay down debt thus enhancing their financial health.
c. *Tax-Efficient Investing*: Many robo-advisors use algorithms for tax loss harvesting-strategically selling your depreciated holdings to offset any potential capital gains and lower your tax bill. This RTM CP tax-efficiency portfolio management is useful for investors, because it guarantees returns optimization, and tax-efficiency optimization with tax-influenced capital gain and losses generated at the same time; thereby, maximizing portfolio performance via automation in post-tax/money individual investment stages by using AI-based platforms.

With the rapid growth in financial service digitalization, the AI-based robo-advisory platforms are due to be a pivotal part of personalized financial planning in the future [20]. Now, they can increasingly make better data-driven personal financial decisions, saving to build their longer-term wealth ahead of time with more ease and precision than ever before through such systems. This growing availability and affordability of AI-based financial solutions highlight a critical paradigm shift in how people interact with wealth management, as financial advice becomes democratized, and the future of finance is more inclusive.

## 13.4 FUTURE TRENDS AND POLICY IMPLICATIONS IN AI-DRIVEN WEALTH MANAGEMENT

### 13.4.1 The Future of AI in Wealth Management and Financial Planning

The fast-paced changes in AI are undoubtedly affecting the future of wealth management and financial planning which is likely to revolutionize algorithmic trading, hyper-personalized financial advisory service, and AI-based behavioural analytics [21]. Features indicative of the next generation of robo-advisory services take shape across the world. One of the most significant recent trends is the emergence of hybrid robo-advisors. These platforms provide the best of both worlds, delivering the automation benefits brought by AI but using actual human financial advisors. Fully automated robo-advisors have gained a lot of traction (e.g., investing based on pre-programmed algorithms), but high-stakes decisions still call for a human touch in at least some respects. Such hybrid advisory models allow AI to take care of mundane processes, like executing fundamental tasks such as asset allocation or portfolio rebalancing but when it comes to high-stakes decision-making, such as during market crises or bespoke tax planning, human advisors – and human judgement – become indispensable [22, 23]. As a model that satisfies the need for automation while preserving the importance of human analysis, this model is likely to take on even greater importance in the future as investors demand variety in the form of investment strategies.

Another major trend is where blockchain technology meets AI-powered robo-advisors [24, 25]. Blockchain has the potential to provide an extra layer of transparency, security, and decentralization, while making investment transactions tamper-proof and easily audited. European regulators are already investigating whether the bitcoin blockchain can help fend off data manipulation or algorithmic bias, while avoiding human error that may enable financial fraud. It is likely to transform the financial system in a way that these platforms will be able to provide decentralized platforms using high integrity, decentralized data that users can trust when using robo-advisory services. In addition, AI is moving towards hyper-personalized financial planning due to deep learning algorithms and behavioural analytics. The traditional risk profiler merely assigns a weighting to different schemas without exploring the deeper questions as to why individuals take risks. These AI have been trained on human factors such as the psychology, spending patterns, and long-term financial ambitions of the individual [26]. The next wave of AI-based financial decisions hopes to completely remove human biases from the equation while directly and continuously adapting to how a human life changes, whether through a job readjustment, a growing family, or sudden economic turmoil. Such systems herald a new era of customized financial advice, and more specific portfolio strategies that target an individual's own financial goals and personal circumstances. With the advent of AI, it is becoming crucial that regulatory frameworks can evolve so that AI-driven wealth management can be made more transparent, ethical, and accountable. Investors want to ensure their own interests are protected, and the same goes for regulatory oversight; it has to evolve to adapt to new technological capabilities but still needs to protect investors and to enforce fairness and security in automated financial services.

## 13.5 POLICY RECOMMENDATIONS FOR AI IN FINANCIAL PLANNING

The proliferation of AI-driven robo-advisory services has in turn shown European regulators to lay down solid governance structures that strike a fine balance between protecting the consumer and promoting technological advancement. There are a few high-level policy recommendation that should be prioritized to grow AI-driven wealth management in a sustainable and responsible way.

a. *AI Model Transparency and Explainability:* The potential for lack of transparency in decision-making is one of the key challenges in using AI in financial services. Making AI-driven decisions deterministic – forces financial institutions to explain exactly how they arrive at decisions and what algorithms are used. It is crucial for building investor trust and confidence, and for ensuring that users know how their investment strategies are created. Transparency measures can also reduce the potential for algorithmic bias, effectively working to ensure that an AI does the ethical thing when it comes to investors.
b. *Stronger AI Governance and Consumer Protection Laws:* Regulators ought to establish ethics guidelines for AI development that require AI systems to meet minimum standards of fairness, accountability, and ethics. There needs to be rigorous auditing of AI models to discover and correct biases. Setting appropriate global ethical guidelines for the application of AI will be essential to the continued success of the pools of money that we collectively invest in as well as ensuring that unscrupulous elements do not take advantage of the many vulnerable investors.
c. *Compliance with European Financial Regulations:* All financial platforms backed up by AI must comply with pre-existing regulations of Europe like MiFID II and GDPR. MiFID II inspires transparent investments and protection of clientele and GDPR enables confidentiality and safety of a range of personal data. Compliance with these regulations is essential for the protection of investors and the responsible implementation of AI in financial services.
d. *Fair AI-based Credit Scoring and Risk Profiling:* Credit scoring systems and risk profiling models powered by AI must be stringently monitored to ensure that they do not discriminate against certain demographic groups. Algorithms should be periodically audited to ensure they are not

unintentionally impeding those with less access to financial services or those historically marginalized. Other important measures to be adopted must be fairness and inclusivity ensuring that everyone has an equal access towards utilizing AI-based financial services, regardless of their socioeconomic background or any other demographic factors.

These measures will provide a safe, responsible, and inclusive financial ecosystem powered by AI. They will contribute towards automating wealth management transforming to become more investor-centric, without diluting the true essence and trust factor of the industry. The future of financial planning is going to be profoundly influenced by AI, and these policy suggestions will be an essential foundation to help ensure that innovation operates in the larger public goals of equity, protection, and consumer safety.

## 13.6 CONCLUSION

AI robo-advisors have revolutionized wealth management by making financial services more accessible, personal, and affordable. With features like active Digital Hybrid (DH) portfolio management, personalized strategies, and behavioural insights, these game-changer platforms are changing the way people invest. Robo-advisors have already witnessed considerable adoption across Europe, propelled by the advancement of technology and regulatory frameworks. For the future, robo-advisors will leverage algorithmic management, blockchain, and hybrid models. AI implementations in financial services must overcome a few barriers and the most important one is driving trust and confidence, which can only be done through ethical governance, compliance with regulatory standards, and protection to the client or investor, thus paving the way for an inclusive and secure financial ecosystem.

## REFERENCES

1. Golić Z. Finance and artificial intelligence: The fifth industrial revolution and its impact on the financial sector. *Zb Rad Ekon Fak Istoc Sarajevu*. 2019;(19):67–81.
2. Met İ, Kabukçu D, Uzunoğulları G, Soyalp Ü, Dakdevir T. Transformation of business model in finance sector with artificial intelligence and robotic process automation. In: *Digital business strategies in blockchain ecosystems*. Springer; 2019. p. 3–29.
3. Wirtz BW, Weyerer JC, Sturm BJ. The dark sides of artificial intelligence: An integrated AI governance framework for public administration. *Int J Public Adm*. 2020; 43(9):818–29.
4. Quarshie MA, Akhtar S, Nawaah D. Barriers to breakthroughs: The crucial role of support services in advancing accounting practices, financial literacy and performance in disability-led SMEs. *Qual Quant*. 2025;59:1–23.
5. El Abiad Z, Abraham R, El-Chaarani H, Skaf Y, Binsaddig RO, Jafar SH. The impact of CEO characteristics on the financial performance of family businesses listed in the Euronext Exchange. *J Risk Financ Manag*. 2024;17(3):129.
6. Bhatia A, Chandani A, Divekar R, Mehta M, Vijay N. Digital innovation in wealth management landscape: The moderating role of robo advisors in behavioural biases and investment decision-making. *Int J Innov Sci*. 2022;14(3/4):693–712.

7. George AS. Robo-revolution: Exploring the rise of automated financial advising systems and their impacts on management practices. *Partners Univ Multidiscip Res J.* 2024;1(4):1–16.
8. Zhang L, Pentina I, Fan Y. Who do you choose? Comparing perceptions of human vs robo-advisor in the context of financial services. *J Serv Mark.* 2021;35(5):634–46.
9. Sironi P. *FinTech innovation: From robo-advisors to goal-based investing and gamification.* Wiley; 2016.
10. Jung D, Dorner V, Glaser F, Morana S. Robo-advisory: Digitalization and automation of financial advisory. *Bus Inf Syst Eng.* 2018;60:81–86.
11. Markowitz H. Modern portfolio theory. *J Finance.* 1952;7(11):77–91.
12. Kamoune A, Ibenrissoul N. Traditional versus behavioral finance theory. *Int J Account Finance Audit Manag Econ.* 2022;3(2–1):282–94.
13. Nawaah D, Asare PY, Quarshie MA. Climate finance and natural capital: Linking global initiatives with local impact. In: *Climate neutrality through smart eco-innovation and environmental sustainability.* Springer; 2025. p. 317–32.
14. Mathur P, Sharma AM. Robo-advisors in investment management. In: *risks and challenges of AI-driven finance.* IGI Global; 2024. p. 121–45.
15. Jafar SH, Kashid AU, Ghosh S, Srividhya S, Sharma D, Bodhankar A. An enhanced performance optimization of ATM networks for cross-border money transfers. In: *2024 15th international conference on computing communication and networking technologies.* IEEE; 2024. p. 1–5.
16. Jafar SH, Oyedele OM, Nawaah D, Bolanle AS. Exploring leadership challenges for adoption of digital innovation and sustainability. In: *Innovation ecosystems and sustainable technologies.* Emerald Publ Ltd; 2025. p. 253–69.
17. Milana C, Ashta A. Artificial intelligence techniques in finance and financial markets: A survey of the literature. *Strateg Change.* 2021;30(3):189–209.
18. Hemachandran K, Rodriguez RV, editors. *The business of the metaverse: How to maintain the human element within this new business reality.* CRC Press; 2023.
19. Jafar SH, Akhtar S, Johl SK. AI in insurance. In: *Artificial intelligence for business.* Productivity Press; 2023. p. 164–73.
20. Malik MY, Jafar SH, Dixit A. Efficiency analysis and macroeconomic determinants of non-tax revenues: Evidence from special category states of India. *Indian Econ J.* 2025. https://doi.org/10.1177/00194662251330385.
21. Challoumis C. How AI is reshaping the way we understand the cycle of money. In: *XIX international scientific conference.* World of Conferences; 2024. p. 569–604.
22. Hemachandran K, George PM, Rodriguez RV, Kulkarni RM, Roy S. Performance analysis of k-nearest neighbour classification algorithms for bank loan sectors. In: *Smart intelligent computing and communication technology.* IOS Press; 2021. p. 9–13.
23. Hemachandran K, Rodriguez RV, Toshniwal R, Junaid M, Shaw L. Performance analysis of different classification algorithms for bank loan sectors. In: *Intelligent sustainable systems: Proc ICISS 2021.* Springer; 2021. p. 191–202.
24. Bonelli MI, Liu J. Artificial intelligence (AI) and virtual reality convergence in financial services: The power of digital twin robo-advisers. In: *International conference on financial technology.* Springer Nature; 2024. p. 137–50.
25. Jafar SH, Hemachandran K, El-Chaarani H, Moturi S, Gupta N, editors. *Artificial intelligence for capital markets.* CRC Press; 2023.
26. Salim M, Khan PA, Jalil NA, Johl SK, Jafar SH, Irfan F, Khan M. Fusion of blockchain and sustainable development goals: A bibliometric analysis for future trends. *KnE Soc Sci.* 2023:633–54.

# 14 AI in Algorithmic Trading and Investment Strategies

*Joseph Tufuor Kwarteng*

## 14.1 INTRODUCTION

### 14.1.1 Algorithmic Trading's Development

The financial markets have evolved over the past few decades from broker-driven, manual trading to algorithmic trading strategies driven by machine intelligence [1]. Historically, traders used their instinct, familiarity with the market, and fundamental analysis when making judgment calls on investments. As financial markets have grown increasingly complex and the volume of electronic transactions soared, relying on this type of manual, judgment-based decision-making is no longer feasible, and automated, data-driven trading models are now essential [2].

Algorithmic trading is the process of making trades without the direct involvement of a human by using statistical methods, machine learning (ML) algorithms, and established mathematical models. These artificial intelligence (AI)-enabled systems can process tremendous volumes of financial data, discover trading signals, and execute millions of trades within a few milliseconds. Over 70% of all trading volume on the main European stock exchanges is currently driven by AI-powered trading algorithms [3–5]. AI-driven trading techniques have become more and more popular among European financial institutions, hedge funds, and investment businesses as a way to minimise market risks, increase profits, and decrease trade inefficiencies. This is primarily due to numerous reasons; AI has become an essential tool in modern financial markets, being able to analyse global economic trends, understand sentiment for financial news and react instantly to changes in the market [6].

### 14.1.2 Key Drivers of AI Adoption in Algorithmic Trading

Algorithmic trading has become more reliant on AI due to various factors, including technology breakthroughs, legal changes, and increasing demand for data-driven decision-making [2, 7]. AI-powered trading systems enhance productivity, optimise financial plans, and ensure compliance with new market regulations. AI has become a necessary tool for financial institutions that seem to be losing their competitive edge in highly volatile markets:

 DOI: 10.1201/9781003611646-14

a. *Market Speed and Efficiency*: Speed and efficiency is one of the essential elements which enhance AI usage in algorithmic trading due to AI-powered models being much faster and efficient [4]. Human cognition limits traditional trading strategies to manual intervention. Conversely, AI algorithms can parse through tons of market data and execute trades in microseconds, making any change in asset price profitable [6]. Quick execution of orders helps to add liquidity in the market and alleviate latency-related risks, the importance of which is high for market stability in general [8].
b. *Advancements in AI and Deep Learning*: AI has greatly expanded the abilities of algorithmic trading systems, particularly in areas such as deep reinforcement learning (DRL), neural networks, and natural language processing (NLP) [9]. For example, deep learning techniques used in these models can identify nonlinear structures in market data, prediction in price movement of assets, and continual learning of trading strategies [10–12]. So, AI-driven trading systems can respond better to the evolutionary nature of the market than traditional rule-driven trading systems.
c. *Expansion of Quantitative Trading in Europe*: Over the years, quantitative trading, defined as the identification of trading opportunities using statistical methods and mathematical models, has evolved remarkably in Europe [13]. AI-enabled investing algorithms are being deployed by European hedge funds and investment firms to optimise investment strategies while utilising both current financial data and former market data. The models powered by the AI allow for a greater overall strategy in risk management and improve trade accuracy while removing human error. The rising use of AI in quantitative trading is consistent with a wider evolution in the global financial markets in line with data-driven investment decision-making [14].
d. *Regulatory Support for AI in Trading*: The role of the regulatory environment has also played a major part in bringing AI within algorithmic trading [4, 15]. Markets in Financial Instruments Directive II (MiFID II) in the European Union has forced automated trading to become more transparent, accountable and risk-managed. Such regulatory for compliance driven by AI will help financial organisations monitor their risk exposure or errors in execution and improve regulatory reporting. AI-powered monitoring systems might improve market integrity, avoid market manipulation cases and keep up with the changing regulations imposed by the finance [11, 16].
e. *Data-Driven Decision-Making and Predictive Analytics*: One of the major advantages of AI in trading is that it can process and analyse large volumes of structured and unstructured data [2]. Traditional trading strategies, which are based on past price behaviour, may not always encompass the complete intricacy of the financial market. Conversely, the breakthrough models utilise several points of data such as current financials, socioeconomic benchmarks and untraditional indicators like social media updates or satellite photos, allowing them to spot undesired correlations and unprecedented signs of market shifts [17]. Thus these predictive functionalities enable a deep-learning powered trading system to predict the market movements with confidence to reduce the risks all while providing traders with good investment opportunities [18, 19].

One of the most important features of AI-enabled trading algorithms is their capability to process and analyse massive amounts of structured and unstructured data [2]. Traditional trading strategies based on price history fail to account for the complete nature of financial markets. On the other hand, the AI models combine a variety of sources of data, such as real-time financial statements, macroeconomic indicators and alternative datasets, such as social media sentiment and satellite images, to find unknown relationships and new signs of market trends [17, 18]. These predictive characteristics provide AI-enabled trading platforms with the ability to predict changes in the market accurately, which ultimately leads to lower risks and more potential investments [20–22].

## 14.2 THEORETICAL FRAMEWORK

### 14.2.1 Understanding AI in Algorithmic Trading

AI-powered algorithmic trading integrates real-time market data, abstractions of deep learning methods and statistical quantitative finance models to optimise trading tactics. Trading strategies rely heavily on moving averages (MAs), technical indicators, and historical price movements. For deeper market insights, however, most modern AI-based trading systems use reinforcement learning, probabilistic modelling and sentiment analysis based on NLP [14]. Early AI models that automated trading strategies in an automated, more primitive way were rule-based AI trading systems that relied on decision trees and if-then rules. ML-based trading algorithms analyse historical trading data through supervised and unsupervised learning methods to identify price trends to offer probabilistic trade predictions. Consequently, more recently, researchers started to focus on DRL. By learning from mistakes, DRL-based trading agents dynamically adapt to the changes in the market in real time. Such state-of-the-art AI-based market-making strategies have significantly improved the speed and accuracy of trading by providing sophisticated decision-making tools to institutional investors [23].

### 14.2.2 Theoretical Models Supporting AI-Driven Trading Strategies

#### 14.2.2.1 Efficient Market Hypothesis (EMH) and AI Trading

The Efficient Market Hypothesis (EMH) states that, since all available information is fully and properly represented in financial markets, it is impossible to regularly beat the market. Nevertheless, this assumption is challenged by AI-driven trading algorithms that identify market inefficiencies that traditional models may overlook. AI trading algorithms can detect anomalies and predict price movements more accurately by processing billions of financial data simultaneously within a sub-second [24]. The EMH, while predicating empirical evidence, would argue that outsmarting the market is improbable, though nevertheless the intrinsic ability of AI to tap into unorthodox data parameters like news sentiment, earnings releases, or social media behaviour demonstrates the potency of AI to arbitrage short-term mispricing in financial markets.

#### 14.2.2.2 Arbitrage Pricing Theory (APT) and Quantitative Trading

The Arbitrage Pricing Theory (APT) claims asset value is influenced by several economic factors, such as GDP growth, interest rates and inflation rates. Applying APT concepts, AI-based quantitative trading models create optimal portfolios using deep learning algorithms and a multifactor regression analysis. These algorithms analyse trends in the markets and macroeconomy to deliver investment opportunities based on their risk share. Using the built-up AI factor investing techniques, traders can dynamically reposition the portfolio through real-time data, resulting in more diverse as well as return-optimised portfolios.

### 14.2.3 AI in High-Frequency Trading (HFT) and Market Microstructure

High-frequency trading (HFT), a more sophisticated form of algorithmic trading, executes large volumes of deals in extremely short time periods, often millisecond exchanges. AI models enhance HFT by predicting order flow trends, recognising liquidity imbalances, and catching mispricing within microseconds. While HFT aided with AI helps in creating liquidity and efficient market, it also increases the questions regarding the market stability and fair play. In 2010, the London Stock Exchange (LSE) experienced a "Flash Crash" in which an algorithmic trading programme based on AI triggered a deep and rapid market sell-off, resulting in billions of dollars being lost in minutes [6]. In European financial authorities, however, the response has been to apply circuit breakers, tighter supervision procedures and even trade halts in order to avoid the kind of disruptions to the market that can arise from the actions of autonomous AI agents [25]. These regulatory moves highlight the need to balance the benefits of AI-enhanced trading with investor protection and the stability of financial markets. The future of algorithmic trading will be based on predictive capabilities that are constantly evolving and improving as AI progresses, but their integration in financial markets will call for a steady iteration of changing regulations to mitigate this risk.

## 14.3 AI-POWERED TRADING, PREDICTIVE MODELLING, AND MARKET SENTIMENT ANALYSIS

### 14.3.1 AI-Driven Investment Strategies in Algorithmic Trading

Algorithmic trading has applied ML to the way financial institutions trade, manage risk and optimise portfolios. AI-based trading strategies analyse large volumes of market data and derive trade execution solutions based on statistical models, ML, and deep learning [26]. Unlike traditional human-led trading, which relies on technical indicators, macroeconomic analysis, and trader intuition, AI-driven algorithms analyse financial news in real-time, social media sentiment, and global market data, making trading decisions in a matter of milliseconds [14]. One of the key advantages of AI-driven trading is its ability to continually learn and improve.

Traditional trading styles require frequent manual adjustments, on the other hand, AI models use adaptive algorithms and reinforcement learning to adjust trade execution based on changing market conditions. These AI strategies allow traders to mitigate slippage expenses, hedge against risk, and capitalise on opportunities in volatile markets. There has always been a more sophisticated use of AI-driven algorithmic trading in the European financial markets. UK-based financial institutions Deutsche Bank and BNP Paribas have rolled the AI-enhanced trading bot onto their proprietary trading desks, the LSE and the Frankfurt-based trades are attributed an ever-greater share [3]. Reacting to this modification, European regulators too have now set forth a risk management framework that restricts the deployment of AI-based trading algorithms to allow for more supervision of AI-driven trading from financial institutions.

### 14.3.2 The Role of Machine Learning in Predictive Market Modelling

Predictive market modelling is one such AI application in algorithmic trading, which can be considered as the prime application of using AI. Treating the price movements of assets as a time series, ML algorithms analyse previous market movements, interest rate changes, earnings announcements, and geopolitical events to predict the direction of asset prices [27]. Unlike traditional econometric models, AI prediction trading systems utilise deep learning techniques such as the long short-term memory (LSTM) models and convoluted neural networks (CNNs) to spot complex trading signals and mappings of trends in the market. Predictive AI trading models outperform traditional models in predicting stock price volatility, identifying trend reversals, and recognising arbitrage opportunities. The HFT firms spread out through Europe incorporated AI-driven predictive analytics as a way to pull in microsecond pricing discrepancies among international exchanges, executing thousands of deals per second [15, 28]. In fact, the Russian invasion of Ukraine in 2022 represented an extraordinary financial event that showcased the effectiveness of AI-based market monitoring. Following this event, many European financial markets were filled with extreme volatility. European hedge funds were able to help institutional investors hedge themselves against the geopolitical risk and limit portfolio losses by using predictive trading algorithms powered by AI that successfully predict major oil price swings, currency devaluations and supply chain outages. As AI for algorithmic trading evolves, financial institutions have started to integrate multi-modal AI models to improve the accuracy of predictions driving investment decision-making. These models combine structured and unstructured data sources, ranging from company filings to satellite imagery to global economic indicators.

### 14.3.3 AI and Sentiment Analysis in Financial Markets

Sentiment analysis is an important type of NLP in AI-driven trading where financial institutions can discover valuable information from news articles, social media feeds, earnings call transcripts and investor sentiment surveys. Real-time analysis of investing confidence and public perception may enable AI trading algorithms to capture buy and sell signals based on shifts in investor sentiment [29, 30]. European finance professionals are increasingly turning to AI-based sentiment analysis tools to assess the impact of breaking news and geopolitical events on financial markets. For example, AI-based sentiment research algorithms detected a significant shift in the perception of investor sentiment related to European banking equities in 2021 due to rumours that the European Central Bank (ECB) may soon be announcing a regulatory influx. Hedge funds and institutional traders used AI sentiment models to adjust their portfolios before official regulatory announcement to minimise loss in the portfolio. Incorporating NLP-based sentiment research into trading algorithms has given traders such a substantial advantage that compared to news that moves the market and changes in investor opinion, they are now able to respond much faster. However, this increasing reliance on AI-driven emotion trading has also raised concerns over AI-driven market manipulation and volatility [31, 32]. Accordingly, EU authorities have created additional compliance standards for how AI can be used in trading techniques.

## 14.4 FUTURE TRENDS AND POLICY IMPLICATIONS

### 14.4.1 The Future of AI in Algorithmic Trading and Investment Strategies

AI-powered algorithmic trading will continue to transform global financial markets over the next decade with emerging blockchain-based trade, AI-driven quantum computing and decentralised finance (DeFi) paving the way for a new wave of financial innovation. As these AI models become more sophisticated, financial institutions are beginning to adopt explainable AI (XAI) frameworks into their trading platforms, ensuring that results from trades generated by AI are easily understood and interpretable. Integration of quantum computing with AI-based trading models is one of the topmost innovations expected in the AI-driven trade. Quantum computers can process market data ten times faster than classical computers [33, 34], so AI trading algorithms may be capable of performing real-time complex portfolio optimisation calculations. With the European Commission funding quantum computing research for financial applications, top European investment companies are already investigating quantum-enhanced trading tactics. Furthermore, blockchain-based trading platforms and DeFi are anticipated to transform AI-powered investing techniques. Smart contracts and automatic liquidity protocols are used by AI-driven DeFi systems to carry out deals in decentralised exchanges (DEXs) without the need for human participation. The effects of AI-driven decentralised trading models are being actively watched by European authorities, especially in relation to market stability, liquidity issues, and regulatory compliance [2]. Financial institutions must address important issues with AI bias, ethical trading practices, and systemic market risks as AI in algorithmic trading advances.

### 14.4.2 Policy Recommendations for AI-Governed Trading Systems

Intensifying role of AI in financial markets puts a burden on policymakers to make them have a stringent set of ethical, legal, and transparency standards in place on AI-driven trading systems. Specific policy recommendations that should be considered:

a. *Stronger AI Regulation in Financial Markets*: European regulators must create AI governance frameworks that require algorithmic trading models to be transparent and require the firms behind AI trading models to openly disclose how their AI trading decisions are made [35, 36].
b. *AI Risk Management Standards*: Regulators, e.g., European Securities and Markets Authority (ESMA) should impose risk management standards that outlaw AI-induced flash crashes, unwarranted market volatility, and algorithmic trading malfunctions [37, 38].
c. *Data Privacy and AI Trading Ethics*: AI trading models need to conform with General Data Protection Regulation (GDPR) guidelines so that traders are not taking advantage of private financial data for an algorithmic trading edge.
d. *Fairness and Anti-Manipulation Measures*: Regulators need to be able to develop compliance measures that inhibit AI-driven trading systems from market manipulation, price fixing, and unfair trading advantages.

These regulations, if adequately implemented, could allow European financial markets to keep AI-driven algo trading a driver of financial innovation over a source of systemic risk or ethics concerns.

## 14.5 CONCLUSION

The use of AI in algorithmic trading and investing techniques has transformed financial markets by making sentiment-based trading, HFT, and predictive market modelling possible. Modern financial organisations cannot function without AI-driven trading techniques because they provide increased accuracy, reduced transaction costs, and enhanced risk management capabilities. However, to maintain market stability and transparency as AI continues to dominate trade, regulatory monitoring, risk governance, and AI ethics must be given top priority. A new age of AI-driven financial market innovation will be ushered in by regulatory developments, quantum computing, and AI-powered DeFi, which will influence algorithmic trading in the future.

## REFERENCES

1. Trivedi SR, Kyal AH. *Effective trading in financial markets using technical analysis.* London, UK: Routledge India; 2020.
2. Ekundayo F. Economic implications of AI-driven financial markets: Challenges and opportunities in big data integration. *Int J Sci Res Arch.* 2024;13:1500–15.

3. Mer A, Singhal K, Virdi AS. A review of the role of artificial intelligence in banking and stock market trading. In: *Finance analytics in business: Perspectives on enhancing efficiency and accuracy*. 2024. p. 175–98.
4. Addy WA, Ajayi-Nifise AO, Bello BG, Tula ST, Odeyem O, Falaiye T. Algorithmic trading and AI: A review of strategies and market impact. *World J Adv Eng Technol Sci*. 2024;11(1):258–67.
5. Quarshie MA, Djimatey R, Akhtar S, Nawaah D. Maximizing financial efficiency through technological synergy: Unleashing ICT for enhanced cash management in SMEs. *J Int Counc Small Bus*. 2025:1–31.
6. Challoumis C. Revolutionizing the financial cycle—The role of artificial intelligence. In: *XIX international scientific conference*. London: Great Britain; 2024. p. 605–39.
7. El Abiad Z, Abraham R, El-Chaarani H, Skaf Y, Binsaddig RO, Jafar SH. The impact of CEO characteristics on the financial performance of family businesses listed in the Euronext Exchange. *J Risk Financ Manag*. 2024;17(3):129.
8. Riordan R, Storkenmaier A. Latency, liquidity and price discovery. *J Financ Mark*. 2012;15(4):416–43.
9. Théate T, Ernst D. An application of deep reinforcement learning to algorithmic trading. *Expert Syst Appl*. 2021;173:114632.
10. Li Y, Bastos J. Deep learning for financial market prediction: A review. *Appl Soft Comput*. 2020;93:106384.
11. Jafar SH, Dhandhukia V, Kumar GB. Application of artificial intelligence in banking: A review. In: *Machine learning for business analytics*. Productivity Press; 2022. p. 145–51.
12. Hemachandran K, Rodriguez RV, editors. *The business of the metaverse: How to maintain the human element within this new business reality*. Boca Raton, FL: CRC Press; 2023.
13. Guo X, Lai TL, Shek H, Wong SPS. *Quantitative trading: Algorithms, analytics, data, models, optimization*. Boca Raton, FL: Chapman and Hall/CRC; 2017.
14. Pillai V. Integrating AI-driven techniques in big data analytics: Enhancing decision-making in financial markets. *Int J Eng Comput Sci*. 2023;12(07):10–18535.
15. Jafar SH, Akhtar S, Johl SK. AI in insurance. In: *Artificial intelligence for business*. Boca Raton (FL): Productivity Press; 2023. p. 164–73.
16. Azzutti A. AI trading and the limits of EU law enforcement in deterring market manipulation. *Comput Law Secur Rev*. 2022;45:105690.
17. Jafar SH, Hemachandran K, El-Chaarani H, Moturi S, Gupta N, editors. *Artificial intelligence for capital markets*. Boca Raton, FL: CRC Press; 2023.
18. Chen Z. Advancing macroeconomic models through artificial intelligence integration. *Appl Comput Eng*. 2024;77:43–8.
19. Rane N, Choudhary S, Rane J. Leading-edge artificial intelligence (AI)-powered financial forecasting for shaping the future of investment strategies [Internet]. SSRN; 2023 [cited May 23, 2025]. Available from: https://ssrn.com/abstract=4640828.
20. Hemachandran K, Rodriguez RV, Toshniwal R, Junaid M, Shaw L. Performance analysis of different classification algorithms for bank loan sectors. In: *Intelligent sustainable systems: Proceedings of ICISS 2021*. Singapore: Springer; 2021. p. 191–202.
21. Boinapalli NR. AI-driven predictive analytics for risk management in financial markets. *Silicon Valley Tech Rev*. 2023;2(1):41–53.
22. Quarshie MA, Akhtar S, Nawaah D. Barriers to breakthroughs: The crucial role of support services in advancing accounting practices, financial literacy and performance in disability-led SMEs. *Qual Quant*. 2025;59:1–23.
23. Khattak BHA, Shafi I, Khan AS, Flores ES, Lara RG, Samad MA, et al. A systematic survey of AI models in financial market forecasting for profitability analysis. *IEEE Access*. 2023;11:125359–80.

24. Rahmani AM, Rezazadeh B, Haghparast M, Chang WC, Ting SG. Applications of artificial intelligence in the economy, including applications in stock trading, market analysis, and risk management. *IEEE Access*. 2023;11:80769–93.
25. Alderighi S, Gurrola-Perez P, Lin K, Speth B. Circuit breakers and other market safeguards [Internet]. SSRN; 2021 [cited May 23, 2025]. Available from: https://ssrn.com/abstract=4562240.
26. Nethravathi N, Samanvitha C, Dharmendra H, Ananthan S. Unleashing the power of AI for intelligent investments: Revolutionizing stock market trading. In: *Advancements in intelligent process automation*. Hershey, PA: IGI Global; 2025. p. 533–52.
27. Plakandaras V, Gogas P, Papadimitriou T. The effects of geopolitical uncertainty in forecasting financial markets: A machine learning approach. *Algorithms*. 2018;12(1):1.
28. Balaji K. Revolutionizing high-frequency trading: The impacts of financial technology and data science innovations. In: *Machine learning and modeling techniques in financial data science*. IGI Global; 2025. p. 103–24.
29. Sahani T. Decoding market emotions: The synergy of sentiment analysis and AI in stock market predictions. *J Next-Gen Res*. 2024. p. 1–11;5:0.
30. Salim M, Khan PA, Jalil NA, Johl SK, Jafar SH, Irfan F, et al. Fusion of blockchain and sustainable development goals: A bibliometric analysis for future trends. *KnE Soc Sci*. 2023:633–54.
31. Omopariola B, Aboaba V. Advancing financial stability: The role of AI-driven risk assessments in mitigating market uncertainty. *Int J Sci Res Arch*. 2021;3(2):254–70.
32. Nawaah D, Asare PY, Quarshie MA. Climate finance and natural capital: Linking global initiatives with local impact. In: *Climate neutrality through smart eco-innovation and environmental sustainability*. Switzerland: Springer Nature; 2025. p. 317–32.
33. Sáez-Ortuño L, Huertas-García R, Forgas-Coll S, Sánchez-García J, Puertas-Prats E. Quantum computing for market research. *J Innov Knowl*. 2024;9(2):101477. https://doi.org/10.1016/j.jik.2024.100510
34. Jafar SH, Kashid AU, Ghosh S, Srividhya S, Sharma D, Bodhankar A. An enhanced performance optimization of ATM networks for cross-border money transfers. In: *2024 15th international conference on computing, communication, and networking technologies (ICCCNT)*. IEEE; 2024. p. 1–5. https://doi.org/10.1109/ICCCNT61001.2024.10725476
35. Lee J. Access to finance for artificial intelligence regulation in the financial services industry. *Eur Bus Organ Law Rev*. 2020;21(4):731–57. https://doi.org/10.1007/s40804-020-00200-0
36. Malik MY, Jafar SH, Dixit A. Efficiency analysis and macroeconomic determinants of non-tax revenues: Evidence from special category states of India. *Indian Econ J*. 2025. https://doi.org/10.1177/00194662251330385
37. Azzutti A. AI governance in algorithmic trading: Some regulatory insights from the EU AI Act. SSRN. 2024 [cited May 23, 2025]. Available from: https://ssrn.com/abstract=4939604.
38. Jafar SH, Oyedele OM, Nawaah D, Bolanle AS. Exploring leadership challenges for adoption of digital innovation and sustainability. In: *innovation ecosystems and sustainable technologies*. Leeds, West Yorkshire, England: Emerald Publishing; 2025. p. 253–69.

# 15 Deep Learning in Stock Forecasting and Market Predictions

*Kotagiri Sai Deepak*

## 15.1 INTRODUCTION

### 15.1.1 The Evolution of Stock Market Forecasting

For decades, predictability of stock price trends has remained one of the leading goals of financial research with investors, analysts, and regulators all searching for reliable models to forecast returns in order to enhance asset pricing, risk management, and investment decisions [1]. Generally, the two predominant techniques of stock prediction have come from the field of technical and fundamental analysis [2]. Fundamental analysis seeks to determine a Company's intrinsic value through examination of its financial statements, earnings reports, industry trends, and macroeconomic conditions. Technical analysis, on the other hand, examines historical stock price data in an attempt to predict future price movements using trend lines, moving average, and contain trade volume patterns. While these techniques have yielded insightful information on stock valuation, they have serious drawbacks. Technical analysis makes the premise that past price patterns will recur, which is not necessarily true in volatile and unpredictable markets, while fundamental research sometimes overlooks the quick price swings caused by investor mood and macroeconomic shocks [3]. Furthermore, the large and intricate statistics that define contemporary financial markets are difficult for both methods to handle. The advent of artificial intelligence (AI) and big data analytics has revolutionised stock market forecasting by providing computational methods that can recognise complex market patterns that are impossible for humans to do [4–6]. An early development in financial modelling was machine learning (ML), which outperformed conventional methods in pattern detection and prediction [7]. However, decision trees, support vector machines, and linear regression were among the shallow learning architectures that were primarily used in early ML models. Although these methods improved forecasts for the stock market, they frequently missed the intricate, nonlinear correlations present in financial data. Equities are constantly affected by external and innovative events such as world events, investor sentiment, and economic policy [8], which also causes difficulties in understanding the evolving nature of stock markets. The advent of deep learning has surpassed these limitations, enabling multi-layer neural networks to learn complex financial structures with significantly greater accuracy. Examples of deep learning architectures like

DOI: 10.1201/9781003611646-15

recurrent neural networks (RNNs), long short-term memory (LSTM) networks, and transformer-based models that have changed stock forecasting due to unifying multiple financial datasets, learning complex interactions, and capturing long-term dependencies. Analysing vast amounts of historical stock prices, macroeconomic indices, sentiment from financial news, and real-time trading data enables these algorithms to provide some of the best accuracy and flexibility in predicting markets. As deep learning evolves, it will transform financial forecasting, delivering increasingly robust and data-driven insights that enhance risk management and investment strategies [9].

### 15.1.2 Deep Learning Adoption in Stock Forecasting and Key Drivers

Deep learning is a subtype of ML with more advanced algorithms and techniques, but their key difference is the way they learn from data, and the dependence on human assistance required. Deep learning can learn directly from raw data without the guidance of any pre-defined rules [10], while ML needs human experts to indicate what features (such as historical stock prices or economic indicators) should be examined [11]. In this way, deep learning can automatically learn patterns in data that would be missed by other human-perceptible methods. Deep learning, on the other hand, was designed to simultaneously work with high volumes of complex data, involving millions of stock trades, financial news, and social media sentiment, whereas ML excels in small datasets with simpler problems. While traditional ML models, such as decision trees and regression, base their predictions on simple rules, they lack the ability to comprehend more complicated interdependencies in the data [12]. Deep learning, by contrast, applies more sophisticated networks capable of processing vast amounts of data and providing more precise predictions. For instance, a simple ML model might predict stock prices based on historical data, but a deep learning model would independently analyse live market data, read through recent financial news and assess bullish or bearish sentiments of investors to predict fluctuations in stock prices. The deep learning ability of automatic learning and processing massive nonlinear multidimensional data makes it a peak technology and potential for stock price prediction and optimal decision-making [13, 14]. Several key factors have driven the adoption of deep learning in stock market forecasting:

a. *Proliferation of Financial Data and HFT*: With the rise of HFT and algorithmic trading, enormous databases have been generated, rich in financial data. Given access to millions of stock transactions, price movements and other data sources, AI-driven models might now piece together market patterns hidden from traditional models [15].
b. *Advances in Neural Network Architecture*: The development of transformer structures and LSTM networks has significantly increased forecasting accuracies [16].
c. *Better at Handling Sequential Data to Enhance Forecast*: These models learn long-term trends and short-term fluctuations (if any) in sequential stock price data.

d. *Installation*: Transformer-based designs have simplified analysis with big data, utilising self-attention approaches as well to enhance prediction accuracy.
e. *Use of Alternative Data Sources*: In addition to traditional financial metrics, deep learning models also incorporate other types of data, such as sentiment analysis from newspapers, social media discussions, and economic reports. Forecasting models driven by AI can build a more holistic and dynamic view of the market by allowing the model to train on both non-structured (textual) data as well as the structured (numerical) data from different sources [17].
f. *Institutional and Regulatory Support*: Financial rules and regulations have helped in the adoption of AI in finance; this is especially true in the European Union [18].
g. *Regulation Inducing the Adoption of AI*: The AI Act from the EU and transparency regulations are forcing investment businesses to have AI-led forecasting models to fit into data-led decision-making procedures. This regulatory pressure has propelled the use of AI in financial analysis.
h. *Enhanced Computational Resources*: Availability of high-performance computing resources like Graphics Processing Units (GPUs) and cloud-based AI frameworks has significantly reduced the training times of deep learning models and addressed the shortcoming of computational resources [19]. Thus, financial institutions could now employ AI-based forecasting with greater accuracy, practicality, and scalability.

As global financial markets evolve towards a more sophisticated and data-driven ecosystem, deep learning will continue to transform investment strategies, risk assessment models and financial decision-making processes. While many advantages come with AI-driven forecasting, issues such as overfitting, model interpretability and regulatory compliance should remain a higher-order problem as the space of AI-powered financial modelling matures. These questions will need to be tackled in order to ensure that the AI-powered forecasting tools help support even more transparent, reliable and efficient financial markets.

## 15.2 THEORETICAL FRAMEWORK

### 15.2.1 Deep Learning Models for Stock Market Prediction

The onset of deep learning, a type of ML, has enhanced the prediction of the stock market as complicated algorithms are able to process large records and identify correlation relations between the variables [20]. Deep learning, unlike traditional statistical methods that use human intervention for almost every stage of the analysis, is capable of using these multi-layered neural networks to provide better predictions from numeric, text, and visual data. The following models are most often used for the prediction of the stock market:

a. *Recurrent Neural Networks (RNN)*: RNN is capable of processing sequential data, thus well-suited to time-series financial data. They are capable of learning short-term aspects and hallmarks of stock prices by keeping hold of knowledge employing from previous timesteps. Quantitative trading firms, for example, use RNNs to predict the direction (up or down) of stock prices at the end of each day, using historical price trends to learn from them just as meteorologists do when using past climate data to predict the future weather pattern [21].
b. *Long Short-Term Memory (LSTM) Networks*: As a variant of RNNs designed to mitigate the vanishing gradient problem, LSTMs have been used for modelling long-range dependencies in financial time-series predictions. They perform exceptionally well in long-term trend and cyclical market states. Investment management firms use LSTMs to foresee changes in monetary policies affect long-run asset prices [22], much like economic analysts examine how shifts in interest rates impact inflation patterns across time. Developments in the data science and AI field continue to reshape industries in 2021 and beyond [23].
c. *Convolutional Neural Networks (CNNs)*: CNNs were first created for image analysis and then applied to financial analysis. It has become useful for chart pattern recognition and technical indicators [24]. CNNs help identify trading signals by extracting key features from stock price movements. An example of CNNs can be seen in hedge funds reading candlestick graphs for patterns; this is like medical AI systems recognising abnormalities in radiological images.
d. *Transformation AI Models (e.g., Transformer, BERT; GPT-4; T5)*: Transformer models use the attention mechanism to understand and evaluate a high volume of textual data, ranging from financial reports, news articles, and sentiment on social media. These models also bolster market trend predictions through natural language processing (NLP) that analyses macroeconomic discussions and investor sentiment. Investment banks use transformer models to evaluate the effect of a central bank statement on market behaviour following the release of a corporate earnings report like how AI-powered search engines rank and extract important information from large text corpora [25].

The use of deep learning in finance is a concern to some purveyors of economic theory: Most economic climates assume that market prices are perfectly informed by the available information or that stock price movements are completely random [26]. The subsequent sections outline these theoretical considerations.

## 15.2.2 Theoretical Models Supporting AI-Driven Market Predictions

### 15.2.2.1 Efficient Market Hypothesis (EMH) and Deep Learning

Fama wrote the original paper on how stock prices fully integrate all public information, making predictive analysis impossible for systematic excess returns [26]. This body of work is widely known as the Efficient Market Hypothesis (EMH). Under this hypothesis, stock prices respond to new information immediately and arbitrage opportunities disappear. For instance, if a multinational corporation announces that its earnings exceed expectations, EMH predicts that its share price already adjusts to reflect the public knowledge of the earnings report and therefore, investors cannot benefit from privy information. On the other hand, deep learning models seem to contradict this hypothesis, by showing evidence of exploitable inefficiencies in financial markets [27, 28]. By analysing alternative data sources such as social media sentiment or satellite images of industrial activities, advanced AI models can recognise hidden trading patterns and price anomalies [29, 30]. For example, hedge funds have managed to apply AI analysing the movements of shipping containers to anticipate supply chain disruptions and consequent commodity price fluctuations which the EMH assumptions would assume is not instantaneously enacted on stocks. These results imply that even when financial markets may be using the information available to them, they are not perfectly efficient and deep learning models are able to mine predictive signals.

#### 15.2.2.2 Random Walk Theory vs. AI-Driven Market Predictability

According to the Random Walk Theory, the movements of stock prices must follow a random walk where their past movements do not impact their future movements [31]. Although the Random Walk Theory has strong theoretical roots, empirical evidence points that deep learning models can catch repetitious structure and statistical dependencies in those financial markets [11, 32]. Leveraging structured and unstructured data in a probabilistic manner, AI-driven algorithms analyse huge datasets to make far more accurate predictions. This includes during the global economic crisis of 2020, where AI models leveraged up-to-the-minute information from stimulus initiatives, consumer attitudes and corporate performance to predict market rebounds faster than traditional financial models. For instance, in the geopolitical environment, sentiment analysis driven by AI has been used to empirically examine whether trade policies or international conflict events influence stock prices, showing that stock returns are not fully random and respond to identifiable causes. Deep learning can never be a sure shot in predicting financial markets but based on large-scale datasets by identifying hidden correlations (not visible to human analysts) it gives a probabilistic edge [33–35]. Furthermore, this contradicts the weak form of the Random Walk Theory because it shows that there are elements of historical trends and macroeconomic factors that affect the movement of stock prices to some degree.

## 15.3 EMERGING FRONTIERS IN DEEP LEARNING FOR FINANCIAL MARKET PREDICTIONS

Even though deep learning for stock forecasting has advanced significantly, there are still several new areas that are not well covered in scholarly works. Although model designs and prediction accuracy have been the subject of much research, other important aspects such as behavioural finance integration, AI-driven market anomalies, and the constraints of current datasets are frequently disregarded [36]. To give a more thorough understanding of deep learning's developing importance in financial markets, this section examines these factors.

### 15.3.1 Behavioural Finance and Deep Learning: Understanding Investor Psychology

Deep learning models that incorporate behavioural finance concepts are one of the least studied but most important areas of AI-driven stock market predictions [36, 37]. Behavioural finance argues that emotions, biases, and cognitive mistakes have a significant impact on financial decisions, in contrast to traditional financial theories that presume rational investor behaviour. The use of behavioural finance in AI-powered market forecasting has been relatively underutilised, despite its influence on stock market movements [38]. The following behavioural data sources can be included in deep learning models:

a. Neurofinance data (e.g., investor reaction time, physiological reactions to market fluctuations).
b. Psycholinguistic sentiment analysis, such as examining the conviction, tone, and hesitancy of earnings calls.
c. Social contagion models that mimic financial market herd dynamics.

For example, algorithms trained to identify FOMO-driven purchasing or panic-induced selling based on investor mood may enhance short-term market forecasts [25]. However, combining knowledge from data science, psychology, and finance need multidisciplinary cooperation to include behavioural finance into deep learning models.

### 15.3.2 Deep Learning and Market Anomalies: Identifying Hidden Patterns Beyond Traditional Models

Anomalies in financial markets that depart from traditional economic theories include:

a. Momentum anomalies, in which previous winners continue to do well in the near term.
b. PEAD, or post-earnings announcement drift, is the phenomenon when stock prices continue to respond to earnings news for a considerable amount of time following announcements.
c. Algorithmic trading-induced intraday price distortions.

Deep learning can reveal previously undiscovered hidden relationships, but standard methods frequently miss these oddities [39, 40]. Researchers may uncover novel market inefficiencies that contradict accepted financial theories by using AI models to train on multi-modal financial data, such as price swings, trading volumes, geopolitical threats, and insider transactions [41, 42]. A new field that is developing is "Explainable AI (XAI) in market anomaly detection." Present-day deep learning models have little interpretability and function as "black boxes" [43]. However, to assist traders and regulators in making better judgements, future AI models must not only produce accurate forecasts but also give rational explanations for market abnormalities.

### 15.3.3 The Data Problem: Biases, Data Gaps, and the Need for Synthetic Financial Datasets

Even though deep learning models need enormous volumes of high-quality data, financial markets face several data-related difficulties:

a. *Survivorship Bias*: Overly optimistic models result from stock market statistics that frequently exclude delisted or insolvent businesses [44].
b. *Absence of High-Frequency Market Data in Developing Nations*: Although research on deep learning mostly uses data from the stock markets in the United States and Europe, emerging countries struggle with insufficient datasets [45].
c. *Limited Historical Data for AI Training*: Stock market data is time-limited and non-stationary (changing over time), in contrast to image recognition tasks that include millions of labelled examples.

An alternative that has not received much attention is synthetic financial datasets, which are AI-generated financial market simulations that replicate real-world market conditions [46]. Generative Adversarial Networks (GANs) simulate stock price changes depending on macroeconomic scenarios [47, 48]. Federated learning, another privacy-preserving technique that allows many financial institutions to collaborate on AI training without revealing personal data, is also gaining popularity [49, 50]. Through the distribution of AI model training among several market participants, federated learning may fight data silos while preserving confidentiality.

## 15.4 CONCLUSION

Deep learning has transformed stock forecasts and market predictions and enabled financial institutions to analyse vast and complex data, discover concealed trade patterns and refine investment techniques with incredible accuracy. The AI-based forecasting models have transformed institutional investment, hedge fund management, and retail financial advice services and are now accepted widely in North America, Europe, Asia, South America, and Africa. As the use of AI in stock forecasting continues to advance, regulatory oversight, ethical governance of AI and transparency of models must all take precedence to ensure market integrity and confidence among investors. Ensuring that deep learning models are fair, accountable, and explainable will be critical to mitigating risks and preventing systemic shocks as financial markets increasingly rely on AI. Moving forward, new technologies such as quantum computing, decentralised finance (DeFi), and multimodal AI analytics will shape the future application of AI in financial forecasting. These advanced technologies strongly augment each other in combining heaps of data having geopolitical, macroeconomic, and real-time market sensitivity into more sophisticated predictive models. Within this context, a new era of smart investment will commence, where AI not just enhances market predictions, but actually reimagines how decisions are made for more resilient and adaptable financial systems.

## REFERENCES


1. Oyedokun O, Ewim SE, Oyeyemi OP. Leveraging advanced financial analytics for predictive risk management and strategic decision-making in global markets. *Glob J Res Multidiscip Stud.* 2024;2(2):16–26.
2. Nti IK, Adekoya AF, Weyori BA. A systematic review of fundamental and technical analysis of stock market predictions. *Artif Intell Rev.* 2020;53(4):3007–57.
3. McDonald M. *Predict market swings with technical analysis.* Vol. 157. Hoboken: John Wiley & Sons; 2002.
4. Kumar G, Jain S, Singh UP. Stock market forecasting using computational intelligence: A survey. *Arch Comput Methods Eng.* 2021;28(3):1069–101.
5. Li J, Ye Z, Zhang C. Study on the interaction between big data and artificial intelligence. *Syst Res Behav Sci.* 2022;39(3):641–8.
6. Quarshie MA, Akhtar S, Nawaah D. Barriers to breakthroughs: The crucial role of support services in advancing accounting practices, financial literacy and performance in disability-led SMEs. *Qual Quant.* 2025;59:1–23.
7. Huang YP, Yen MF. A new perspective of performance comparison among machine learning algorithms for financial distress prediction. *Appl Soft Comput.* 2019;83:105663.
8. El Wassal KA. The development of stock markets: In search of a theory. *Int J Econ Financ Issues.* 2013;3(3):606–24.
9. Oko-Odion C, Okunuga A, Okunbor OI. Revolutionizing financial risk assessment through deep learning-driven business analytics for maximized ROI and resilience. *World J Adv Res Rev.* 2025;25(1):2444–61. https://doi.org/10.30574/wjarr.2025.25.1.0327
10. Zhang GP. Time series forecasting using a hybrid ARIMA and neural network model. *Neurocomputing.* 2003;50:159–75.
11. Chatzis SP, Siakoulis V, Petropoulos A, Stavroulakis E, Vlachogiannakis N. Forecasting stock market crisis events using deep and statistical machine learning techniques. *Expert Syst Appl.* 2018;112:353–71.
12. De Ville B. Decision trees. *Wiley Interdiscip Rev Comput Stat.* 2013;5(6):448–55.
13. Nosratabadi S, Mosavi A, Duan P, Ghamisi P, Filip F, Band SS, et al. Data science in economics: Comprehensive review of advanced machine learning and deep learning methods. *Mathematics.* 2020;8(10):1799.
14. El Abiad Z, Abraham R, El-Chaarani H, Skaf Y, Binsaddig RO, Jafar SH. The impact of CEO characteristics on the financial performance of family businesses listed in the Euronext Exchange. *J Risk Financ Manag.* 2024;17(3):129.
15. Ekundayo F. Economic implications of AI-driven financial markets: Challenges and opportunities in big data integration. *Int J Sci Res Arch.* 2024;13:1500–15.
16. Kabir MR, Bhadra D, Ridoy M, Milanova M. LSTM–Transformer-based robust hybrid deep learning model for financial time series forecasting. *Science.* 2025;7(1):7.
17. Chakraborty M, Parida P. Comprehensive study of AI-driven market forecasting models and their applicability. In: *2024 international conference on advancements in smart, secure. and intelligent computing (ASSIC).* Piscataway, NJ: IEEE; 2024. p. 1–5.
18. Lee J. Access to finance for artificial intelligence regulation in the financial services industry. *Eur Bus Organ Law Rev.* 2020;21(4):731–57.
19. Mahmoudi SA, Belarbi MA, Mahmoudi S, Belalem G, Manneback P. Multimedia processing using deep learning technologies, high-performance computing cloud resources, and big data volumes. *Concurr Comput Pract Exp.* 2020;32(17):e5699.
20. Nabipour M, Nayyeri P, Jabani H, Mosavi A, Salwana E, Shahab S. Deep learning for stock market prediction. *Entropy.* 2020;22(8):840.
21. Nelson DM, Pereira AC, De Oliveira RA. Stock market's price movement prediction with LSTM neural networks. In: *2017 International Joint Conference on Neural Networks (IJCNN).* Piscataway, NJ: IEEE; 2017. p. 1419–26.

22. Petrozziello A, Troiano L, Serra A, Jordanov I, Storti G, Tagliaferri R, La Rocca M. Deep learning for volatility forecasting in asset management. *Soft Comput.* 2022; 26(17):8553–74.
23. Campbell J, Koffi BA. The role of AI-powered financial analytics in shaping economic policy: A new era for risk management and national growth in the United States. *World J Adv Res Rev.* 2024;23(3):2816–25.
24. Yu H, Yang LT, Zhang Q, Armstrong D, Deen MJ. Convolutional neural networks for medical image analysis: State-of-the-art, comparisons, improvement and perspectives. *Neurocomputing.* 2021;444:92–110.
25. Hill JE, Harris C, Clegg A. Using Bing AI search for data extraction in systematic reviews. *Res Synth Methods.* 2024;15(2):347–53. https://doi.org/10.1002/jrsm.1689
26. Fama EF. The behaviour of stock-market prices. *J Bus.* 1965;38(1):34–105.
27. Hsu MW, Lessmann S, Sung MC, Ma T, Johnson JE. Bridging the divide in financial market forecasting: Machine learners vs. financial economists. *Expert Syst Appl.* 2016;61:215–34.
28. Hemachandran K, Rodriguez RV, editors. *Artificial intelligence for business: An implementation guide containing practical and industry-specific case studies.* Boca Raton: CRC Press; 2023.
29. Jafar SH, Oyedele OM, Nawaah D, Bolanle AS. Exploring leadership challenges for adoption of digital innovation and sustainability. In: *Innovation ecosystems and sustainable technologies.* Leeds, West Yorkshire, England: Emerald Publishing; 2025. p. 253–69.
30. Jafar SH, Akhtar S, Johl SK. AI in insurance. In: *Artificial intelligence for business.* Boca Raton, FL: Productivity Press; 2023. p. 164–73.
31. Joshi A, Mehta D. Random walk and price convergence in the commodities market in India. *J Commer Account Res.* 2023;12(2):18–26.
32. Hemachandran K, George PM, Rodriguez RV, Kulkarni RM, Roy S. Performance analysis of k-nearest neighbour classification algorithms for bank loan sectors. In: *Smart intelligent computing and communication technology.* Amsterdam, Netherland: IOS Press; 2021. p. 9–13.
33. Hemachandran K, Rodriguez RV, editors. *The business of the metaverse: How to maintain the human element within this new business reality.* Boca Raton: CRC Press; 2023.
34. Kejriwal M. *Artificial intelligence for industries of the future.* Cham: Springer; 2023.
35. Quarshie MA, Djimatey R, Akhtar S, Nawaah D. Maximizing financial efficiency through technological synergy: Unleashing ICT for enhanced cash management in SMEs. *J Int Counc Small Bus.* 2025:1–31.
36. Olubusola O, Mhlongo NZ, Daraojimba DO, Ajayi-Nifise AO, Falaiye T. Machine learning in financial forecasting: A US review: Exploring the advancements, challenges, and implications of AI-driven predictions in financial markets. *World J Adv Res Rev.* 2024;21(2):1969–84.
37. Nawaah D, Asare PY, Quarshie MA. Climate finance and natural capital: Linking global initiatives with local impact. In: *Climate neutrality through smart eco-innovation and environmental sustainability.* Cham: Springer Nature Switzerland; 2025. p. 317–32.
38. Kotecha N. Artificial intelligence in the stock market: The trends and challenges regarding AI-driven investments. *Open J Bus Manag.* 2025;13(2):709–34.
39. Ching T, Himmelstein DS, Beaulieu-Jones BK, Kalinin AA, Do BT, Way GP, et al. Opportunities and obstacles for deep learning in biology and medicine. *J R Soc Interface.* 2018;15(141):20170387.
40. Jafar SH, Hemachandran K, El-Chaarani H, Moturi S, Gupta N, editors. *Artificial intelligence for capital markets.* Boca Raton: CRC Press; 2023.

41. Avramelou L, Nousi P, Passalis N, Tefas A. Deep reinforcement learning for financial trading using multi-modal features. *Expert Syst Appl.* 2024;238:121849.
42. Salim M, Khan PA, Jalil NA, Johl SK, Jafar SH, Irfan F, et al. Fusion of blockchain and sustainable development goals: A bibliometric analysis for future trends. *KnE Soc Sci.* 2023:633–54.
43. Somani A, Horsch A, Prasad DK. Interpretability in AI-based financial decision-making: Challenges and solutions. In: *2023 IEEE International Conference on Artificial Intelligence (ICAI).* Piscataway, NJ: IEEE; 2023. p. 135–42.
44. Anand A, Verma R. Blockchain-based fintech: Emerging paradigms and regulatory challenges. *Finan Innov.* 2024;10(1):45–60.
45. Cheung KC, Mehta K, Prasad DK. Comparative analysis of AI-enabled trading strategies: Risk-return dynamics in global markets. *J Risk Financ Manag.* 2024;17(2):88.
46. Zhang Y, Zhao L, Li H. A survey on data-driven financial risk forecasting: From traditional statistics to deep learning. *Neurocomputing.* 2023;527:126–42.
47. Raj R, Sharma S, Banerjee T. ESG investing and AI: A transformative synergy for sustainable finance. *Sustain Financ Invest.* 2024;6(1):1–15.
48. Banerjee A, Das A. Explainable AI in finance: Transparency, trust, and regulatory compliance. *J Financ Data Sci.* 2024;6(3):52–67.
49. Kumar P, Sharma V, Kaur J. Artificial intelligence and investor sentiment: A critical study of behavioral finance trends. *J Behav Financ.* 2023;24(4):278–90.
50. Rao S, Singh A, Joseph J. AI governance in financial institutions: Ethics, compliance, and strategy. *J Financ Regul Compliance.* 2024;32(1):91–109.

# 16 AI Applications for Anti-Money Laundering and Compliance in Financial Institutions

*Donkor Nawaah and Rockson Mintah*

## 16.1 INTRODUCTION

The rapid evolution and increasing sophistication of financial crimes like fraud, money laundering, and regulatory non-compliance have raised serious doubts about the effectiveness of traditional financial security measures. Rule-based compliance frameworks have served their purpose for some time, but they are now utterly inadequate in the context of how financial institutions operate today [1–3]. These historic methodologies are ineffective, reactive, and rigid resulting in excessive false positives which are hardly well-suited to combat the more sophisticated and adaptive types of fraud to come. Therefore, not only is a strong compliance and anti-money-laundering solution built around artificial intelligence (AI) necessary, but its adoption is urgent, as this tool can effectively help ensure protection of the financial system. AI solutions have transformed the development of internal risk management and regulatory compliance for financial institutions [2]. Based on these capabilities, it can improve the detection and prevention of financial crimes with real-time transaction monitoring, smart anomaly detection, risk-based Customer Due Diligence (CDD), and predictive fraud prevention. Using natural language processing (NLP), unstructured data can be extracted and analysed in a more useful way. While machine learning (ML) models can accommodate the more complex patterns and changes in strategies employed by malicious actors, predictive analytics enables businesses to deal with potential threats before they become greater problems.

This chapter examines the emerging trend of ML, NLP, and predictive analytics being applied to current Anti-Money Laundering (AML) systems and how it is helping to make the world a more secure place. It explains why previous expert systems failed and how AI-enabled alternatives are shifting the compliance paradigm. As regulations are changing rapidly, AI technologies are playing a key role in the detection of suspicious activity and later applying these prevention mechanisms to fraud. Still, there are many obstacles to navigate when considering using AI for finance compliance. The major issues in this area are data privacy, ethical decision-making challenges faced by automation, discrimination from AI model bias, and constraints on the full-scale regulation of AI technologies. These challenges need to

DOI: 10.1201/9781003611646-16

be addressed to ensure that AI applications in AML remain effective as well as ethical. Despite ongoing debates about the explainability of AI models and the broader ethical implications of reliance on automated systems, it is apparent that AI has a critical role in financial crime prevention. The world is likely to see developments in areas such as adaptive compliance automation, AI-driven regulatory real-time reporting tools and blockchain-enabled AML mechanisms in the future. Such developments are likely to pave a more secure, transparent, and efficient global financial infrastructure. Against this background, the chapter aims to provide an overview of the growing sophistication of financial crimes and the subsequent demand for AI-driven AML and compliance solutions. It explores the impact of ML, NLP, and predictive analytics to revolutionize preventing financial crime, enhance regulatory compliance, and critically addresses issues and future directions which gives you a comprehensive understanding of how technology is reshaping financial crime prevention and regulatory compliance.

## 16.2 AI-POWERED AML MODELS AND TECHNIQUES

With the rise of sophisticated financial crimes such as fraud, money laundering, and non-compliance with regulations, financial institutions are leveraging AI-driven AML solutions to enhance compliance and risk management [4–6]. By replacing conventional rule-based compliance frameworks, which are mostly reactive and ineffective, with intelligent, adaptable, proactive detection models, AI has completely changed the way we conduct AML methods. This theoretical framework explores the core AI models and methods used in AML compliance, emphasizing their analytical capabilities, practical applications, and regulatory significance. AML models driven by AI scale and enhance the detection of financial fraud by leveraging ML, deep learning, graph analytics, reinforcement learning, and NLP. These methods provide an easier, yet far more data-driven approach towards identifying any forms of illegal financial activities.

### 16.2.1 Supervised and Unsupervised Machine Learning for AML

ML forms the backbone of risk assessment, transaction monitoring, and fraud detection. Supervised and unsupervised learning models both tremendously enhance the ability of financial institutions to detect and mitigate potential money laundering risks [7] through:

a. *Supervised Learning Models*: These are models that learn from previous data (labelled) to identify previously learned behaviour of fraud. They export the ability to detect known fraud methods, transaction laundering operations, and repeated definitions.
b. *Unsupervised Learning Models*: These models find anomalies in financial transactions without pre-defined labels, unlike supervised models. Such algorithms that analyse trends in transactions, consumer behaviour, and flow of funds to identify discrepancies play a critical role in detecting new and unknown money laundering activities.

### 16.2.2 Graph-Based AI for Transaction Monitoring

Financial crimes sometimes involve convoluted layers of secret transactions in which money flows illegally from one bank account to others, shell corporations, and foreign financial institutions [8–10]. Graph algorithms use graph theory and network analytics to:

a. Blockchain visualization which involves mapping a network of transactions and uncover relationships among things that seem unrelated.
b. Detectors of unusual patterns in fund transfers that may lead to money laundering.
c. Identify circular money flows that are widely used in the layering and integration stages of money laundering.

These methods reduce the likelihood of money laundering tactics escaping notice by making it easier for authorities and financial institutions to trace illegal money flows more effectively.

## 16.3 AI IN REGULATORY COMPLIANCE AND FINANCIAL CRIME DETECTION

The adaptation of AI is changing the market of financial crime culture and regulatory compliance, which enables financial institutions to track transactions, verify clients' identities and detect the movements of clients that may be involved in crime in real-time [11–13]. AI increases productivity minimizes the chances of fraud, and ensures compliance is achieved with higher accuracy and timeliness using automation and ML.

### 16.3.1 AI-Driven Transaction Monitoring and Anomaly Detection

The use of AI for AML compliance, particularly real-time transaction monitoring and anomaly detection, is among the most sensitive use cases for the application of AI [14–16]. Traditional AML systems, which rely on fixed rule-based structures that ascertain suspicious behaviours based on specific thresholds. However, these systems generate thousands of false positives, overwhelming compliance teams (and reducing the effectiveness) of the fraud protection system. AI AML solutions use ML and deep learning algorithms to process and analyse enormous amounts of financial transactions to identify subtle anomalies that might be related to potential money laundering/financial crime behaviour. Transaction monitoring systems powered by AI rely on the following:

a. *Anomaly Detection Algorithms*: AI models identify transactions that are different from known behaviour patterns and flag them for further investigation.

b. *Pattern Recognition and Predictive Modelling*: AI detects theft laundering patterns like layering and placement and dirty money structuring in various personal accounts.
c. *Graph Processing AI for Network Analysis*: The graph analytics captures complex financial networks, mapping unusual connections between account holder, shell company, and overseas entity.

In Europe, the EU mandates using AI-based transaction monitoring via the 6th Anti-Money Laundering Directive (6 AMLD) [17]. Financial institutions such as Deutsche Bank and Barclays utilize AI-powered tools to analyse transactions that help them spot unusual fund transfers across multiple jurisdictions. A good example of this application can be seen in the use of AI-based risk scoring models done by throughout the year by JPMorgan Chase and Bank of America, measuring content within the AML compliance investigations and lowering false positive investigations by as much as 30%–50% [18, 19]. In Asia, for example, Singapore's DBS Bank has integrated AI-driven abnormality detection models into its existing data infrastructure to analyse cross-border money flows and identify illicit transactions related to underground banking networks [20]. AI-enabled anomaly detection can help financial institutions reduce compliance-related expenses, stay in line with the regulatory authorities and improve the quality of risk identification.

### 16.3.2 AI in Know Your Customer (KYC) and Customer Due Diligence (CDD)

AI is revolutionizing Know Your Customer (KYC) and CDD processes by automating identity verification and risk assessment [21–23]. The most common components of AML compliance are KYC and CDD, which ensure that a financial institution assesses the associated risk profiles of new and existing customers properly. AI makes KYC/CDD better in the following ways:

a. *KYC Onboarding*: AI-based facial recognition, biometric authentication, and document verification enable automation of identity verification.
b. *Behavioural Risk Scoring*: AI models assess customer transaction behaviours along with their financial histories to classify individuals into relevant risk buckets.
c. *AI-Powered Adverse Media Screening*: NLP sifts through a wide array of worldwide news media, judicial documents, and regulatory watchlists to identify any persons associated with fraud, corruption, or criminal conduct.

Fintech firms (such as Revolut and N26) use AI-based KYC compliance to deploy ML methods to automatically verify customer identities, with the onboarding process being cut down from a few days to a few minutes [24]. This is a technology common in Europe. In Africa, digital banks such as Flutterwave and Opay use AI-based KYC verification technology to reduce identity fraud and other illicit banking-related activities or KYC violations, thereby balancing the scale between inclusive finance and regulatory compliance. The worldwide acceptance of AI-enabled KYC/CDD solutions reinforces their value proposition in balancing the trade-off between minimizing exposure to financial crime risks and providing a superior customer journey, as well as achieving compliance in a cost-effective manner.

### 16.3.3 AI in Suspicious Activity Reporting (SAR) and Regulatory Compliance Automation

Whenever there are indicators that money laundering may be occurring, financial institutions must file Suspicious Activity Reports (SARs) with regulators. AI streamlines SAR processes by automating the detection, documenting, and investigation of questionable transactions. The SAR automation makes use of the AI technology in various aspects, such as:

a. *Smart Case Managements*: AI can prioritize alerts by risk levels, allowing compliance teams to target and work on suspicious transactions only when the risk is real. NLP tools based on AI analyse the content of legal text, documentation of compliance reports, and investigation summaries to minimize human error in SAR submissions.
b. *AI for Predicting Risk Scoring for Regulatory Audits*: Help regulators to narrow down on at-risk banks and financial firms by identifying financial institutions which are more prone to compliance behaviour flagged as high-risk.

AI-powered SAR automation in the United States is slashing AML compliance reporting times for large banks to ensure faster regulatory response time. Financial Crimes Enforcement Network (FinCEN), however, is one of the most active backers of AI-powered automation in compliance, especially as it pertains to U.S. banks. In Latin America, Brazil's Central Bank adopted AI-based analysis tools for SAR to monitor financial transactions associated with illegal wealth associated with organized crime groups and drug cartels [25]. AI-powered SAR reporting, a shot in the arm for global financial security, allows financial institutions to meet their regulatory requirements in a streamlined manner.

## 16.4 FUTURE TRENDS AND POLICY IMPLICATIONS

### 16.4.1 The Future of AI in AML and Financial Compliance

Given the ongoing evolution of money laundering, as well as financial crime tactics, AI-driven AML compliance will keep on growing through levels of sophistication. Future trends may include:

a. *AI and Blockchain Integration for AML Compliance*: AI-driven AML will get access to an immutable transaction record, and this will mean transparency in financial transactions.

b. *Explainable AI (XAI) in AML Compliance*: Regulators are pushing for AI models to become more interpretable and auditable so that institutions can gain a full understanding of how their AI-driven AML decisions are made.
c. *AI to Streamline Cross-Border Compliance*: ML-based compliance platforms will stream international funds to real-time compliance monitoring, to comply with AML regulations in real time.
d. *AML Risk Analysis via Quantum Computing*: Financial institutions are looking at quantum AI models to deal with complex money laundering networks, enhancing fraud prediction.

### 16.4.2 Policy Recommendations for AI-Governed AML Compliance

AI adoption is happening quickly, and the foundations of policy around AI need to be built to ensure that AI-based technology delivers on the promise of enhanced financial security and stability in the AML compliance space (and beyond). The key recommendations for policymakers are:

a. *Standardization of Global AI AML Compliance*: International regulators should create a common set of guidelines for AI-driven AML which will guarantee inter-state collaboration in combatting financial crime.
b. *Guidelines on Use of Ethical AI in AML*: AI-powered AML tools will fall under General Data Protection Regulation (GDPR) and other data protection laws, leading to the possibility of discriminatory compliance, thereby prohibiting the use of AI-based customer risk profiling.
c. *Auditable AI-based AML Models*: All supervisory authorities will need to ensure AI-based AML systems are explainable, transparent, and accountable, to avoid bias and collusion errors.
d. *AI AML Collaboration between the Public and the Private*: Governments and financial institutions need to collaborate to run AI-driven public-private AML intelligence-sharing initiatives which can help in making the detection of financial crimes more efficient.

Such policy safeguards will enable regulators to ensure that AI-driven AML compliance is simultaneously ethical, effective, and harmonized with global standards for financial security.

## 16.5 CONCLUSION

Risk management, regulatory compliance, and financial crime detection in financial institutions have all been transformed by AI-driven AML compliance. Financial crime risks have been decreased and compliance efficiency greatly increased because of AI-powered transaction monitoring, KYC/CDD automation, and predictive risk assessment models. As evidence of their widespread influence on financial security, AI-powered AML solutions have been embraced across Europe, the Americas, Asia, and Africa. Nonetheless, to avoid prejudice, data abuse, and unjust risk profiling, AI-driven compliance frameworks must continue to be open, moral, and compliant with legal requirements. To ensure that AI-driven financial security continues to be a fundamental component of the contemporary financial ecosystem, XAI, blockchain integration, and international regulatory harmonization will all influence the future of AI in AML compliance.

## REFERENCES


1. Edge ME, Sampaio PRF. The design of FFML: A rule-based policy modelling language for proactive fraud management in financial data streams. *Expert Syst Appl.* 2012;39(11):9966–85.
2. Aziz LAR, Andriansyah Y. The role of artificial intelligence in modern banking: An exploration of AI-driven approaches for enhanced fraud prevention, risk management, and regulatory compliance. *Rev Contemp Bus Anal.* 2023;6(1):110–32.
3. Quarshie MA, Akhtar S, Nawaah D. Barriers to breakthroughs: The crucial role of support services in advancing accounting practices, financial literacy and performance in disability-led SMEs. *Qual Quant.* 2025;59:1–23.
4. Agorbia-Atta C, Atalor I. Enhancing anti-money laundering capabilities: The strategic use of AI and cloud technologies in financial crime prevention. *World J Adv Res Rev.* 2024;23(2):2035–47.
5. Koduru L. Driving business success through AI-driven fraud detection innovations in AML and risk monitoring systems. In: *Driving business success through eco-friendly strategies.* Hershey, PA: IGI Global Scientific Publishing; 2025. p. 115–30.
6. Quarshie MA, Djimatey R, Akhtar S, Nawaah D. Maximizing financial efficiency through technological synergy: Unleashing ICT for enhanced cash management in SMEs. *J Int Counc Small Bus.* 2025:1–31.
7. Chen Z, Van Khoa LD, Teoh EN, Nazir A, Karuppiah EK, Lam KS. Machine learning techniques for anti-money laundering (AML) solutions in suspicious transaction detection: A review. *Knowl Inf Syst.* 2018;57:245–85.
8. Sharman JC. Shopping for anonymous shell companies: An audit study of anonymity and crime in the international financial system. *J Econ Perspect.* 2010;24(4):127–40.
9. Pacini C, Hopwood W, Young G, Crain J. The role of shell entities in fraud and other financial crimes. *Manag Audit J.* 2019;34(3):247–67.
10. Jafar SH, Hemachandran K, El-Chaarani H, Moturi S, Gupta N, editors. *Artificial intelligence for capital markets.* Boca Raton: CRC Press; 2023.
11. Narsina D, Gummadi JCS, Venkata SSMGN, Manikyala A, Kothapalli S, Devarapu K, et al. AI-driven database systems in FinTech: Enhancing fraud detection and transaction efficiency. *Asian Account Audit Adv.* 2019;10(1):81–92.
12. Rahmani FM, Zohuri B. The transformative impact of AI on financial institutions, with a focus on banking. *J Eng Appl Sci Technol.* 2023;5(192):2–6.
13. Nawaah D, Asare PY, Quarshie MA. Climate finance and natural capital: Linking global initiatives with local impact. In: *Climate neutrality through smart eco-innovation and environmental sustainability.* Cham: Springer Nature Switzerland; 2025. p. 317–32.
14. Ray A. Applying AI in anti-money laundering operations. *J AI Robot Workplace Autom.* 2021;1(2):197–209.
15. Tsapa JA. Artificial intelligence use cases for banking anti-money laundering. *J Artif Intell Mach Learn Data Sci.* 2023;1:259–64.
16. Malik MY, Jafar SH, Dixit A. Efficiency analysis and macroeconomic determinants of non-tax revenues: Evidence from special category states of India. *Indian Econ J.* 2025:00194662251330385.
17. Pavlidis G. Deploying artificial intelligence for anti-money laundering and asset recovery: The dawn of a new era. *J Money Laund Control.* 2023;26(7):155–66.

18. Rier SJ. More money more problems: Examining the impact of the Anti-Money Laundering Act of 2020 on banks and regulators. *NC Bank Inst.* 2022;26:89.
19. Velez SB. Regulatory compliance requirement and practices. In: *Compliance and financial crime risk in banks: A practitioners guide.* Bingley: Emerald Publishing Limited; 2024. p. 3–13.
20. Wewege L, Lee J, Thomsett MC. Disruptions and digital banking trends. *J Appl Finance Bank.* 2020;10(6):15–56.
21. Khare P, Srivastava S. Transforming KYC with AI: A comprehensive review of artificial intelligence-based identity verification. *J Emerg Technol Innov Res.* 2023; 10(12):525–30.
22. Parate S, Josyula HP, Reddi LT. Digital identity verification: Transforming KYC processes in banking through advanced technology and enhanced security measures. *Int Res J Mod Eng Technol Sci.* 2023;5(9):128–37.
23. Jafar SH, Kashid AU, Ghosh S, Srividhya S, Sharma D, Bodhankar A. An enhanced performance optimization of ATM networks for cross-border money transfers. In: *2024 15th international conference on computing, communication, and networking technologies (ICCCNT).* Piscataway, NJ: IEEE; 2024. p. 1–5.
24. Salerno E. *Digital transformation in the financial industry* (Doctoral dissertation). Torino, Italy: Politecnico di Torino.
25. Gupta A, Dwivedi DN, Shah J. *Artificial intelligence applications in banking and financial services.* Cham: Springer Nature; 2023.

# 17 Ethical Considerations for AI in Financial Services

*Prashant Subhash Chougule and Siddharth Nanda*

## 17.1 INTRODUCTION AND OVERVIEW

### 17.1.1 Introduction

Artificial intelligence (AI) has emerged as a transformative force within the dimensions of many industries and already, its integration into Financial Services (FS) has led to notable improvements in risk management, fraud detection, personal banking, and investment strategies. Despite this, it has opened Pandora's box of ethical considerations necessary to ensure AI's responsible, sustainable, and ethical use within FS. Ethical AI frameworks ensure that these technological innovations achieve their objectives while aligning with the wider societal values and regulatory standards.

Primarily, integration of ethical frameworks in AI deployment will ensure fairness and avoid discrimination. AI algorithms have the potential to reproduce biases present in previous data if they are not carefully designed and monitored. This might result in unjust treatment based on economic position, gender, or ethnicity, which could lead to biassed credit rating, discriminatory lending, and unequal financial inclusion [1]. Secondly, financial systems cannot function in a trustworthy manner without the assumption of transparency and accountability, which is often compromised due to "Black-box" nature of AI systems, wherein, decisions are made without clear explanations, leading to reduced trust among stakeholders, regulators, and customers [2, 3]. Thirdly, ethical integration of AI in FS is important for risk mitigation and compliance with legal and regulatory frameworks and by incorporating ethical AI principles like data privacy, consent, and security into FS systems, financial institutions can confidently navigate regulatory landscapes and reduce risks of breaches and penalties [4, 5].

Finally, this integration of ethical considerations into AI development and deployment life cycle fosters sustainable finance, which aims to support economic growth without compromising on social and environmental considerations. Based on this discussion, the chapter objectives are.

a. To critically examine the ethical challenges inherent in the integration of AI in FS.
b. To critically examine the important regulatory and compliance frameworks (Global) which guide ethical AI deployment in FS.
c. Highlight ways in which responsible, transparent, and socially aligned AI adoption in FS can be achieved.

DOI: 10.1201/9781003611646-17

## 17.2 ETHICAL CHALLENGES IN AI-POWERED FINANCIAL SERVICES

### 17.2.1 Bias, Fairness, Transparency, and Explainability

Systemic biases inherited from past input data used as training data can frequently affect AI-powered financial models, resulting in biassed judgements and outcomes in domains such as credit scoring, lending, fraud detection, processing insurance applications, etc. This typically happens due to imbalanced training and validation datasets, skewed feature selection and structural inequalities prevalent in financial systems [6, 7]. Automated credit assessment algorithms sometimes have inherently favoured majority groups and men, reinforcing historical disparities in financial inclusion [8]. Socio-economic biases have also been found to be prevalent, where AI algorithms systematically favour high income groups, mis-associating financial stability with supposed wealth rather than actually analysing individual creditworthiness [9, 10].

Integrating fairness in AI-powered FS packages is a complex and evolving discussion due to the challenges posed by the multi-dimensional nature of fairness itself. It is difficult to arrive at a singular objective fairness standard applicable to all areas under AI-FS integration due to various interpretations of fairness by various stakeholders. A second challenge is the often-unavoidable trade-off between bias and accuracy, whereby reducing bias in algorithms may cause accuracy loss in outcomes [11]. In one instance, feature selection of biased features leads to proxy discrimination, as variables that correlate with characteristics such as zip codes (which proxy for race or income) may inadvertently preserve bias in outcomes [12]. The escape route from this mess is for FS providers to demand and institutionalize Human-In-The-Loop (HITL) interventions as well as periodic algorithm impact assessments and adversarial debiasing methods [13]. With its ability to scale and efficiency, AI-based credit scoring and lending models can enhance financial inclusion while simultaneously raising concerns of fairness, accountability, and transparency. Our credit scoring algorithms have, for a long time, been accused of continuing some systemic biases and this problem has only been worsened by the increasing use of non-traditional data sources (e.g., social media activity, browsing history, habits of mobile usage) that AI-powered packages have introduced. These could also introduce covert biases into lending decisions [14]. The black-box nature of AI credit scoring makes appealing against such decisions extremely difficult as applicants do not have access to how their loan applications were rejected or accepted [15], causing governance bodies to insist on Explainable AI (XAI) frameworks in credit assessment.

### 17.2.2 Accountability and Responsibility

The ever-growing adoption of AI-driven financial systems raises difficult questions about how to fix accountability for AI-powered decisions and outcomes, and on whom to fix that accountability, especially in cases of erroneous outcomes, financial losses, or discriminatory practices. Traditional financial decision-making systems relied on human agency and oversight, regulatory frameworks, and predetermined accountability and responsibility whereas AI-powered decision-making models utilize autonomous machine learning algorithms that continuously adapt to new input data [16]. This causes accountability to be dispersed over developers, 3rd party AI vendors in addition to regulatory bodies and financial institutions [17]. Another important issue is the legal status of AI – whether AI can be considered as an entity legally responsible for its actions or whether the developers or deployers (FS providers) should bear the accountability for the same [18].

AI-driven financial decision-making further complicates ethical oversight as AI-driven systems can execute trades, approve loans, or flag accounts with minimal human input, but their opacity may hinder recourse, especially where high-stakes or vulnerable population are involved and to mitigate these risks, financial firms must adopt XAI, maintain HITL controls, and ensure decision logic auditability. Even though regulatory frameworks like the EU AI Act are mandating these steps, organizational governance must hurry to keep pace. Legal liability in cases of AI-related misconduct, such as unjust credit denials or market manipulations via trades execution is under-developed and effective risk management strategies require institutions to define internal accountability structures, document algorithmic decisions, and anticipate ethical failings. Emerging legal instruments indicate a gradual shift towards holding institutions accountable even for partially autonomous systems [19].

### 17.2.3 Data Privacy and Security

AI systems need granular, sensitive financial data to function effectively with hyper-personalization and risk detection. This raises ethical concerns about consent, data stewardship, and misuse. The aggregation of behavioural, transactional, and biometric data introduces possible risks of surveillance and exploitation [11]. Also, when financial institutions harness AI packages to extract insights from customer data for commercial gain, questions arise about inferred data (i.e., patterns or predictions about user behaviour generated via derived unrelated information) which can lead to opaque profiling and discriminatory targeting. AI-enabled financial surveillance for compliance or fraud detection, though justified in some contexts, may undermine privacy and autonomy when deployed without sufficient transparency and/or oversight [20, 21]. In limited regulation environments, such tools may be used to target low-income or marginalized users. Ethical deployment must use privacy-preserving technologies like differential privacy and federated learning to strike a balance between security, inclusivity, and civil rights.

In response to escalating concerns over AI-powered financial data processing, global regulators enacted stringent data protection laws to regulate AI integration in FS. The European Union's Data Protection Regulation (GDPR), the CCPA, or California Consumer Privacy Act, in the United States, and industry-specific financial rules such as PSD2 and BASEL III all require stringent data collecting, processing, and storage [22]. For example, GDPR requires AI-driven financial models to minimize data, limit purpose and get user consent. Automated decision-making systems must be explainable and allow human intervention. Failure to comply may result in significant fines, reputational damage, and potential lawsuits.

## 17.3 REGULATORY AND GOVERNANCE FRAMEWORKS FOR ETHICAL AI IN FINANCIAL SERVICES

The rapid adoption of AI in FS necessitated the rapid adoption of robust global regulatory and governance frameworks to ensure transparency, fairness, and ethical compliance [23]. Financial institutions already operated in a highly regulated environment. The seriousness has risen further where AI-driven decisions can impact credit scoring, fraud detection, investment management, and compliance monitoring. As a result, governance systems that reduce risks associated with algorithmic bias, transparency, privacy violations, and financial stability are being established by regulatory agencies, business executives, and international organizations.

### 17.3.1 Global Regulatory Landscape

Regulatory bodies worldwide are introducing AI-specific financial regulations to ensure accountability, fairness, and compliance. The European Union's Artificial Intelligence Act (EU AI Act) is one of the most comprehensive regulatory frameworks, classifying AI applications into risk categories and imposing regulatory requirements based on the same [24]. Similarly, in the US Algorithmic Accountability Act, it is mandated that AI deployers (AKA FS providers) conduct regular AI Impact Assessments to detect bias, discrimination, and other such vulnerabilities [25, 26]. The Financial Stability Board (FSB) and the Bank of International Settlement (BIS) have also issued guidelines on AI ethics, accountability, and data privacy to improve financial stability and prevent systemic risks.

In Asia, the Monetary Authority of Singapore (MAS) has developed FEAT (Fairness, Ethics, Accountability, and Transparency) principles to guide ethical adoption in banking and FinTech sectors [27]. Similarly, China's Personal Information Protection Law (PIPL) and AI governance frameworks impose strict compliance measures in financial AI applications, particularly connected with customer data privacy and cybersecurity risks [28]. All of these represent a global insistence on AI accountability, necessitating FS providers to align their AI policies with their ethical and legal obligations.

### 17.3.2 Ethical AI Frameworks

Many international stakeholders have come together to create ethical AI frameworks to guide responsible AI adoption in FS. The OECD AI principles emphasize human-centric AI, fairness, and robustness, ensuring that AI models in FS operate with standardized levels of transparency and explainability [29]. At the same time, the IEEE Ethically Aligned Design Framework outlines best practices for AI accountability, protection of data, engagement of stakeholders, prevention of algorithmic discrimination and opaque decision-making in FS [30]. The EU High Level Expert Group on AI (HLEG) has proposed the Ethics guidelines for trustworthy AI and pushed for bias mitigation, fairness-aware AI and transparency in financial institutions [31]. Additionally, to maintain auditability and regulatory compliance, the BASEL Committee on Banking Supervision (BCBS) has advocated for the use of XAI in financial risk modelling, AI-powered lending, credit scoring, and fraud detection procedures [31].

### 17.3.3 Industry Best Practices

Leading financial institutions have implemented robust AI governance models that emphasize risk assessment, fairness auditing, and explainability. AI ethics boards have become a key component of responsible AI governance, ensuring that AI-powered financial systems undergo rigorous ethical reviews before deployment, while institutions like HSBC, J P Morgan, Citibank, etc., have already adopted fairness-aware AI models and are using adversarial debiasing techniques and algorithmic impact assessments to detect, flag, and deal with bias in credit decisions and trading algorithms.

Additionally, AI Risk Management Frameworks (AI-RMFs) help financial institutions assess model interoperability, detection of biases, and compliance with AI-specific regulatory requirements. Many banks are investing in XAI solutions to mitigate the Blackbox aspects of AI-powered decision-making processes. Privacy preserving AI techniques, like federated learning, differential privacy, etc., are being deployed by financial institutions to protect customer data while empowering AI-enabled financial analytics.

## 17.4 CONCLUSION

### 17.4.1 Main Findings

a. The ethical integration of AI with FS is a necessity as well as a challenge because as FS providers move ahead, they must strive to balance innovation, efficiency, and profitability with ethical responsibility and legal accountability.
b. While AI has transformed key areas of credit risk assessment, fraud detection, algorithmic trading, and customer service, it has also raised concerns about bias, fairness, accountability, and transparency.
c. Identified key ethical risks include discriminatory biases in credit scoring, unfair lending practices, lack of transparency in AI-powered financial decisions and outcomes, and data privacy violations, further escalating the risk of financial exclusion, systemic discrimination, and market manipulation.
d. In the absence of robust AI accountability frameworks, regular fairness audits, and strict regulatory oversight (harnessing HITL aspects) there is always the possibility that AI-powered FS packages may exacerbate economic disparities rather than bridge them.
e. The rise of AI-driven Decentralized Finance (AI-DeFi) and AI-Blockchain integrations presents further ethical challenges, including regulatory loopholes, cyber vulnerabilities, and algorithmic financial surveillance.
f. Regulatory bodies (like the European Union with its AI Act, the US Algorithmic Accountability Act, and the MAS with their FEAT principles)

are shaping governance structures to ensure transparency, accountability, and consumer protection in AI-powered financial solutions and even though, financial institutions are proactively adopting XAI, AI Ethics boards, AI-RMFs and fairness-aware AI practices to align AI integration with ethical principles and regulatory standards, these good efforts will need to be continuous, adaptive, and also globally coordinated to have lasting impact and keep pace with evolving risks and technological advancements.

### 17.4.2 Recommendations and Future Directions

a. The ethical considerations of AI-FS integration must be proactively addressed through interdisciplinary collaboration and cooperation between policymakers, FS providers, AI development teams, and various regulatory bodies.
b. There must be a shift in focus to developing human-centred, human-empowered AI models that are free from bias and aligned with ethical FS-related regulations.
c. Future research should explore scalable AI fairness mechanisms, bias mitigation strategies, and ethical impact measurements and assessments to ensure that AI-powered FS remain transparent, inclusive, and trustworthy.

The FS industry can harness AI's transformative potential without compromising consumer rights, financial stability, and societal trust only by embedding ethics-by-design principles into AI design, development, and deployment while integrating it into FS.

## REFERENCES


1. O'Neil C. *Weapons of math destruction: How big data increases inequality and threatens democracy.* New York: Crown Publishing Group; 2016.
2. Mittelstadt BD, Allo P, Taddeo M, Wachter S, Floridi L. The ethics of algorithms: Mapping the debate. *Big Data Soc.* 2016;3(2):2053951716679679.
3. Jafar SH, Akhtar S, Johl SK. AI in insurance. In: *Artificial intelligence for business.* Boca Raton: Productivity Press; 2023. p. 164–73.
4. European Union. *European Commission white paper on artificial intelligence – A European approach to excellence and trust.* Brussels: EU; 2021. Available from: https://digital-strategy.ec.europa.eu/en/library/white-paper-artificial-intelligence-public-consultation-towards-european-approach-excellence-and
5. Quarshie MA, Akhtar S, Nawaah D. Barriers to breakthroughs: The crucial role of support services in advancing accounting practices, financial literacy and performance in disability-led SMEs. *Qual Quant.* 2025;59:1–23.
6. Leslie D. *Understanding artificial intelligence ethics and safety: A guide for the responsible design and implementation of AI systems in the public sector.* London: The Alan Turing Institute; 2019. https://doi.org/10.5281/zenodo.3240529
7. Nawaah D, Asare PY, Quarshie MA. Climate finance and natural capital: Linking global initiatives with local impact. In: *Climate neutrality through smart eco-innovation and environmental sustainability.* Cham: Springer Nature Switzerland; 2025. p. 317–32.

8. Bajracharya A, Khakurel U, Harvey B, Rawat DB. Recent advances in algorithmic biases and fairness in financial services: A survey. In: *Proceedings of the future technologies conference*. Cham: Springer; 2022. p. 809–22.
9. Zetzsche DA, Arner DW, Buckley RP. Decentralized finance. *J Financ Regul.* 2020; 6(2):172–203.
10. Quarshie MA, Djimatey R, Akhtar S, Nawaah D. Maximizing financial efficiency through technological synergy: Unleashing ICT for enhanced cash management in SMEs. *J Int Counc Small Bus.* 2025:1–31.
11. Lepri B, Oliver N, Letouzé E, Pentland A, Vinck P. Fair, transparent, and accountable algorithmic decision-making processes: The premise, the proposed solutions, and the open challenges. *Philos Technol.* 2018;31(4):611–27.
12. Prince AE, Schwarcz D. Proxy discrimination in the age of artificial intelligence and big data. *Iowa Law Rev.* 2019;105:1257.
13. Oguntibeju OO. Mitigating artificial intelligence bias in financial systems: A comparative analysis of debiasing techniques. *Asian J Res Comput Sci.* 2024;17(12):165–78.
14. Thiruma Valavan A. AI ethics and bias: Exploratory study on the ethical considerations and potential biases in AI and data-driven decision-making in banking. *World J Adv Res Rev.* 2023;20(2):197–206.
15. Hassija V, Chamola V, Mahapatra A, Singal A, Goel D, Huang K, et al. Interpreting black-box models: A review on explainable artificial intelligence. *Cogn Comput.* 2024; 16(1):45–74.
16. Gualdi F, Cordella A. Artificial intelligence and decision-making: The question of accountability. In: *Proceedings of the Annual Hawaii international conference on system sciences.* Hawaii: IEEE Comp Soc Press; 2021. p. 2297–306.
17. Zetzsche DA, Buckley RP, Arner DW, Barberis JN. Artificial intelligence and financial regulation: Ethical and compliance perspectives. *Stanford J Law Bus Finance.* 2020;25(1):1–48.
18. Boppiniti ST. Artificial intelligence in financial markets: Algorithms and applications. SSRN; 2021. Available from: https://ijiert.org
19. Borges G. Liability for AI systems under current and future law: An overview of the key changes envisioned by the proposal of an EU-directive on liability for AI. *Comput Law Rev Int.* 2023;24(1):1–8.
20. Xu J, Yang T, Zhuang S, Li H, Lu W. AI-based financial transaction monitoring and fraud prevention with behaviour prediction. *Appl Comput Eng.* 2024;77:218–24.
21. Jafar SH, Kashid AU, Ghosh S, Srividhya S, Sharma D, Bodhankar A. An enhanced performance optimization of ATM networks for cross-border money transfers. In: *2024 15th international conference on communication and network technology (ICCCNT).* Piscataway, NJ: IEEE; 2024. p. 1–5.
22. Awwal-Bolanta O, Anakanire OC. Artificial intelligence and data privacy: Evaluation of the innovations, legal frameworks and technological protection. *J Law Glob Policy.* 2025;9:36–49
23. Jafar SH, Oyedele OM, Nawaah D, Bolanle AS. Exploring leadership challenges for adoption of digital innovation and sustainability. In: *Innovation ecosystems and sustainable technologies.* Bingley: Emerald Publ Ltd; 2025. p. 253–69.
24. Passador ML. AI Act and the ECB: Steering financial supervision in the EU. SSRN; 2024. Available from: https://ssrn.com/abstract=4603959
25. Mökander J, Juneja P, Watson DS, Floridi L. The US Algorithmic Accountability Act of 2022 vs. the EU Artificial Intelligence Act: What can they learn from each other? *Minds Mach.* 2022;32(4):751–58.
26. Malik MY, Jafar SH, Dixit A. Efficiency analysis and macroeconomic determinants of non-tax revenues: Evidence from special category states of India. *Indian Econ J.* 2025. https://doi.org/10.1177/00194662251330385

27. Gorian E. Deployment of AI in banking: Comparison of Russian and Singaporean approaches. *Eur Proc Soc Behav Sci.* 2021;111:340–7.
28. Calzada I. Citizens' data privacy in China: The state of the art of the Personal Information Protection Law (PIPL). *Smart Cities.* 2022;5(3):1129–50.
29. Yeung K. Recommendation of the council on artificial intelligence (OECD). *Int Legal Mater.* 2020;59(1):27–34.
30. Shahriari K, Shahriari M. IEEE standard review—Ethically aligned design: A vision for prioritizing human wellbeing with artificial intelligence and autonomous systems. In: *2017 IEEE Canada international humanitarian technology conference (IHTC).* Piscataway, NJ: IEEE; 2017. p. 197–201.
31. Corrêa NK, Santos JW, Del Pino C, Pinto EP, Barbosa C, de Oliveira N. Worldwide AI ethics: A review of 200 guidelines and recommendations for AI governance. *Patterns.* 2023;4(10).

# 18 Artificial Intelligence in Healthcare Finance

## *Developing Sustainable Financial Models*

*Emmanuel Asare Tettey*

## 18.1 INTRODUCTION: THE CONVERGENCE OF ARTIFICIAL INTELLIGENCE AND HEALTHCARE FINANCE

Artificial intelligence (AI) solutions for healthcare finance are transforming how organizations manage financial resources by helping optimize costs, reduce fraud, and enhance financial sustainability. Funding healthcare remains a key challenge in many countries due to inefficient payment systems, rising health costs, and administrative barriers hindering reimbursement from insurance [1–3]. AI technologies such as machine learning, natural language processing, robotic process automation (RPA), and predictive analytics are providing some critical solutions to these persistent issues. Financial stability is crucial for any healthcare organization to ensure quality patient care delivery. If they have zero financial sustainability, hospitals and clinics might struggle to pay healthcare professionals or keep up with supplies, let alone invest in new medical technology. For example, postponed payments from insurers created cash flow crises for private hospitals in India during 2023, in some cases resulting in shelving payments to healthcare workers [4–7]. Similarly, the National Hospital Insurance Fund (NHIF) in Kenya reported losing KSh 10 billion, or around $70 million, as a result of inefficiencies and false claims, which had a significant effect on funding for public hospitals [8, 9]. AI is being used more and more by healthcare finance professionals to improve their financial decision-making [5]. AI-powered solutions can more accurately predict hospital expenses, identify irregularities in financial transactions, and automate tedious administrative duties. In order to keep medical treatments cheap for a range of socioeconomic groups, AI-driven models are also making it simpler for insurance firms and hospitals to customize patient payment plans [10] In addition to increasing transparency in healthcare finance, the transition from manual financial procedures to AI-driven solutions is guaranteeing that organizations can continue to be financially sustainable over the long term [11].

## 18.2 THE AI REVOLUTION IN HEALTHCARE FINANCE

The increased use of AI in healthcare finance can be attributed to the rapid advancements in data processing and large datasets that enable more accurate financial forecasts [12]. Traditional hospital finance relied heavily on manual bookkeeping and

DOI: 10.1201/9781003611646-18

human-led data analysis, which were susceptible to error and inefficiency [13, 14]. In contrast, AI-based systems can read massive amounts of financial data in real time and identify patterns that human analysts could not identify [15]. One of the major AI technologies transforming healthcare finance is machine learning, which allows computers to learn from the past to predict future outcomes based on historical data [3, 16]. Revenue Cycle Management (RCM) can use machine learning algorithms that help hospitals estimate for cash flow, optimize billing cycles, and stop revenue leakage. To illustrate with an example, AI-based financial predictions enabled public hospitals in São Paulo, Brazil, to increase their revenue collection by 23% and cut their operating expenses by 18% [17, 18]. These improvements had allowed hospitals to save money and reinvest in better medical options and infrastructure, compared with the previous state of healthcare. Another powerful AI technology used in healthcare finance is natural language processing, which enables robots to understand and analyse human language [19]. Natural language processing is used to analyse unstructured financial data such as insurance claims and patient bills to detect fraud. In Australia, the implementation of an AI-powered fraud detection system found more than AU$2.2 billion (approximately $1.6 billion) worth of fraudulent transactions by Medicare in 2020 [20–22]. The technology used natural language processing to examine millions of medical claims in a matter of seconds, finding suspicious patterns that would have taken months for human auditors to find.

Another AI-powered tool that is assisting healthcare finance professionals in minimizing manual labour is RPA. Software applications that can manage repetitive operations like billing, processing insurance claims, and payment reconciliation are referred to as RPA. For instance, Apollo Hospitals in India reduced administrative effort and operating expenses by 22% by automating 60% of its billing and claims procedures with an AI-driven RPA system [23–25]. This made it possible for hospital employees to devote more time to patient care rather than tedious financial paperwork. Another AI-powered tool that is helping hospitals and insurance companies foresee financial issues before they materialize is predictive analytics. AI systems can predict patient payment patterns by evaluating past data, which enables hospitals to develop flexible financial arrangements for patients who might find it difficult to pay for their care up front. Predictive analytics driven by AI assisted NHIF in Kenya in identifying patients who were at risk of payment default, enabling the organization to introduce other payment plans that resulted in a 30% decrease in non-payment rates [26]. AI is helping to keep healthcare accessible and inexpensive, in addition to increasing the effectiveness of financial operations. Hospitals may better distribute resources by using AI-powered cost optimization techniques, which guarantee that money is spent on necessary medical services rather than sitting about inefficiently.

## 18.3 SUSTAINABLE FINANCIAL MODELS IN AI-DRIVEN HEALTHCARE FINANCE

The formulation of sustainable financial models is one of the most important areas where AI can contribute to making healthcare finance more sustainable while simultaneously ensuring the continued financial health of healthcare institutions

[27, 28]. The typical financial models create inefficiencies where hospitals focus on volume rather than value because of fee-for-service billing [29]. Which resulted in overcharging of medical bills, over-utilization and increase in costs of the services to the patients. However, AI-driven financial models are redirecting healthcare finance into a value-based care model rewarding hospitals based on patient outcomes instead of several procedures [30, 31]. In value-based financial models, healthcare providers are paid according to treatment effectiveness as opposed to volume of services rendered. The shift from volume to value, whereby society is willing to pay for outcomes rather than services, is an essential step, and AI hastens this transition, processing the data available from patients' long-term health records to find the most effective therapies at the lowest cost. In Brazil, predictive analytics in healthcare enabled public hospitals to enhance chronic disease patient treatment plans, minimizing unnecessary medical treatments and generating 15% in cost savings [32, 33].

Predictive budgeting is another popular AI-related financial model, with hospitals adopting predictive algorithms for budgeting to predict future expenses, allowing better allocation of resources. The conventional budgeting process is always based on estimations which sometimes does not reflect the reality of budget needs exactly. On the other hand, predictive budget models powered by AI rely on historical financial data and hospital operational habits to make better estimates of the hospital budget. Bupa Health implemented AI augmented budgeting systems in Australia that enabled better planning for hospital expenditure, netting AU$50 million ($36 million) in savings in 2022 alone [34, 35]. Additionally, AI is used to create patient-specific models of care that will guarantee affordability for patients from varying economic backgrounds. Care approaches that use financial payment assessment powered by AI create individualized payment strategies that are designed to reduce the burden of the cost of care at this point in time for the patient by evaluating their financial history, medical requirements, and other insurance coverage status. Patient affordability models powered by AI brought in by Narayana Health in India improved accessibility to high-cost treatment by having adaptive payment plans that shifted depending on a patient's paying capacity [36–38]. Creating healthy financial sustainability models is not only a boon for hospitals and insurance companies; It is a critical factor for patient access. Use AI to optimize financial management, enabling healthcare institutions to lower unnecessary spending and minimize financial fraud while ensuring the right funds are used in the most needed areas.

## 18.4 AI-DRIVEN COST OPTIMIZATION AND REVENUE CYCLE MANAGEMENT

Proper cost optimization and revenue management are the foundation which strengthens the financial health of any healthcare organization. While previously, hospitals, insurance providers, and other health set-ups tracked, processed, and derived maximum throughput out of their finances either through manual efforts or using ERP packages, the use of AI-based solutions for cost-optimization and RCM is now changing healthcare finance management from a machine brain perspective. The standard RCM procedure is an in-depth process that begins with patient registration, billing, and insurance verification and lasts until payment collection. These processes can be slow, error-prone, and costly. AI assists healthcare institutions to run smoother, reduce expenses, and have an advanced financial sustainability.

### 18.4.1 Predictive Analytics for Cost Reduction and Fraud Detection

The predictive analytics utilizes AI algorithms to analyse past financial data to forecast upcoming trends [39, 40]. Predictive analytics also features prominently in healthcare finance when it explores areas in which money may be saved and in which fraud may be mitigated. Traditional fraud detection methods depend upon a slow manual audit that could last months but often they do not work for more subtle and less obvious forms of financial malfunction. On the other hand, AI-enabled fraud detection solutions will recognize patterns that can indicate early criminal activity and will evaluate millions of transactions in seconds instead of hours. In India, for instance, the Insurance Regulatory and Development Authority of India (IRDAI) identified fraudulent health insurance claims amounting to over ₹200 crores (US 24 million approximately) in 2022, with the advantage of routine operation of AI-enabled fraud detection systems [41, 42]. Such patterns triggered alerts on the AI system, and it enabled authorities to act on the fraudulent practice immediately. For example, the National Health Insurance Fund (NHIF) in Kenya used predictive analytics based on AI for their claims which minimized operational inefficiencies and fraudulent claims [43]. Using historical claims data, the AI detected that certain hospitals were claiming with uncanny frequency, which prompted further investigations that revealed several cases of insurance fraud [26]. Predictive analytics was able to reduce fraudulent claims by 25% thereby saving NHIF Millions in dollars [44].

### 18.4.2 Enhancing Billing Efficiency with AI-Driven Automation

One of the leading causes for revenue loss for any healthcare provider is the billing inefficiencies. Coding mistakes, incorrect insurance claims and delayed reimbursement financially stress many hospitals. Automation powered by AI is assisting healthcare organizations in managing their billing processes with high levels of precision, low administrative burden and faster payment cycles. The Medicare system in Australia had an AI-powered automated billing system that accelerated the time between claims being submitted and providers being paid by 45% [45]. With the help of automation for checking the insurance claims and billing patients over an automated system, the hospitals were to reduce the manual errors and manage their cash flows efficiently. Similarly, India-based Apollo Hospitals embraced AI-fuelled RPA for billing, claims, and patient invoicing [46]. Using an AI-driven system to assign the correct medical codes, Apollo Hospitals was able to reduce claim rejection rates by 30% and improve the efficiency of revenue collection [46].

### 18.4.3 Real-Time Financial Monitoring for Improved Decision-Making

Healthcare administrators can enjoy the benefits of real-time financial monitoring to track revenue, expenses, and payment trends as they happen. Financial dashboards powered by AI offer insight into the financial health of an institution so that decision-makers can proactively mitigate financial risks. For instance, in Britain, AI-based financial monitoring systems were used in public hospitals to prevent unauthorized use of expenditure and find revenue leaks [47]. Through real-time data analysis of the hospital day-to-day, the system highlighted aspects of the care pathway and treatments in which expenses exceeded those usually considered effective, allowing us to reduce operational costs by 18% in 2022 [48, 49]. In addition to detecting fraudulent transactions, AI-driven financial monitoring can also help private hospitals anticipate cash flow fluctuations. For example, in Australia, Bupa Health utilizes AI-enabled analytics to measure financial performance which allows executives to make data-driven decisions that maximize resource allocation while minimizing excess spending. Incorporating AI in cost optimization and RCM will allow healthcare organizations to maintain financial viability, mitigate fraud, and keep essential clinical services available to the patient population [50, 51].

## 18.5 RISK MANAGEMENT AND AI: STRENGTHENING FINANCIAL STABILITY

### 18.5.1 AI-Powered Risk Assessment Models

Hospitals, insurance companies, and financial administrators conduct risk assessments to predict possible monetary losses, fraud, and inefficiencies in operations, making risk assessment a crucial element in the field of healthcare finance. Conventional risk assessment approaches depend on historical data and manual reviews, resulting in a slow process and human errors. On the other hand, AI-based risk assessment models utilize machine learning and big data analytics to real-time identify financial risks and recommend actions to avoid them. For example, AI-powered risk assessment tools have enabled some of the best private hospitals in India to forecast default rates for patients and enhance financial planning [51]. One of India's premier hospital networks, Max Healthcare, implemented an AI-based risk model to identify the income level of patients, the payment behaviours of previous medical bills, and the insurance history to assess the chance of payment default [52]. Using this model, the hospital was able to proactively provide financial assistance to patients they determined were most at risk and stem revenue losses. In Kenya, the NHIF has rolled out AI-based risk models to review hospital claims and detect discrepancies. This has decreased fraudulent payouts and boosted long-term financial sustainability for the fund [26].

### 18.5.2 Fraud Detection and Prevention in Healthcare Finance

Financial fraud is one of the biggest challenges in global health systems with annual losses amounting to billions of dollars [53, 54]. Fraudulent actions are overcharging, double claims, false claims towards insurance and charging non-existent procedures. With the help of AI, fraud detection system examines and analyses different financial transactions and patient records for fraud, in real time. In Brazil, the government used an AI-based fraud detection system to detect more than $500 million dollars' worth of medical fraud in 2022 [55, 56]. The system identified practitioners who were billing for an abnormally large number of claims for this high cost infrequently performed treatments. Thus, it ended with investigations and prosecutions of the fraudsters. Likewise, in Australia, the Medicare Benefits Scheme (MBS), implemented AI fraud detection algorithms that screen millions of medical claims daily and resulted in a 30% decrease in fraud in the first year [57]. The use of AI-powered fraud detection has emerged as a critical factor in maintaining the financial stability of healthcare providers and insurers.

### 18.5.3 Ethical and Regulatory Considerations in AI Adoption

The use of AI in healthcare finance presents moral and legal issues even if it has tremendous advantages for risk management and fraud detection. The fairness and accuracy of AI-driven financial judgements is a significant ethical problem. Because AI models are educated on historical data, they may unjustly refuse financial assistance to specific patient groups if the data contains biases [58]. One such instance was an Indian investigation which found that some AI-based financial models used by insurance companies had discriminatory trends, in which claims by poor patients were systematically rejected. This was because the data used for training were biased, connecting low-income patients with high financial risk [59]. This has led to regulators now calling for AI models to undergo thorough assessments, to ensure fairness and transparency. The laws that govern the use of AI in healthcare finance are also in transition. In Europe, the General Data Protection Regulation (GDPR) has laid out strict guidelines regarding the use of AI in financial-related decisions, ensuring responsibility and transparency [60]. Similar legislation is in development in Australia, India, and Kenya to protect against unethical use of AI in healthcare finance [61].

## 18.6 PERSONALIZED FINANCIAL PLANNING FOR PATIENTS

### 18.6.1 AI-Powered Insurance Recommendations and Claims Processing

A major obstacle in the field of healthcare finance is making sure that people can afford medical care [2]. AI-powered insurance recommendation systems propose the best insurance plans based on a patient's health, financial history, and previous insurance claims. To evaluate consumer profiles and provide individualized health insurance plans, for instance, Acko General Insurance in India employs AI-powered algorithms. For those with lower incomes who previously had trouble finding inexpensive insurance, this has improved access to insurance [62]. AI is also revolutionizing the handling of insurance claims by automating approvals and cutting down on delays. AI-powered claims processing at Jubilee Health Insurance in Kenya cut down on processing time by 40%, guaranteeing that patients are paid more quickly [63]. In 2023, Jubilee Health Hospitals are using predictive modelling to project future patient care costs and create flexible payment options in line with those estimates [64]. Low-income patients now have greater access to care in Brazil because of AI-powered affordability models that allow hospitals to provide zero-interest payment plans for costly procedures [55]. Value-based care, in which hospitals are paid according to treatment results rather than the quantity of treatments completed, is replacing fee-for-service models, and AI is helping to accelerate this transition [65]. AI-powered patient outcome tracking technologies have helped hospitals cut healthcare expenses by 15% by eliminating needless operations [66].

## 18.7 CHALLENGES AND ETHICAL CONSIDERATIONS IN AI-DRIVEN HEALTHCARE FINANCE

### 18.7.1 Data Privacy, Security, and Ethical Concerns

AI-driven financial models rely on vast amounts of sensitive patient data, making data protection a critical challenge. In India, the Personal Data Protection Bill (2023) enforces stricter privacy measures to prevent the misuse of patient financial data by AI systems [66]. Also, bias in the algorithm causing bias in financial decision-making can lead to injustice. An example of this is in Kenya, where an AI-based insurance approval system used biased training data that caused claims from rural patients to be rejected at an 8% higher rate than urban patients [26]. Governments, in turn, are introducing fairness audits for financial models powered by AI to ensure that these models are fair [67]. To regulate AI in healthcare finance, several countries are creating legal frameworks to increase transparency. The adoption of ethical principles in AI systems is another critical step being taken, such as with Australia's Artificial Intelligence Ethics Framework which requires regular audits of the systems, and similar regulations are also expected in India and Brazil [68]. These initiatives underscore the worldwide effort to regulate AI responsibly in the healthcare finance sector.

## 18.8 FUTURE OUTLOOK: AI AND THE NEXT GENERATION OF HEALTHCARE FINANCIAL MODELS

Models completely embedded with AI, automated billing and live patient finance will be the standard for healthcare finance in the future. In India, Apollo Hospitals has already started to pilot AI-driven self-sufficient finance systems that are capable of managing hospital revenue without human interference. In addition, Blockchain technology along with AI is changing financial security by generating immutably safe records. In Brazil, hospitals are slashing costs as claims are removed as false using blockchain-enabled AI. Governments and business leaders need to collaborate to ensure that the implementation of AI in healthcare financing is ethical and effective. For instance, the Australian government established the AI Healthcare Finance Task Force to track how AI has helped the healthcare sector build financial resilience. Advancing AI will make Healthcare Finance management more resilient, efficient, and transparent.

## 18.9 CONCLUSION: PAVING THE WAY FOR A SUSTAINABLE AI-DRIVEN FINANCIAL FUTURE

AI is transforming healthcare finance by decreasing fraud, increasing productivity, and lowering costs. Adoption of AI-powered financial models will guarantee healthcare's long-term viability. Data privacy, algorithmic bias, and legal compliance, however, require close attention. Healthcare organizations may increase financial stability, affordability, and transparency by adopting AI-powered financial solutions, guaranteeing a better future for all.

## REFERENCES

1. Gopal G, Suter-Crazzolara C, Toldo L, Eberhardt W. Digital transformation in healthcare – Architectures of present and future information technologies. *Clin Chem Lab Med.* 2019;57(3):328–35.
2. Kumar AS, Chen LC, Choudhury M, Ganju S, Mahajan V, Sinha A, et al. Financing health care for all: Challenges and opportunities. *Lancet.* 2011;377(9766):668–79.
3. El Abiad Z, Abraham R, El-Chaarani H, Skaf Y, Binsaddig RO, Jafar SH. The impact of CEO characteristics on the financial performance of family businesses listed in the Euronext Exchange. *J Risk Financ Manag.* 2024;17(3):129.
4. Bhatia M, Banerjee K, Dixit P, Dwivedi LK. Assessment of variation in cesarean delivery rates between public and private health facilities in India from 2005 to 2016. *JAMA Netw Open.* 2020;3(8):e2015022.
5. Rodriguez RV, Sinha S, Tripathi S. Impact of Artificial Intelligence on the health protection scheme in India. *Public Adm Policy.* 2020;23(3):273–81.
6. Hemachandran K, Rodriguez RV, editors. *Artificial intelligence for business: An implementation guide containing practical and industry-specific case studies.* Boca Raton: CRC Press; 2023.
7. Quarshie MA, Akhtar S, Nawaah D. Barriers to breakthroughs: The crucial role of support services in advancing accounting practices, financial literacy and performance in disability-led SMEs. *Qual Quant.* 2025;59:1–23.
8. Jung J. Social health insurance for informal sector on the path to universal health coverage: A case of Kenya National Hospital Insurance Fund (NHIF). *Korea Assoc Int Dev Coop.* 2021;13(2):45–68.
9. Njuguna BK. *Assessment of expenditure and budget impact analysis of post-kidney transplant care at Kenyatta National Hospital* [dissertation]. Nairobi: University of Nairobi; 2022.
10. Ingole BS, Ramineni V, Krishnappa MS, Jayaram V. AI-driven innovation in Medicaid: Enhancing access, cost efficiency, and population health management. *arXiv preprint*; 2024. https://doi.org/10.48550/arXiv.2410.21284.
11. Varghese A. AI-driven solutions for energy optimization and environmental conservation in digital business environments. *Asia Pac J Energy Environ.* 2022;9(1):49–60.
12. Dash S, Shakyawar SK, Sharma M, Kaushik S. Big data in healthcare: Management, analysis and future prospects. *J Big Data.* 2019;6(1):1–25.
13. Asante A, Wasike WS, Ataguba JE. Health financing in sub-Saharan Africa: From analytical frameworks to empirical evaluation. *Appl Health Econ Health Policy.* 2020; 18:743–6.
14. Jafar SH, Akhtar S, Johl SK. AI in insurance. In: Hemachandran K, Rodriguez RV, editors. *Artificial intelligence for business.* New York: Productivity Press; 2023. p. 164–73.
15. Jafar SH, Oyedele OM, Nawaah D, Bolanle AS. Exploring leadership challenges for adoption of digital innovation and sustainability. In: *Innovation ecosystems and sustainable technologies.* Bingley: Emerald Publishing; 2025. p. 253–69.

16. Lu Y. Artificial intelligence: A survey on evolution, models, applications and future trends. *J Manag Anal.* 2019;6(1):1–29.
17. Oliveira JD, Wendt A, Cueto M, Massuda A, Lima LD. From health sector reform to universal health coverage in Brazil: A global health policy analysis. *Int J Health Policy Manag.* 2023;12:7520.
18. Mrazek M, O'Neill F. *Artificial intelligence and healthcare in emerging markets.* Washington (DC): World Bank Group; 2020.
19. Wang YH, Lin GY. Exploring AI-healthcare innovation: Natural language processing-based patents analysis for technology-driven roadmapping. *Kybernetes.* 2023;52(4):1173–89.
20. Australian National Audit Office. Audits of the Financial Statements of Australian Government Entities for the Period Ended 30 June 2020: Auditor-General Report No. 25, 2020–21 [Internet]. Canberra: ANAO; 2020 [cited May 29, 2025]. Available from: http://nla.gov.au/nla.obj-2912989562
21. Bello OA, Olufemi K. Artificial intelligence in fraud prevention: Exploring techniques and applications challenges and opportunities. *Comput Sci IT Res J.* 2024;5(6):1505–20.
22. Yamaguti Mondego D. *The use of artificial intelligence to enhance user satisfaction in cloud-based payment systems in Australia* [dissertation]. Rockhampton: CQUniversity; 2024.
23. Sinha A, Ranajee R, Dutta S. Apollo 24/7 – A chink in Apollo Hospitals' armour? *Emerald Emerg Mark Case Stud.* 2023;13(4):1–36.
24. Panigrahi P. *A study on bill payble management at Apollo Hospital, Bhubaneswar* [dissertation]. Bhubaneswar: BIITM; 2023.
25. Hemachandran K, George PM, Rodriguez RV, Kulkarni RM, Roy S. Performance analysis of k-nearest neighbour classification algorithms for bank loan sectors. In: *Smart intelligent computing and communication technology.* Amsterdam: IOS Press; 2021. p. 9–13.
26. National Health Insurance Fund. *Annual national insurance report.* Nairobi: Ministry of Health; 2022.
27. Hemachandran K, Rodriguez RV, Toshniwal R, Junaid M, Shaw L. Performance analysis of different classification algorithms for bank loan sectors. In: *Intelligent sustainable systems: Proceedings of ICISS 2021.* Singapore: Springer; 2021. p. 191–202.
28. Bhatnagar M, Sehajpal S. Leveraging AI for financial sustainability in healthcare: Advancing SDG 3. In: *Sustainability, innovation, and consumer preference.* Hershey (PA): IGI Global; 2025. p. 411–26.
29. Miller HD. From volume to value: Better ways to pay for health care. *Health Aff.* 2009;28(5):1418–28.
30. Vesty G, Kokshagina O, Jansson M, Cheong F, Butler-Henderson K. Accounting, valuing and investing in health care: Dealing with outdated accounting models. *Meditari Account Res.* 2023;31(1):52–77.
31. Jafar SH, Hemachandran K, El-Chaarani H, Moturi S, Gupta N, editors. *Artificial intelligence for capital markets.* Boca Raton: CRC Press; 2023.
32. Castro MC, Massuda A, Almeida G, Menezes-Filho NA, Andrade MV, de Souza Noronha KVM, et al. Brazil's unified health system: The first 30 years and prospects for the future. *Lancet.* 2019;394(10195):345–56.
33. Tentori M, Ziviani A, Muchaluat-Saade DC, Favela J. Digital healthcare in Latin America: The case of Brazil and Mexico. *Commun ACM.* 2020;63(11):72–77.
34. Braithwaite J, Churruca K, Clay-Williams R, Cutler H, Ellis LA, Long JC, et al. Health policy in Australia. In: *Research handbook on health care policy.* Cheltenham: Edward Elgar; 2024. p. 347–73.
35. Carter SM, Aquino YSJ, Carolan L, Frost E, Degeling C, Rogers WA, et al. How should artificial intelligence be used in Australian health care? Recommendations from a citizens' jury. *Med J Aust.* 2024;220(8):409–16.

36. Narayanamurthy G, Moser R, Sutter Y, Shainesh G. Indian healthcare value chain – Status quo not a sustainable solution. *J Asia Bus Stud.* 2017;11(4):481–506.
37. Mazumdar-Shaw K. Leveraging affordable innovation to tackle India's healthcare challenge. *IIMB Manag Rev.* 2018;30(1):37–50.
38. Salim M, Khan PA, Jalil NA, Johl SK, Jafar SH, Irfan F, et al. Fusion of blockchain and sustainable development goals: A bibliometric analysis for future trends. *KnE Soc Sci.* 2023:633–54.
39. Okeleke PA, Ajiga D, Folorunsho SO, Ezeigweneme C. Predictive analytics for market trends using AI: A study in consumer behavior. *Int J Eng Res Updates.* 2024;7(1):36–49.
40. Quarshie MA, Djimatey R, Akhtar S, Nawaah D. Maximizing financial efficiency through technological synergy: Unleashing ICT for enhanced cash management in SMEs. *J Int Counc Small Bus.* 2025:1–31.
41. Nagarajan S, Duggal E. Life insurance industry in India: The inside story. In: *Modeling economic growth in contemporary India.* Bingley: Emerald Publishing; 2024. p. 81–108.
42. Mallikarjun G. Role of IRDAI in promoting e-commerce in insurance sector while ensuring policyholder protection. *Int J Cyber Law Policy.* 2022;10:136.
43. Mwangi GT, Musembi M, Kamau J, Obunga F. Digital transformation strategy and performance of e-claims systems at National Health Insurance Fund, Kenya. *Strateg J Bus Change Manag.* 2024;11(2):1616–40.
44. Onyango MN. *Application of machine learning to detect fraudulent maternal medical claims* [dissertation]. Nairobi: University of Nairobi; 2024.
45. Barrett OOP. New development: Whither the strategic direction of public audit in an era of the 'new normal'? *Public Money Manag.* 2022;42(2):124–8.
46. Agarwal Y, Jain M, Sinha S, Dhir S. Delivering high-tech, AI-based health care at Apollo Hospitals. *Glob Bus Organ Excell.* 2020;39(2):20–30.
47. Soltan AA, Kouchaki S, Zhu T, Kiyasseh D, Taylor T, Hussain ZB, et al. Rapid triage for COVID-19 using routine clinical data for patients attending hospital: Development and prospective validation of an artificial intelligence screening test. *Lancet Digit Health.* 2021;3(2):e78–87.
48. Tortorella GL, Fogliatto FS, Sunder MV, Cawley Vergara AM, Vassolo R. Assessment and prioritisation of Healthcare 4.0 implementation in hospitals using Quality Function Deployment. *Int J Prod Res.* 2022;60(10):3147–69.
49. Ritto AP, de Araujo AL, de Carvalho CRR, De Souza HP, Favaretto PMES, et al. Data-driven, cross-disciplinary collaboration: Lessons learned at the largest academic health center in Latin America during the COVID-19 pandemic. *Front Public Health.* 2024;12:1369129.
50. Nawaah D, Asare PY, Quarshie MA. Climate finance and natural capital: Linking global initiatives with local impact. In: *Climate neutrality through smart eco-innovation and environmental sustainability.* Switzerland: Springer Nature; 2025. p. 317–32.
51. Jafar SH, Kashid AU, Ghosh S, Srividhya S, Sharma D, Bodhankar A. An enhanced performance optimization of ATM networks for cross-border money transfers. In: *2024 15th International Conference on Computing Communication and Networking Technologies (ICCCNT).* Piscataway, NJ: IEEE; 2024. p. 1–5.
52. Pan R, Budhiraja S, Jha V, Mathur P, Pan R. Transforming healthcare: The role of artificial intelligence in revolutionising patient care. *Med J.* 2024;1:30–2.
53. Mackey TK, Liang BA. Combating healthcare corruption and fraud with improved global health governance. *BMC Int Health Hum Rights.* 2012;12:1–7.
54. Malik MY, Jafar SH, Dixit A. Efficiency analysis and macroeconomic determinants of non-tax revenues: Evidence from special category states of India. *Indian Econ J.* 2025:00194662251330385.
55. da Silva JB, Magalhaes HM. Initiatives in cancer control from Brazil's Ministry of Health. *Lancet Oncol.* 2013;14(5):385–6.

56. Massuda A, Dall'Alba R, Chioro A, Temporão JG, Castro MC. After a far-right government: Challenges for Brazil's Unified Health System. *Lancet.* 2023;401(10380):886–8.
57. Barrett AOP. New development: Whither the strategic direction of public audit in an era of the 'new normal'? *Public Money Manag.* 2022;42(2):124–8.
58. Hoffman S, Podgurski A. Artificial intelligence and discrimination in health care. *Yale J Health Policy Law Ethics.* 2019;19:1.
59. Thakur M. Compliance related to fintech: An overview of the Indian legal system. In: *E-banking, fintech, & financial crimes: The current economic and regulatory landscape.* Cham, Switzerland: Springer; 2024. p. 121–32.
60. Hamon R, Junklewitz H, Sanchez I, Malgieri G, De Hert P. Bridging the gap between AI and explainability in the GDPR: Towards trustworthiness-by-design in automated decision-making. *IEEE Comput Intell Mag.* 2022;17(1):72–85.
61. World Health Organization. *Ethics and governance of artificial intelligence for health.* Geneva: World Health Organization; 2021.
62. Satuluri RK, Radhika R. Digital transformation in Indian insurance industry. *Turk J Comput Math Educ.* 2021;12(4):310–24.
63. Mosiori, I. (2023). *Effect of emerging technologies on performance of medical insurance providers in Nairobi City County, Kenya* [Unpublished MBA thesis]. United States International University–Africa. Available from: https://erepo.usiu.ac.ke/bitstream/handle/11732/7867/Mosiori/Isaiah/MBA/2023.pdf?isAllowed=y&sequence=1 USIU eRepo
64. Sumaya MK, Allen RM. The application of operations research information system tools in hospital operations management in developing nations: A systematic literature review. *Univ Dar es Salaam Libr J.* 2023;18(1):134–51.
65. Ray JC, Kusumoto F. The transition to value-based care. *J Interv Card Electrophysiol.* 2016;47:61–68.
66. Hossain MA, Arafat MS, Desai K, Akter S, Asha AI. The economic impact of AI-driven remote patient monitoring: A business intelligence perspective on healthcare cost optimization. *Int Interdiscip Bus Econ Adv J.* 2025;6(05):39–67.
67. Agu EE, Abhulimen AO, Obiki-Osafiele AN, Osundare OS, Adeniran IA, Efunniyi CP. Discussing ethical considerations and solutions for ensuring fairness in AI-driven financial services. *Int J Frontier Res Sci.* 2024;3(2):001–9.
68. World Health Organization. *Tracking universal health coverage: 2023 global monitoring report.* Geneva: World Health Organization; 2023.

# 19 Blockchain and AI in Finance

## *Synergies for a Digital Economy*

*Muneer Shaik and Mukundamgari Rishik Reddy*

## 19.1 INTRODUCTION

The last few decades have seen an unprecedented pace of growth in the world of digital technologies, leading to transitions in the way societies, businesses, and governments operate [1, 2]. Initially starting with internet banking and recently progressing into mobile payments, technology has slowly become the backbone of the global financial ecosystem. While this evolution continues to grow, artificial intelligence (AI) and blockchain emerge as two of the most potent forces fuelling the next stage of evolution. AI, with its capacity to process and analyse big data, predict future outcomes, and automates decision-making, has already begun reshaping industries ranging from healthcare to transportation and finance [3, 4]. But the technology underlying this phenomenon retains high potential to change the way how we transactions and records without central authorities, this is what blockchain is, technologies well-known for its decentralization, transparency, and security. Collectively, these technologies are moving forward in terms of data independence. However, it seems the most exciting part of the current phase is that the AI and blockchain are converging in the field of financial services. This convergence is more than the coalescence of two digital tools; it speaks to an integration in which AI could imbue the intelligence and efficiency of blockchain systems and provide secure and verifiable environments for AI operations. There is an emerging combination of financial applications such as decentralized finance (DeFi), smart contracts powered by AI, robo-advisory and credit scoring powered by AI, all in the context of blockchain platforms. This chapter explores the ways in which these technologies are converging, the potential advantages, challenges and threats they present, and possible pathways this convergence will follow in the future.

### 19.1.1 AI Fundamentals

One must have a basic understanding of blockchain and AI to explore the complexities of these topics as discussed in this chapter. AI are algorithms that allow for the automatic handling of a range of tasks [5]. The terms such as machine learning

 DOI: 10.1201/9781003611646-19

(ML), natural language processing (NLP), and deep learning (DL) are often related to AI. AI engages in tasks that would typically require human intelligence: problem-solving and decision-making. ML, one of the most important fields in AI, gives computer systems the ability to learn in an unstructured way, without being explicitly programmed to perform a certain task. It leverages vast data sets to identify patterns and make predictions. NLP, on the other hand, is a form of AI where computers are programmed to understand and generate human-like text, moving beyond the traditional use of numerical and logical data [6]. DL which is a part of ML involves training models on large sets of labelled data. These models further refine themselves to that will help them take up advanced tasks like speech recognition, stock market predictions, and facial recognition [7, 8].

AI can be categorized into two major categories: Narrow AI and General AI [9]. Narrow AI is designed to perform the best on specific activities like facial recognition, internet searches, autopilot systems in cars, etc., which is currently in application (DL falls in this criteria). In contrast, General AI, which theoretically possesses cognitive and intellectual abilities like the human mind, remains a concept and is yet to be realized [10]. The applications of AI are vast, ranging from speech recognition to comprehending and responding to human language, continuously learning from experts and new data, and making recommendations or predictions. Essentially, it simulates human activities. In BFSI sector, AI is increasingly being integrated into daily processes and systems. Key implementations include KYC automation, chatbots, CRM systems, credit risk management, predictive analytics, and fraud detection systems.

### 19.1.2 Blockchain Fundamentals

Blockchain is a chronological set of blocks connected like a chain, each containing a list of transactions. It serves as a decentralized, immutable ledger where the executed transactions are stored and tracked across a business network. Transactions are validated only when most participants in the network agree on them [11]. One of the fundamental pillars of blockchain is its integrity, once information is recorded, it cannot be erased. Key features of blockchain include traceability, decentralization, anonymity, and distributed consensus for transactions within the network [12].

#### 19.1.2.1 Smart Contracts: An Emerging Use Case

One of the major applications of blockchain technology are the smart contracts. These are immutable digital contracts that have a set of conditions which are to be met for the contract to be executed [12, 13]. By eliminating intermediaries, smart contracts automate the transaction process, reduce transaction costs, and create a faster and more efficient system. Applications of smart contracts span various domains, including cryptocurrencies. For instance, Ethereum, a cryptocurrency platform using blockchain utilizes smart contracts to execute currency sales only when pre-defined conditions are satisfied, further enhancing the automation process.

#### 19.1.2.2 Key Features of Blockchain

a. *Immutability*: If a transaction is recorded on the blockchain's network, it cannot be removed. Each block acts as a permanent record, with immutability ensured by the decentralized nature of the system and cryptographic hashing.
b. *Distributed Consensus*: All nodes or participants in the blockchain collectively decide on the validity of transactions. This decentralized decision-making ensures the system's fault tolerance and reliability, even if some participants do not agree [14].

#### 19.1.2.3 Levels of Blockchain Operation

Blockchain can operate at different levels, each with unique characteristics:

a. *Public Blockchain*: A secure and transparent blockchain network where anyone can join and participate in activities such as reading, writing, and adding blocks [15]. This decentralized, community-driven system ensures immutability.
b. *Private Blockchain*: Is a restricted blockchain network accessible only to verified participants. Entry into this network requires identity verification and authentication. Unlike public blockchains, private blockchains are centralized, allowing the network owner to edit, modify, or change information as needed [15].
c. *Consortium Blockchain*: This a network of blockchain that is run by organization(s). It is a hybrid model combining the likes of both public and private blockchains, with controlled access and shared governance among the participating organizations [15].

Having covered AI and blockchain technologies, the remaining sections of the chapter focus on how these two technologies complement each other and examine how their combined strengths can drive transformative change in the finance industry.

## 19.2 SYNERGIES: BLOCKCHAIN AND AI

Blockchain and AI complement each other perfectly by addressing each other's weaknesses and amplifying their respective strengths. Let us explore how these two technologies create a synergistic balance, leveraging their unique capabilities to bring transformative potential to various industries.

### 19.2.1 Centralized AI and Decentralized Blockchain: The Optimal Combination

Blockchain is democratizing AI, creating a transformative shift in how AI is developed and monetized [16]. One of the core challenges with centralized AI, whether it involves major players like Amazon, Meta, or Google generating massive amounts of data for informed decision-making or large language models like ChatGPT, is the vulnerability of centralized systems. There are serious privacy concerns, including risks of tampering, hacking, and manipulation. The centralization of data also concentrates power in the hands of a few, raising ethical and security challenges. Here, blockchain's decentralization value proposition steps in, fostering the concept of decentralized AI. In this model, AI utilizes digitally signed data from a trusted, shared source to perform analysis, make predictions, and support decision-making. Meanwhile, blockchain ensures the secure storage and transaction of this data [17]. Additionally, smart contracts are pivotal in facilitating seamless access to and hence the decision-making processes.

#### 19.2.1.1 Key Benefits of Decentralized AI through Blockchain

a. *Enhanced Reliability of AI Models*: The ledgers which are decentralized record transactions on a peer-to-peer (P2P) basis, increasing trust in AI-driven decision-making processes. Blockchain's traceability enhances transparency, fostering public trust in the outcomes derived from AI [17].
b. *Improved Data Security*: In a decentralized system, data is not stored in a single location, reducing the risk of breaches. Furthermore, the digital signing of data ensures enhanced privacy and credibility, strengthening trust in the process of decision-making and bolstering the effectiveness of AI-driven insights.

### 19.2.2 Enhancing AI Transparency with Blockchain's Immutability

One of blockchain's core features is immutability. Once a transaction enters the network (particularly in public blockchains), it is nearly impossible to erase. In contrast, AI, especially the DL models, are often mocked for its black box nature. Models like these are opaque, making it difficult to trace the sources of their information or explain their decision-making processes [17]. The accountability of these models is often questioned due to its lack of transparency. Integrating blockchain into AI's decision-making processes can address these challenges. Blockchain's transparency ensures that predictions, decisions, or other results produced by AI models can be scrutinized and verified. This integration plays a vital role in regulating DL models, ensuring their safe and responsible use.

### 19.2.3 The Synergy of AI's ML Capabilities and Blockchain's Data Management Strengths

After examining the individual technologies, blockchain, AI, ML, and its subsets like DL, it becomes evident how these systems complement each other. DL is heavily data-dependent, requiring vast amounts of reliable and credible information to make accurate predictions. Blockchain addresses this need by providing a systematic and secure way to collect, store, and manage data within specific networks or locations. With blockchain's smart contracts, data access and control can be regulated, ensuring data integrity while making large volumes of trustworthy data available for AI systems to process and leverage [18]. This seamless integration helps overcome existing challenges in both technologies, amplifying their combined potential.

### 19.2.4 Heightened Efficiency Due to Integration

Key industries are integrating advanced blockchain systems in their business and are also investing a lot in these industries [2, 19]. But there lies a crucial problem with how they store their data. For example, they don't handle queries (that search for data) well and are slow at it [20]. As the blockchain grows with requiring storing more and more data and supporting more and more applications, frequent searches (queries) become necessary. But as these systems are faster in writing speeds than reading, the search is slowed down which creates a bottleneck for query inefficiency. To solve this, AI can improve how blockchains store data. For instance, one research project introduced an AI-based TTA-CB protocol. This uses a Particle Swarm Optimization (PSO) algorithm to choose the best data providers [20]. This makes blockchain systems more secure, distributed, and efficient.

## 19.3 APPLICATIONS IN FINANCE

The complementarity of blockchain technology and AI has been studied. The use of real-world applications in the financial sector will be explored in this section. The conversation starts with an exploration of the revolutionary impacts of blockchain on financial services and continues into a discussion around the role of AI in modern finance. This sets the stage for the next part, which provides real-world examples of companies leveraging the complementary nature of both technologies to their advantage.

### 19.3.1 Applications of Blockchain in Finance

#### 19.3.1.1 Fundraising in Secondary Markets

Blockchain is revolutionizing the secondary market for private fundraising with new avenues for liquidity and investment opportunities. This change is best represented by the NASDAQ Private Equity Exchange launched in 2013 [21]. The exchange offers pre-IPO services to private companies who want to raise funds from secondary markets, providing a mechanism to access liquidity for private companies as well as an avenue for private investors and funds to source capital deployment. This partnership seeks to implement intelligent contracts into the exchange processes to provide practical benefits of decentralization, traceability, and efficiency [21]. With the inclusion of blockchain technology, NASDAQ has enhanced the platform's transparency, security, and automation, thereby reducing the mediating entities in the entire fundraising process.

#### 19.3.1.2 Cryptocurrency

Cryptocurrency, often referred to as crypto, is a digital currency secured by cryptography, utilizing various algorithmic and cryptographic methods to encrypt its entries [21]. It represents one of the most innovative applications of blockchain technology. The decentralization inherent in cryptocurrencies empowers them with the unique attribute of immutability, free from control by any central authority or government.

Cryptocurrencies are revolutionizing finance and banking, challenging the traditional model where centralization was fundamental to the system. They offer a decentralized approach that enables faster, more secure, and transparent transactions across borders. Among the myriad cryptocurrencies, Bitcoin stands as the most renowned, often considered a pioneer in this space. Ethereum provides another layer of functionality to the blockchain using smart contracts, allowing a fully decentralized financial products and services [22]. Other alternatives that stand out from the rest such as Tether, Binance Coin, or Solana also contribute with different applications and benefits within the ecosystem.

#### 19.3.1.3 Decentralized Finance

So, blockchain technology and cryptocurrencies are not only challenging the traditional banking method; they are also disrupting another important domain of finance, or lending and borrowing. DeFi, as it is often called, is the movement to make traditional financial activities happen using the cryptocurrencies we have today. The traditional role of banks in lending and borrowing activities was to act as intermediaries, providing trust, credit checks, and loan contracts. However, DeFi removes these intermediaries and allows P2P transaction directly with the smart contracts. Such smart contracts automate the enforcement of the terms of the agreement, ensuring faster, clearer, and cheaper transactions. DeFi loans, where you place your cryptocurrency assets as collateral to receive loans in other currencies, are becoming the industry standard thanks to platforms like Compound and Aave. This innovation facilitates peer-to-peer lending and borrowing of cryptocurrencies without the involvement of traditional banks, thereby creating a significant new space for investors, financiers, and early adopters to participate in decentralized financial activities [23].

#### 19.3.1.4 Asset Tokenization

Asset tokenization is a method that allows real-world assets to be broken down into smaller, tradable units known as tokens, which are then represented on blockchain networks. This allows multiple investors to own a fraction of the assets, opening up the market for a high-value asset to many smaller investors, thereby facilitating ownership, transfer, and trading with greater efficiency [24, 25]. With asset tokenization, a wide range of physical assets, such as real estate, fine art, gold, and even mining operations that can be tokenized [4]. By tokenizing these assets and opening them up to a global, decentralized network, geographic and financial barriers are removed [24]. Therefore, tokenization greatly improves access to these markets and attracts investment all over the world, thus providing liquidity and pushing the investment geography of these assets.

### 19.3.2 Applications of AI in Finance

#### 19.3.2.1 Security and Intelligence Systems

AI has spearheaded the response against cybersecurity hurdles in the ever-evolving digital space. ML models have changed the game, allowing for large volumes of data to be analysed quickly, where trends and outliers can be flagged. These models have the capability to continuously learn from earlier analyses and datasets which improves their accuracy. Such flexibility enables AI to identify fraud at an early stage and highlight it before it can grow, thus protecting the finances of these institutions. AI-driven integration of security systems not only reinforces digital defences but also provides a proactive method of addressing cyber threats, thus delivering another strong layer of protection in the financial ecosystem in Fintech 2024 [11].

#### 19.3.2.2 AI and Algorithmic Trading Systems

ML models can process a wide range of data that is generated in mere seconds from markets, finding trends that allow them to construct trading systems that produce profits. These algorithms need to constantly learn over time as new data comes in and analysing it from multiple sources like daily stock data, new sites, social media and historical data. These systems make it possible to discover patterns and trends, which facilitate data-driven decision-making that is more accurate for increasing the returns of the users [26]. This speedy execution of trades is one of the most fundamental benefits of AI in trading that helps humans to give a very quick response, which they cannot in any case match. Moreover, these systems are highly autonomous and need little supervision, as they can act on an order without the need for human involvement, if certain criteria are defined by the trader or the investor. Unlike humans who often make trading decisions in a reactive manner due to emotions like fear or greed, an AI will tackle trading scenarios in an objective and consistent manner. This translates into relatively rational and lucrative results granting a competitive advantage in financial markets [26].

#### 19.3.2.3 Risk Management and Lending Solutions

AI is now embedded as an essential component within credit risk management systems at leading financial institutions, especially multinational banks that span various geographies with complex portfolios. AI systems help mitigate losses from defaults on loan obligations by providing enhanced solutions. ML models are proficient at large data volume analyses, pattern recognition and can determine the creditworthiness of borrowers with incredible precision. When lending institutions capitalize on these capabilities, they can ensure that their loan approvals are based on data-driven decisions and avoid defaulting risks effectively. AI-enabled analysis helps to boost the accuracy of credit risk assessments which is a crucial aspect of protecting the organizational financial stability.

#### 19.3.2.4 Robo-advisory Services

One of the promising applications of AI is, no doubt, robo-advisory services. These platforms are driven by advanced AI models and behave like an online financial advisor using algorithms to suggest financial securities customized to varying user interests [27]. All this is backed by extensive user analytics, from risk profiles to time horizons to preferences. The core data processing mechanisms are like those used in algorithmic trading systems with complete accuracy and efficiency. One of the most useful features of robo-advisors is auto-portfolio rebalancing. That is, as the market shifts, the portfolio rebalances itself to this. In layman's terms, it means buying and selling of the securities according to the risk appetite and financial goals of the respective investor, without the need for manual work. This feature presents a differentiating and compelling value to investors who want their portfolios to be consistently managed over time. The benefits of these robo advisors is that they cost less. Advisory fees are usually less than 1%, allowing individuals to gain access to financial markets, thus making investing democratized [26]. Robo-Advisors allow people with less capital, or financial literacy, access to the stock market without needing to worry about managing investments. These numbers reflect the rising interest in these platforms, with robo-advisors expected to see their assets under management (AUM) grow to $2.3 trillion by 2024 [28]. That growth echoes the power of AI, making advanced investment management possible for everyone.

## 19.4 THEORETICAL FRAMEWORK

The integration of AI and blockchain not just represents a technological transition but a drastic shift in the way of value creation, mediation and governance in modern economies. While much can be envisioned about the potential of these technologies, the true impact lies in their systemic deployment and scaling. Crucially, the influence of these technologies does not exist in isolation it is shaped by a web of interdependent factors, including institutional acceptance, organizational capability, regulatory frameworks, and the broader socio-economic context. In this light, we propose the Techno-Financial Synergy Framework (TFSF): a model that captures and structurally maps the interaction between technological enablers, organizational readiness, institutional conditions, and innovative transformational outcomes in the adoption of emerging technologies in finance.

### 19.4.1 Foundation Theories

Four major streams of theory make up the TFSF articulating how emerging technologies (e.g., AI and blockchain) and systems of innovation interface with organizations and institutions:

a. *Socio-Technical Systems Theory*: It treats organizations as systems of people and technology [29]. It indicates that social, institutional, and technological components of an organization need to align for large-scale change to succeed. Change in one aspect influences the others, hence all need to evolve in harmony.
b. *Dynamic Capabilities Theory*: This refers to an organization's ability to accommodate, learn, and transform in very changeable environments [30]. When we look through the lens of AI and blockchain, it translates into the need to remain agile, reskill the internal workforce and continuously challenge existing business processes, to stay ahead of the competition and remain relevant.
c. *Institutional Theory*: It focuses on the influence of template structures such as laws, rules, regulations, and cultural norms in the adoption of new

technologies [31]. Depending on how misaligned the changes brought by AI and blockchain are with the trajectory of the institutions, the institutions can either promote or inhibit innovation.

d. *Theory of Modular Innovation*: This theory states that technologies such as AI and blockchain are modular, that is they can be decomposed down into smaller parts and then recombined in different structural entities [32]. That flexibility leads to rapid, more decentralized innovation, but it also comes with the necessity for clear rules, and the need for systems to make sure everything fits and works right.

### 19.4.2 The Techno-Financial Synergy Framework (TFSF)

The TFSF is a five-layer model about the integration of AI and blockchain in the financial sector. This covers a few key areas such as the underlying technologies, internal capabilities, external environment, value pathways and the macro implications of integration.

#### 19.4.2.1 Technological Core (Dual Enablers)

Grounding the framework are two compelling technologies for transformation:

a. Distributed ledgers, smart contracts, and consensus mechanisms make up blockchain infrastructure by providing tools for secure and tamper-proof transactions.
b. AI, ML, predictive analytics, NLP, and anomaly detection or risk detection tooling.

These technologies complement each other. AI can, for instance, help create better smart contracts and execute them, and in turn, blockchain can provide the transparent, traceable foundation to AI models and data, so they operate safely.

#### 19.4.2.2 Strategic Capabilities (Organizational Readiness)

This layer addresses internal needs of the organization to implement and scale with these technologies:

a. *Digital Talent and Innovation Mindset*: Companies need teams that are willing to adapt and explore without boundaries when it comes to new technologies and across departments.
b. *Data Standards and Interoperability*: Well-defined protocols for data sharing, storage and access, such as open API architecture and compliance with data specifications and norms (like GDPR or RBI guidelines).
c. *Security and Risk Frameworks*: Well-established systems to safeguard digital activities, particularly for decentralized working or trust less settings.

These capabilities position firms to transition from experimentation to transformation at scale.

#### 19.4.2.3 Institutional Environment (External Constraints and Enablers)

This layer considers how policies, laws, and institutions affect the uptake of AI and blockchain:

a. *Regulatory Sandboxes and Test Zones*: Intriguing zones that offer an atmosphere with more flexible legal guidelines for start-ups and fintech to test run new verticals of technology.
b. *Smart Contracts to Have Legal Certainty*: Jurisdictions must enforce such contracts at law.
c. *Data Privacy*: Laws that demand the local storage of data, require firms to ensure the responsible processing of personal information.
d. *Sector-Specific Norms*: Guidelines issued by sector regulators will help define the legal and ethical boundaries of deployment of these technologies across sectors.

Such conditions will determine not only the speed but also the path of technology adoption in finance.

#### 19.4.2.4 Value Creation Mechanisms (Transformational Pathways)

When the technological foundation, organizational readiness, and institutional environment are in play, financial systems begin to truly transform. The most immediate benefit is reinforcement of trust and security, courtesy of the immutable record-keeping of blockchain, and the transparent, explainable decision-making capability of AI. They combine to create a degree of responsibility and traceability that traditional systems have a hard time providing. Operational processes, especially with smart contracts that execute or trigger workflows without manual intervention, become significantly more efficient through automation. This saves cost, time, and friction. In addition, AI allows for greater personalization and intelligence of financial services using machinery such as risk profiling, behavioural analysis and real-time data to deliver unique products to individuals or businesses. This personalization goes hand in hand with peer-to-peer models made possible by blockchain that are eating away at the edges of the intermediary empire. Emerging systems like DeFi are enabling users to use financial services directly, eliminating traditional banks and brokers.

#### 19.4.2.5 Outcome Dimensions (System Level Effects)

When AI and blockchain come together, the benefits are no longer only incremental; they completely change the nature of financial ecosystems. Perhaps the most important possible result is improved financial inclusion. It enables new low-cost, AI-powered services that allow populations that were previously underserved or excluded from access to the benefits of microloans, savings tools, and access to credit assessments like never before. Simultaneously institutional disruption is inevitable where banks and regulators as well as intermediaries are forced to redefine their place in the world with whom they will partner and how they earn a living in this upcoming paradigm. Yet another important outcome is the empowerment of consumers who will exert more control over the use of their data, the degree to which their privacy is invaded, and the services they receive. Within these systems, people can explore financial options with greater independence and transparency. Finally, the confluence of automation and transparency results in stronger markets: those that can sense aberrations and self-correct instantaneously while attenuating systemic risks. In this way, AI and blockchain do not merely upgrade existing financial structures; they lay the groundwork for a more inclusive, adaptable, and robust digital economy.

## 19.5 CHALLENGES

### 19.5.1 Computational Complexity

Combining the complex blockchain and AI increased the computational complexity, primarily due to the intensive resources that blockchain and DL AI models consume. Training DL models is highly expensive, with costs influenced by dataset size, model parameters, and training volume, for instance, training a model with 110 billion parameters can range from $2.5K to $50K [33]. AI models such as GPT-3 demand substantial computational power, consuming approximately 1,287 MWh, equivalent to yearly energy consumption of 120 American homes [34]. Similarly, blockchain's consensus protocols, such as Proof of Work, are notorious for consuming high energy resources, with Bitcoin's annual usage comparable to that of small nations [35]. Latency further complicates integration, as blockchain networks like Bitcoin and Ethereum experience transaction confirmation delays, making them unsuitable for real-time AI applications like autonomous driving and high-frequency trading, which require millisecond-level responses [36]. Additionally, storage constraints present a major hurdle, DL models often consist of hundreds of billions of parameters, requiring vast storage capacities, while blockchain networks operate with limited on-chain storage, with Ethereum block sizes measured in kilobytes, making direct storage of AI models impractical. It is these factors that, in unison, compound the challenge of deploying AI and blockchain in a manner that is harmonious in the real world.

### 19.5.2 Scalability

Integrating blockchain with AI still faces the critical challenge of scalability. A consensus mechanism assures that the operations handled by the blockchain are secure, meaning that most of the nodes in the network must agree on the transaction before it gets validated. But the quest for speed often puts this agreement process under pressure, which may cause mistakes in the best case or create "forks" of the blockchain in the worst case, when the network is torn in two versions. Moreover, decentralized information passes through several nodes which generates latency in communication, which is critical to handle high transaction volumes in low times. This bottleneck increases operational latency while placing huge demands on resources, thereby exacerbating the computational overhead of AI-blockchain integration.

### 19.5.3 Interoperability

The major challenge to blockchain being integrated with AI is interoperability as both technology works in different eco-systems having different protocols, consensus mechanisms, and data structures. Blockchain networks have their unique ways of validating transactions, and similarly, AI models are constructed using different frameworks designed for specific purposes. Such divergence creates a challenge in having a common communication standard with both systems. What makes it more difficult to integrate blockchain with AIs is the lack of common protocols to govern the interaction between them. In order for data to be exchanged among systems, data formats and structures must be compatible, and any mismatch between them can affect the integrity and reliability of that data, which will, in turn, impede the efficiency of AI-embedded blockchain applications [11].

### 19.5.4 Regulatory Compliance

One major challenge faced by blockchain and AI application in the financial sector is that the existing regulations in the financial sector cannot fit well with the effective implementation of blockchain and AI technology. Decentralization, automation, and high-volume data management introduce complexities that are not suited to conventional regulation. The immutable character of blockchain threatens privacy, while AI's absence of accountability in decision-making makes legal adherence incredibly difficult. Moreover, regulations are slow in catching up with tech developments, which remains particularly grey in case of cross-border transactions and AI-powered financial decisions. This requires the development of adaptive policies that promote innovation while ensuring adherence to the law and ethics, which must be a collaborative process between regulators and industry stakeholders [11].

## 19.6 CONCLUSION AND FUTURE OUTLOOK

The intersection of blockchain and AI is not just a technological revolution; it will be a paradigm shift, setting a new standard in trust, transparency, and efficiency. The convergence of blockchain's immutable ledge and AI's analytical powers is about to make the future of finance faster, smarter, and more robust in ways that will be collectively beneficial to individuals and institutions alike. However, there are multiple roadblocks such as computational complexity, scalability, interoperability, and regulatory compliance that need to be solved before these technologies can achieve their greater utility. In the near future, blockchain-anchored data will enable AI-powered models to identify fraud, manage the market risk, and ensure regulatory compliance instantly and with unmatched accuracy. Technologies such as zero-knowledge proofs; and homomorphic encryption, will solve decades-old trade-offs between security and data privacy, allowing for transparent but private financial systems. Scalability and interoperability breakthroughs will unlock mass adoption, making cross-border payments effortless, tokenized assets more liquid and financial services increasingly individualized. From lending to global trade, automated smart contracts will eliminate inefficiencies and outcome accountability like never before. Doing so will take the work of policymakers and workers as well as the leaders across industry to take the ethical considerations and regulatory clarity to help create the innovation incentive structures that allow innovation to occur without risking public trust. The merging of blockchain and AI is not a futuristic dream but a present occurrence. The question is not if this transformation will take place, but if we are prepared for it. This is the start of the financial revolution that is only growing and spreading stronger.

## REFERENCES


1. Tapscott D, Williams AD, Herman D. Government 2.0: Transforming government and governance for the twenty-first century. *New Paradigm*. 2008;1(15):1–21.
2. Quarshie MA, Akhtar S, Nawaah D. Barriers to breakthroughs: The crucial role of support services in advancing accounting practices, financial literacy and performance in disability-led SMEs. *Qual Quant*. 2025;59:1–23.
3. Jafar SH, Kashid AU, Ghosh S, Srividhya S, Sharma D, Bodhankar A. An enhanced performance optimization of ATM Networks for Cross-border Money Transfers. In: *2024 15th International Conference on Computing Communication and Networking Technologies (ICCCNT)*. Piscataway, NJ: IEEE; 2024. p. 1–5.
4. Malik MY, Jafar SH, Dixit A. Efficiency analysis and macroeconomic determinants of non-tax revenues: Evidence from special category states of India. *Indian Econ J*. 2025:00194662251330385.
5. Mathew D, Brintha NC, Jappes JW. Artificial intelligence powered automation for industry 4.0. In: *New horizons for Industry 4.0 in modern business*. Cham: Springer; 2023. p. 1–28.
6. Brown M. Machine learning, explained. MIT Sloan [Internet]. 2021 [cited January 25, 2025]. Available from: https://mitsloan.mit.edu/ideas-made-to-matter/machine-learning-explained
7. Holdsworth J, Scapicchio M. What is deep learning? IBM [Internet]. 2024 [cited January 25, 2025]. Available from: https://www.ibm.com/think/topics/deep-learning
8. Nawaah D, Asare PY, Quarshie MA. Climate finance and natural capital: Linking global initiatives with local impact. In: *Climate neutrality through smart eco-innovation and environmental sustainability*. Cham: Springer; 2025. p. 317–32.
9. Babu MV, Banana KR. A study on narrow artificial intelligence—An overview. *Int J Eng Sci Adv Technol*. 2024;24:210–9.
10. Kumar A. Types of AI | Artificial intelligence type [Internet]. Simplilearn.com; 2025 [cited January 25, 2025]. Available from: https://www.simplilearn.com/tutorials/artificial-intelligence-tutorial/types-of-artificial-intelligence
11 Rane N, Choudhary S, Rane J. Blockchain and Artificial Intelligence (AI) Integration for Revolutionizing Security and Transparency in Finance. SSRN Scholarly Paper No. 4644253. 2023.
12. Crosby M, Pattanayak P, Verma S, Kalyanaraman V. *Blockchain technology: Beyond bitcoin. Sutardja Center Technical Report*. Berkeley: UC Berkeley; 2016.
13. Jafar SH, Akhtar S, Johl SK. AI in insurance. In: *Artificial intelligence for business*. Boca Raton, FL: Productivity Press; 2023. p. 164–73.
14 Zavala R. Blockchain components—Distributed consensus protocol [Internet]. Encora; 2025 [cited January 26, 2025]. Available from: https://insights.encora.com/insights/distributed-consensus-protocol-a-key-component-of-blockchain
15. Seth S. Public, private, and permissioned blockchains compared. Investopedia [Internet]. 2024 [cited January 26, 2025]. Available from: https://www.investopedia.com/news/public-private-permissioned-blockchains-compared/

16. Lee S. AI meets decentralization: How blockchain is democratizing AI. Forbes [Internet]. 2024 [cited January 26, 2025]. Available from: https://www.forbes.com/sites/digital-assets/2024/11/11/ai-meets-decentralization-how-blockchain-is-democratizing-ai/
17. Kuznetsov O, Sernani P, Romeo L, Frontoni E, Mancini A. On the integration of artificial intelligence and blockchain technology: A perspective about security. *IEEE Access.* 2024;12:3881–97.
18. Witt L, Fortes AT, Toyoda K, Samek W, Li D. Blockchain and artificial intelligence: Synergies and conflicts. *arXiv preprint.* 2024. https://doi.org/10.48550/arXiv.2405.13462
19 Tymoshchenko D. 8 Blockchain use cases in key industries | 2025 guide [Internet]. Acropolium; 2024 [cited January 26, 2025]. Available from: https://acropolium.com/blog/use-cases-for-blockchain-technology-adoption-across-major-industries/
20. Rajarajeswari S, Arunachalam M, Nachiyappan S, Kumar SS, Viswabharathy AM. Convergence of artificial intelligence and blockchain in finance and governance. In: *Applications of blockchain and artificial intelligence in finance and governance.* Boca Raton, FL: CRC Press; 2024.
21 Nasdaq. Nasdaq and chain to partner on blockchain technology initiative [Internet]. Nasdaq; 2015 [cited January 26, 2025]. Available from: https://ir.nasdaq.com/news-releases/news-release-details/nasdaq-and-chain-partner-blockchain-technology-initiative
22. Hayes A. Tort Law: what it is and how it works, with examples. Investopedia [Internet]. 2024 [cited January 27, 2025]. Available from: https://www.investopedia.com/terms/t/tort-law.asp
23. Oliverethan. How cryptocurrencies are reshaping the banking industry. Nasscom [Internet]. 2025 [cited January 27, 2025]. Available from: https://community.nasscom.in/communities/blockchain/how-cryptocurrencies-are-reshaping-banking-industry
24. Bhardwaj C. Asset tokenization on blockchain: Future of asset management. Appinventiv [Internet]. 2019 [cited January 27, 2025]. Available from: https://appinventiv.com/blog/blockchain-assets-tokenization/
25. Pratt MK. 10 blockchain use cases in finance that show value. TechTarget [Internet]. 2023 [cited January 27, 2025]. Available from: https://www.techtarget.com/searchcio/feature/5-blockchain-use-cases-in-finance-that-show-value
26. Turton A. AI is revolutionizing algo trading but markets must remain vigilant. ION [Internet]. 2024 [cited January 27, 2025]. Available from: https://iongroup.com/blog/markets/ai-is-revolutionizing-algo-trading-but-markets-must-remain-vigilant/
27. Kinza Y. What is a robo-advisor? Everything to know before using one. TechTarget [Internet]. 2025 [cited January 27, 2025]. Available from: https://www.techtarget.com/searchenterpriseai/definition/robo-advisor
28. Statista. Robo-advisors—Worldwide | Statista market forecast [Internet]. 2024 [cited January 27, 2025]. Available from: https://www.statista.com/outlook/fmo/wealth-management/digital-investment/robo-advisors/worldwide
29. Trist E. The evolution of Socio-Technical Systems. Ontario Ministry of Labour; 1981 [cited January 27, 2025]. Available from: https://www.lmmiller.com/blog/wp-content/uploads/2013/06/The-Evolution-of-Socio-Technical-Systems-Trist.pdf
30. Teece DJ, Pisano G, Shuen A. Dynamic capabilities and strategic management. *Strateg Manag J.* 1997;18(7):509–33.
31. Scott RW. Institutional theory: Contributing to a theoretical research program [Internet]. 2004 [cited January 27, 2025]. Available from: https://www.researchgate.net/publication/265348080_Institutional_Theory_Contributing_to_a_Theoretical_Research_Program
32. Clark KB, Baldwin CY. Modularity after the Crash. SSRN Scholarly Paper No. 270292. 2001. Available from: https://papers.ssrn.com/sol3/papers.cfm?abstract_id=270292

33. Sagar M. Why deep learning is a costly affair. Analytics India Mag [Internet]. 2020 [cited January 27, 2025]. Available from: https://analyticsindiamag.com/deep-tech/deep-learning-costs-cloud-compute/
34. Leon M. Escalating AI energy demands and need for sustainable solutions. *WSEAS Trans Syst.* 2024;23:444–57. https://doi.org/10.37394/23202.2024.23.46
35. Walther CC. The hidden cost of AI energy consumption. Knowledge at Wharton [Internet]. 2024 [cited January 27, 2025]. Available from: https://knowledge.wharton.upenn.edu/article/the-hidden-cost-of-ai-energy-consumption/
36. Shafay M, Ahmad RW, Salah K, Yaqoob I, Jayaraman R, Omar M. Blockchain for deep learning: Review and open challenges. *Clust Comput.* 2022;26(1):Article 1. https://doi.org/10.1007/s10586-022-03582-7

# 20 AI-Driven Socially Responsible Investing

## *Tools for Impact Measurement*

*Leticia Bosu*

## 20.1 INTRODUCTION

Socially responsible investing (SRI) has evolved from being a niche strategy to a mainstream investment in the last two decades to keep up with the growing demand for investment that creates social and environmental impact along with financial return [1, 2]. SRI incorporates environmental, social, and governance (ESG) factors of firms into the risk and return dilemma faced by investors and aims to change the direction of capital to the companies which positively influence sustainability, corporate governance and social justice [3, 4]. This change signals that the belief that financial performance and sustainability are two sides of the same coin, not competing drivers of long-term economic development and risk mitigation, is gathering momentum. SRI has traditionally been characterized by ethical screening and negative investment criteria, where an investor avoids investing in societal and environmental harmful sectors [5, 6]. Historically, SRI portfolios have avoided companies that have very high ethical and sustainability risks such as fossil fuel extraction, tobacco production and weapons manufacture. Meanwhile, the rise of international sustainability movements, the understanding of climate risks, and growing stakeholder activism have vastly broadened the definition of SRI. Rather than focusing only on the economic cost to society of certain industries and activities, there is now a market for investments that can make a positive impact that can be measured, such as renewable energy, social enterprises, and corporate sustainability programmes [7, 8]. By contrast, this proactive approach, known popularly as impact investing, seeks to invest in economies generating financial and competitive returns while contributing to the advancement of many aspects of sustainable development goals.

This would help tackle one of the big issues facing SRI, namely the difficulty of assessing the impact of investments made with an ESG focus. Trustworthy ESG assessment is critical to ensure that investments are actually beneficial to sustainability goals and are not just a form of "greenwashing"; the fraudulent practice of presenting an exaggerated image of corporate environmental and social commitments [9]. Traditional ESG evaluation methods are based on either self-reported ESG data, third-party ESG ratings, or manual assessments by investment managers, driven by

DOI: 10.1201/9781003611646-20

the opinions of relatively few ESG researchers [10–12]. Then there are plenty of limitations of each of the methods above, and this limits the reliability and effectiveness of ESG performance measurement.

ESG data that is self-reported is popular, but it is typically incomplete, inconsistent, and biased. While companies do report sustainability metrics, they often focus on the "positive" aspects of their performance, only including more pleasant reports, which can lead to misreporting the actual environmental or social impacts. Self-reported data is untrustworthy in the absence of standardized reporting frameworks and independent verification. In addition, third-party ESG rating agencies like MSCI, Sustainalytics, and FTSE Russell calculate ESG scores and data for dozens of companies using different criteria [13, 14]. But the methodologies employed by these agencies differ fundamentally from each other which accounts for the variation in ratings for the same company. Also, several of the rating models do not contain live data that could help to make them less effective in capturing new, potential sustainability risks and environmental violations. Manual assessments performed by fund managers to complement automated systems are valuable, albeit time-intensive, and prone to human bias. The large uncertainty of qualitative ESG analysis can lead to inconsistencies, causing companies and industries to be difficult to compare objectively in sustainability performance.

Artificial intelligence (AI) capabilities have also emerged as revolutionary tools that can transform the practice of ESG analysis, make the impact measurement easier [12, 15], introduce new ways to identify sustainability risk and improve decision-making while investing. This means AI-based models have an advantage of taking a more objective, time-efficient, and scalable approach to ESG evaluation using a larger set of real-time data from various sources [16]. They can assess ESG performance in a comprehensive manner, for instance, by allowing models to evaluate sustainability reports, financial disclosures, and social media sentiment and government regulatory data. With automated data collection and analysis, AI also lowers the risk of human error and the occurrence of bias, ensuring that your investment decisions are based on correct and timely information.

In addition, AI helps detect corporate greenwashing, i.e., checking specific claims made by a corporation about their sustainability efforts to independent sustainability indicators [17, 18]. It helps in addressing the mismatch between what a company claims for ESG and its real impact on the environment and society, as machine learning (ML) algorithms can help to differentiate between the real sustainability among companies and green washing. This capability not only increases the transparency of ESG investing but also improves investor confidence in sustainable finance initiatives. AI-based predictive analytics not only improve existing ESG assessments, but they also provide a wide-ranging indication of future sustainability risks [19, 20]. Using AI models trained on historical ESG data and trend lines, it is possible to predict future environmental as well as social and governance risks that could affect corporate performance [15]. By doing this, the investors will be able to predict the future financial risks of ESG and therefore make better decisions regarding their portfolios to avoid financing unsustainable business. AI-powered ESG analytics are a huge step forward in SRI. With the ultimate goal of enabling investors to make fully informed choices that align with their risk-return aspirations as well as sustainability targets, AI enables real-time analysis of data, greater transparency, and predictive insights to power data-driven decision-making. With the increasing need for responsible investing, AI in ESG assessment will play a vital role to ensure that capital goes to real sustainable and impactful investment.

## 20.2 THEORETICAL FRAMEWORK

### 20.2.1 AI-Powered Tools in Socially Responsible Investing

AI has transformed investing in ESG factors by powering SRI investors. Using technology-driven analytic models, AI-powered analytics enhance impact measurement, risk assessment, and investment decision-making [21]. Natural language processing (NLP) is one of these models that provides ESG sentiment analysis by scanning thousands of sources from news articles, company disclosures, and even social media content. This enables the identification of sustainability controversies, climate-related breaches, and ethical issues as they unfold to provide investors real-time data to the sustainability intent of corporations when it comes to ESG. This brings us to another important progress in satellite imagery and remote sensing which serves as an independent credible tool to measure environmental impacts. It also allows for an independence verification of corporate sustainability claims through AI-driven analysis of satellite data to detect deforestation, carbon emissions, and land-use changes. It does so by limiting investors' dependence on self-reported ESG indicators that are generally inconsistent or prone to greenwashing. Besides the instant analysis, predictive AI models are responsible for ESG risk forecasting. AI using past ESG information and trend data and analytics indirectly identifies risks around sustainability, allowing investors to earmark companies that are more likely to face some environmental or governance issues [15]. They enhance sustainable long-term investment planning through the integration of sustainability-related financial risks into the financial system. The integration of blockchain with AI has also created an additional layer of transparency in the field of ESG. Blockchain-enabled AI platforms monitor supply chain provenance/ethics, track carbon credits [22], and verify corporate sustainability commitments to ensure the security and immutability of ESG impact validation. Together, this combination of AI and blockchain boosts investor confidence by providing immutable records of corporate ESG performance, thus minimizing any possibility of misinformation or greenwashed sustainability claims.

### 20.2.2 Theoretical Models Supporting AI in SRI

Several financial and investment theories offer a conceptual basis for using AI as an SRI input or output. Consider stakeholder theory, which states that businesses should consider all stakeholder interests, including those of investors, employees, communities, and the environment, not just shareholder returns [23]. Benefiting from AI, ESG models can understand the true alignment of a company with the interests of its stakeholders by examining its sustainability reports and governance policies. Originally meant to maximize risk-adjusted returns, Modern Portfolio Theory

(MPT) is being augmented to include ESG [24]. Incorporating sustainability risks into portfolio optimization via AI-driven SRI models leads to investment strategies that simultaneously seek to optimize returns and social impact. With the addition of AI-powered ESG risk factors, MPT expands to account for non-traditional risk factors such as climate risk and social responsibility metrics. Furthermore, the Efficient Market Hypothesis (EMH) adds that all relevant information has already been incorporated in the price of assets. Nonetheless, AI-driven ESG analytics question this belief by identifying unseen sustainability risks that typically escape traditional financial models. Using deep learning and sentiment analysis, AI identifies ESG-related material risks earlier than they are recognized by the market, consequently generating an informational advantage for investors in sustainable finance [25].

### 20.2.3 AI in SRI Across Continents

From continents apart, the emergence of AI-enhanced SRI strategies shows the global reach of this force. In North America, asset managers are using these AI-powered climate risk assessment models to incorporate ESG into pension and mutual fund investments [15]. Taking climate risks into account is part of this approach, which makes portfolios more resilient over the long term. Regulatory stimuli like EU SFDR have driven AI-driven ESG rating methodologies in Europe. With these models review corporate sustainability pledges with examples, compliance with straightforward environmental and governance regulations. AI-driven ESG platforms provide European investors with data-based insights that help them comply with regulations while optimizing their portfolios for sustainable and ethical investing. Research is conducted in Asia around carbon foot printing monitoring systems such as pollution and sustainability for corporate responsible behaviour using AI. AI-Powered ESG Solutions for International Investment Strategies to Meet Divergent Net-Zero Commitments across Countries (e.g., Japan, China, India, in particular) [26]. Using AI-Driven ESG Analysis to Aid Investors in Adjusting to Rapidly Changed Climate Policies across Borders AI enabling impact investing platforms fund renewable energy and social enterprises in Africa [27, 28]. AI technologies evaluate financial inclusion indicators and microinsurance projects, guaranteeing that capital flows are aligned with sustainable economic growth. AI-driven environmental-monitoring instruments in South America are used for tracking Amazon rainforest deforestation, so investors can sidestep funds associated with environmental damage [29]. It ensures that investment is responsible from the outset, while encouraging sustainable future land-use. AI is an integral part of the nature of SRI movement – the global implementation of AI emphasizes the future of SRI.

## 20.3 INCORPORATING CUTTING-EDGE TECHNOLOGY IN ETHICAL INVESTING METHODS

### 20.3.1 AI in ESG Data Collection and Analysis

The availability and reliability of ESG data represent the main issue in SRI. Not surprisingly is the fact that most ESG measures are self-reported by corporations, in an often inconsistent, unaudited, easily greenwashed fashion [30]. Most data providers that deal with ESG ratings heavily rely on mechanical assessments with a playlist of criteria that are limited [13], laden with subjectivity, slow to update, and the data coverage remains constrained. From real-time impact monitoring and automated sentiment analysis to predictive sustainability metrics, AI is revolutionizing ESG data collection [31]. ML web crawlers and NLP models crawl millions of diverse sources; company filings, government databases, media reports, and social media, to derive salient ESG sentiments [32]. This provides for a greater depth of aggregate ESG data than mere self-disclosures. Against greenwashing, a sentiment analysis powered by AI cross compares corporate sustainability statements with independent third-party data references. AI also identifies gaps, going as far as debunking overinflated ESG claims, encouraging companies to come forth with honest sustainability stories [33]. In addition, Earth observation (satellite imagery and other forms of remote sensing) adds to ESG transparency by offering independent verification of environmental impacts [34]. It uses AI to assess deforestation, pollution, carbon emissions, among others, and offers an impartial criteria-based measure of corporate environmental performance. The AI resources also include the ML models that operate the foundations of ESG risk prediction. The models utilize historical data on sustainability to forecast upcoming environmental violations, workplace problems, and governance collapses before they turn into scandals in the media. That ability to make predictions allows investors to set their portfolios in advance, in a way that helps them hedge against sustainability-related financial risks.

### 20.3.2 AI in Portfolio Optimization for Socially Responsible Investing

With the promise of achieving optimal balance across sustainability criteria and financial performance, AI is transforming portfolio optimization in SRI. Unlike traditional portfolio models which prefer profit over ESG, AI-driven investing solutions employ corporate social responsibility (CSR) indicators, carbon footprint assessments and ESG ratings as the basis for their portfolio selection process. Through AI-backed portfolio management, one can construct risk-adjusted sustainable and responsible investment portfolios thereby ensuring the sustainable equities are yielding maximum returns on the lowest net sustainability risk. In addition, AI-driven robot-advisors for automated impact fund management allow investors to customize the impact investing portfolio in line with their risk aversion threshold and ethical preferences. Another aspect of AI-enhanced SRI is dynamic ESG portfolio rebalancing. AI implicitly monitors the portfolio ESG performance with the continuous portfolio monitoring, thereby automatically reallocating the portfolio when underperforming ESG stocks threaten its assigned weight [35, 36]. This, in turn, may better align SRI portfolios with changing sustainability measures. In addition, AI improves the prediction of ESG trends at the market level and helps investors understand shifts in corporate governance behaviour, consumer demand for sustainable goods, and government regulatory structures [15]. These data can be actionable for the investor, enabling them to ensure relatively greater resilience of their portfolio to risk stemming from changing sustainability dynamics.

### 20.3.3 AI in Social and Governance Impact Measurement

Social and governance (S&G) variables are more complex to quantify than carbon emissions and other environmental indicators. AI is modernizing the ways of impact assessment through observation of company policies, ethical labour practices and diversity efforts well as their degree of governance transparency [15]. NLP-based algorithms scour company disclosures and Human Resource Policies to identify companies with potential labour violations, hiring biases or governance flags. Data on board composition is analysed by machine-learning algorithms to gauge progress on diversity and inclusion across the workplace. In the same vein, AI-based systems for evaluating supply chain ethics also identify risks associated with coercive labour, poor working conditions and human rights violations [37]. Such approaches give investors access to information on the verification of CSR compliance. Additionally, by detecting businesses at risk of fraud, CEO malfeasance, or regulatory non-compliance, predictive AI models evaluate governance risks. Investors can foresee governance shortcomings before they affect financial performance because of this skill. Investors may make sure that their portfolios support moral business practices that go beyond environmental concerns by utilizing AI-driven social and governance impact studies.

## 20.4 FUTURE TRENDS AND POLICY IMPLICATIONS

### 20.4.1 The Future of AI in Socially Responsible Investing

The future of ethical investment will be shaped by several new developments, including AI-powered SRI and impact measurement:

a. *Blockchain with AI for ESG Impact Verification*: AI will use blockchain technology to produce unchangeable ESG data, guaranteeing auditable and transparent impact reporting [38].
b. *Quantum AI in Sustainable Finance*: AI-driven ESG forecasting models will be improved by quantum computing, giving investors better long-term sustainability projections [39].
c. *AI in Climate Risk-Adjusted Investing*: By integrating climate change risks into portfolio management, sophisticated AI models can help investors minimize financial losses from natural disasters [40].
d. *Hyper-Personalized Impact Investing Driven by AI*: Fintech systems driven by AI will provide completely personalized sustainable portfolios, enabling individual investors to align their investments with ethical considerations.

These developments will strengthen AI's influence on the direction of ethical investment in the future.

### 20.4.2 Policy Recommendations for AI-Governed SRI

Strong governance frameworks must be put in place by legislators as AI usage in SRI increases to guarantee moral, open, and responsible AI-driven ESG research. Important suggestions consist of:

a. *Standardized AI-Driven ESG Reporting Regulations*: To guarantee that impact indicators produced by AI are reliable and consistent, governments must establish international standards for AI-based ESG research.
b. *AI Bias Audits in ESG Risk Scoring*: To avoid algorithmic prejudice against developing markets or smaller businesses, regulators should require bias audits in AI-powered ESG rating models.
c. *Cross-Border AI Collaboration in Sustainable Finance*: To ensure meaningful cross-border transparency in impact investment, financial authorities are required to establish global AI-powered platforms for sustainability monitoring.
d. *AI Ethical Principles in ESG Data Collection*: AI-based ESG tracking systems must be designed to comply with privacy regulations, as AI should not infringe on the rights of enterprises or individuals when analysing impact data.

Once these regulatory measures are integrated, AI-powered SRI will ensure protection of investors and regulatory integrity, subsuming into itself a fierce project that advocates investment with ethics.

## 20.5 CONCLUSION

The rise of AI-driven platforms has led to SRI transformations through automated portfolio optimization, real-time ESG impact assessment, and enhanced transparency in ethical investing. This is indicative of their global reach on responsible finance as AI-powered ESG analytics have been adopted in North America, Europe, Asia, South America, and Africa. In the future, AI-driven SRI will be shaped by blockchain integration, quantum computing and bespoke sustainable investment, only ensuring the fact that ethics and money will work hand in hand to create a more sustainable world.

## REFERENCES


1. Gangi F, Meles A, Daniele LM, Varrone N, Salerno D. Socially responsible investment (SRI): From niche to mainstream. In: *The evolution of sustainable investments and finance: Theoretical perspectives and new challenges*. Springer International Publishing; 2021. p. 1–58.
2. Quarshie MA, Akhtar S, Nawaah D. Barriers to breakthroughs: The crucial role of support services in advancing accounting practices, financial literacy and performance in disability-led SMEs. *Qual Quant*. 2025;59:1–23.

3. Fung HG, Law SA, Yau J. *Socially responsible investment in a global environment.* Cheltenham: Edward Elgar Publishing; 2010.
4. El Abiad Z, Abraham R, El-Chaarani H, Skaf Y, Binsaddig RO, Jafar SH. The impact of CEO characteristics on the financial performance of family businesses listed in the Euronext Exchange. *J Risk Financ Manag.* 2024;17(3):129.
5. Berry TC, Junkus JC. Socially responsible investing: An investor perspective. *J Bus Ethics.* 2013;112:707–20.
6. Hemachandran K, Rodriguez RV, editors. *Artificial intelligence for business: An implementation guide containing practical and industry-specific case studies.* Boca Raton: CRC Press; 2023.
7. Brest P, Born K. When can impact investing create real impact. *Stanford Soc Innov Rev.* 2013;11(4):22–31.
8. Jafar SH, Akhtar S, Johl SK. AI in insurance. In: Hemachandran K, Rodriguez RV, editors. *Artificial intelligence for business.* Boca Raton: Productivity Press; 2023. p. 164–73.
9. Aliano M, Cestari G, Madonna S. Greenwashing. In: *Sustainable finance for SMEs: The role of capital for sustainable and inclusive growth.* Cham: Springer Nature Switzerland; 2024. p. 103–24.
10. Jafar SH, Oyedele OM, Nawaah D, Bolanle AS. Exploring leadership challenges for adoption of digital innovation and sustainability. In: *Innovation ecosystems and sustainable technologies.* Bingley: Emerald Publishing Limited; 2025. p. 253–69.
11. Visalli F, Patrizio A, Lanza A, Papaleo P, Nautiyal A, Pupo M, et al. ESG data collection with adaptive AI. In: *ICEIS (1).* Setúbal, Portugal: SCITEPRESS – Science and Technology Publications, Lda.2023. p. 468–75.
12. Hemachandran K, George PM, Rodriguez RV, Kulkarni RM, Roy S. Performance analysis of k-nearest neighbour classification algorithms for bank loan sectors. In: *Smart intelligent computing and communication technology.* Amsterdam: IOS Press; 2021. p. 9–13.
13. Dell'Erba M, Doronzo M. Sustainability gatekeepers: ESG ratings and data providers. *Univ Pa J Bus Law.* 2023;25:355.
14. Quarshie MA, Djimatey R, Akhtar S, Nawaah D. Maximizing financial efficiency through technological synergy: Unleashing ICT for enhanced cash management in SMEs. *J Int Counc Small Bus.* 2025:1–31.
15. Rane N, Choudhary S, Rane J. Artificial intelligence enhanced environmental, social, and governance (ESG) strategies for financial services and investment sectors. In: *Social, and governance (ESG) strategies for financial services and investment sectors.* Elsevier BV; 2024.
16. Thielmann LS. *Smart Circularity: Exploring the Impact of Artificial Intelligence on the Circular Economy: Building Block C: Cross-Sector Collaboration* [Master's thesis]. Lisbon: Universidade NOVA de Lisboa; 2023.
17. Moodaley W, Telukdarie A. Greenwashing, sustainability reporting, and artificial intelligence: A systematic literature review. *Sustainability.* 2023;15(2):1481.
18. Jafar SH, Hemachandran K, El-Chaarani H, Moturi S, Gupta N, editors. *Artificial intelligence for capital markets.* Boca Raton: CRC Press; 2023.
19. Nost E, Colven E. Earth for AI: A political ecology of data-driven climate initiatives. *Geoforum.* 2022;130:23–34.
20. Salim M, Khan PA, Jalil NA, Johl SK, Jafar SH, Irfan F, et al. Fusion of blockchain and sustainable development goals: A bibliometric analysis for future trends. *KnE Soc Sci.* 2023:633–54.
21. Pillai V. Integrating AI-driven techniques in big data analytics: Enhancing decision-making in financial markets. *Int J Eng Comput Sci.* 2023;12(07):10–8535.
22. Han H. *The impact of artificial intelligence (AI) and blockchain adoption in corporate governance: Ethical perspectives* [dissertation]. London: Brunel University; 2023.

23. Orts EW, Strudler A. The ethical and environmental limits of stakeholder theory. *Bus Ethics Q.* 2002;12(2):215–33.
24. Lukomnik J, Hawley JP. *Moving beyond modern portfolio theory: Investing that matters.* London: Routledge; 2021.
25. Lim T. Environmental, social, and governance (ESG) and artificial intelligence in finance: State-of-the-art and research takeaways. *Artif Intell Rev.* 2024;57(4):76.
26. Olawade DB, Wada OZ, David-Olawade AC, Fapohunda O, Ige AO, Ling J. Artificial intelligence potential for net zero sustainability: Current evidence and prospects. *Next Sustain.* 2024;4:100041.
27. Nawaah D, Asare PY, Quarshie MA. Climate finance and natural capital: Linking global initiatives with local impact. In: *Climate neutrality through smart eco-innovation and environmental sustainability.* Cham: Springer Nature Switzerland; 2025. p. 317–32.
28. Singh S, Yadav S, Singh A, Krishna YJ, Singh A. Harnessing technology for a sustainable future in finance: The role of artificial intelligence in promoting environmental responsibility. In: *Anticipating future business trends: Navigating artificial intelligence innovations: Volume 2.* Cham: Springer Nature Switzerland; 2024. p. 367–78.
29. Andrae S. The use of artificial intelligence to curb deforestation in the Brazilian rainforest: Methods, infrastructure, and implications. In: *Artificial intelligence and data science for sustainability: Applications and methods.* Hershey: IGI Global Scientific Publishing; 2025. p. 81–122.
30. Hira A. *The smoke and mirrors game of global CSR reporting: Issues and fixes.* London: Anthem Press; 2023.
31. Jafar SH, Kashid AU, Ghosh S, Srividhya S, Sharma D, Bodhankar A. An enhanced performance optimization of ATM networks for cross-border money transfers. In: *2024 15th international conference on computing communication and networking technologies (ICCCNT).* Piscataway, NJ: IEEE; 2024. p. 1–5.
32. Perdices D, Ramos J, Garcia-Dorado JL, Gonzalez I, de Vergara JE. Natural language processing for web browsing analytics: Challenges, lessons learned, and opportunities. *Comput Netw.* 2021;198:108357.
33. Puaschunder JM. Focusing COVID-19 bailout and recovery. *Ohio State Bus Law J.* 2021;16:91.
34. Gopal S, Pitts J. Satellite remote sensing: Pioneering tools for environmental insight and sustainable investment. In: *The FinTech revolution: Bridging geospatial data science, AI, and sustainability.* Cham: Springer Nature Switzerland; 2025. p. 275–315.
35. Tamura Y. *How can we promote impact/ESG investing? Clarifying the skeptical reasons and benefits of addressing impact & ESG investing in the age of artificial intelligence* [dissertation]. Cambridge: Massachusetts Institute of Technology; 2023.
36. Malik MY, Jafar SH, Dixit A. Efficiency analysis and macroeconomic determinants of non-tax revenues: Evidence from special category states of India. *Indian Econ J.* 2025. https://doi.org/10.1177/00194662251330385
37. Bohlens C. Navigating AI and children's rights in corporate practices: Ethical AI integration in corporate responsibility. In: *Human values, ethics, and dignity in the age of artificial intelligence.* Hershey: IGI Global Scientific Publishing; 2025. p. 239–84.
38. Almadadha R. Blockchain technology in financial accounting: Enhancing transparency, security, and ESG reporting. *Blockchains.* 2024;2(3):312–33.
39. Roger JDD. AI-driven financial modeling techniques: Transforming investment strategies. *J Appl Bus Econ.* 2024;26(4):63–74.
40. Indiazi C. The roles of AI on predictive analytics in managing climate change risks in reinsurance. *Gospodarka i Innowacje.* 2025;55:39–49.

# 21 Financial Management and AI

## *A New Dawn for Companies*

*Murage Jane Karuana and R. V. Palanivel*

## 21.1 INTRODUCTION

Financial management is a wide range of functions performed in an organization which includes budget development, financial reporting, taxation, investment analysis, payroll, and communication with stakeholders [1]. Historically, many of these tasks have been very manual which is not only tedious but also prone to error. In addition, the growing complexity of global markets, compliance obligations, and consumer expectations has rendered the conventional form of financial management increasingly unsustainable. Within financial operations, artificial intelligence (AI) is already rethinking how things get done. The definition of AI is the simulation of human intelligence in machines that are programmed to think like humans and mimic their actions capable of reasoning, learning, and decision-making [1] and it has swiftly moved from being a theoretical concept to an implementation-ready tool in 21st-century financial systems [2]. The three often have different goals but given the way AI can help with pattern recognition, natural language processing, and autonomous decision-making, AI enable smarter, faster, and scalable financial operations [3]. The difference between conventional financial management and AI-powered financial management systems is a dichotomy. Traditional approaches are reactive; understand what some trends are and react accordingly. By anticipating results and recommending the best choices, AI, in contrast, makes it much easier to manage proactively. AI allows a more advanced approach compared to previous systems. An example is legacy systems that only detect financial fraud ex-post, while AI is capable of identifying suspicious behaviour in real-time, hence avoiding damages [4]. The following sections explore the use of AI in finance and conclude with a detailed discussion of its advantages, challenges, and limitations. The chapter ends with a set of recommendations for how states can extract the most strategic benefit from AI while minimizing its dangers.

## 21.2 FINANCIAL MANAGEMENT AI APPLICATIONS

AI is already a practical technology used in many financial sectors, not just a futuristic idea. Key AI applications with practical applications are described in the ensuing subsections.

 DOI: 10.1201/9781003611646-21

### 21.2.1 Investment Predictive Analysis

Investment forecasting is one of the most potent uses of AI. To spot patterns and predict changes in the market, machine learning models examine enormous information, such as past price, market sentiment, and macroeconomic variables [4]. AI models process information more quickly and accurately than human analysts. Weng et al. [5] show that AI algorithms outperform conventional econometric models in predicting asset price movements and portfolio risks. Investment platforms with AI support give businesses a competitive edge by facilitating real-time market response tactics.

### 21.2.2 Financial Chatbots and Customer Interaction

AI-enabled chatbots are transforming customer service by providing 24/7 personalization at scale [6]. NLP interprets customer queries and answers within seconds. AI systems offer 24/7 assistance, providing seamless interactions whenever customers need them, no matter a human agent's working hours. This way, some complicated concerns can be forwarded to human agents, which ensures that service quality is retained, even while efficiency is maximized. This high degree of availability makes customers happy and saves on service costs.

### 21.2.3 Fraud Detection and Risk Management

Traditional analytics-based fraud detection systems are rule-based and use thresholds to identify anomalies, and these approaches can be easily circumvented by cunning adversaries. Conversely, AI systems learn from new data and the models are probably changing all the time. It enables to analyse massive transactions and identifies anomalies, thus presenting it as an active approach to manage risk [7, 8]. For example, AI models used in a study reduced fraud detection time by over 60% compared with legacy systems [9]. This is especially beneficial for industries like banking and insurance where the cost of fraud is high and increasing.

### 21.2.4 Automated Tax Planning

AI: Automating tax-related tasks including but not limited to data entry, calculation, classification, and reporting to improve accuracy and compliance [9]. Regular tax processing involves several layers of departmental approvals and tedious manual verifications, which makes it inefficient. With fewer ways for a human to make an error, AI reduces the risk of non-compliance and penalties, a key consideration for multinational organizations that do business in multiple tax jurisdictions.

### 21.2.5 Market Sentiment Analysis

Sentiment analysis has emerged as an important use case for AI-driven systems, using machine learning algorithms to analyse consumer opinions as expressed from various sources such as social media, reviews, and news stories. It enables companies to measure market perceptions with immediacy [10]. While conventional customer feedback mechanisms, such as surveys, are scope-limited in their timeliness and frequency, AI tools use continuous monitoring. Likewise, public sentiment understanding can direct financial communications and investment decisions in a timely manner, when the product is launched or a financial crisis is happening.

### 21.2.6 Projecting the Performance of Organizations

AI systems estimate cash flows, revenue patterns, and operational efficiency by using past data [11]. This aids in resource allocation and long-term planning. Conventional forecasting is based on spreadsheet analysis and linear models, both of which have limitations due to sluggish updates and cognitive bias. AI, on the other hand, uses multivariate models that adapt dynamically to fresh data inputs, increasing accuracy and dependability.

### 21.2.7 Automating Typical Financial Activities

Financial reconciliations, payroll calculations, and invoice processing are just a few of the repetitive operations that AI is excellent at automating [12–15]. In addition to increasing accuracy and speed, this frees up human resources for critical tasks. For instance, it has been demonstrated that in certain organizations, Robotic Process Automation (RPA) can cut reporting cycle times by as much as 70% [4]. Automation greatly reduces operating expenses and guarantees consistency.

### 21.2.8 Customer Segmentation and Personalization

AI can utilize the data the bank has access to analyse the behaviour, preferences, and transaction history of each customer and accordingly provide tailored financial products and services [16–19]. Conventional segmentation methods such as demographic profiling tends to be static and high-level. With AI, there is micro-level segmentation in real-time, which leads to better engagement, higher customer retention and more revenue.

## 21.3 ADVANTAGES OF USING AI FOR FINANCIAL MANAGEMENT

### 21.3.1 Improved Efficiency of Operations

By automating tasks, AI minimizes the manual effort to be done, as a result making the best use of resources [20]. Zhan et al. [3] discovered that the productivity of organizations using AI improved by 40–60%. Tasks, such as ledger entries, bank reconciliations, and reporting, are automated, which both accelerates operations speedy and minimizes human error. Moving away from transactional work to strategic tasks in this way frees up finance functions to perform high-value parts of their work.

### 21.3.2 Building Decision-Making on Predictions

AI improves the decision quality by providing real-time data analytics and predictive modelling to the customer. Trend detection and proactive financial projection enable companies to be more responsive and agile in their actions [21]. Mullangi [4] also states that access to the right data at the right time helps in better decision-making, either at an operational level or at a strategic level. AI systems supported by contextual, scenario-based analysis aids long-term planning better than traditional tools.

### 21.3.3 Best Customer Experiences

With AI, customer journeys get enriched with personalized suggestions, quicker responses, and self-services [22]. Seamless customer experiences through chatbots, virtual assistants, and intelligent help desks increase satisfaction and loyalty. This leads to a transformation from reactive customer service to proactive customer engagement.

### 21.3.4 Advanced Risk Management

These AI systems act as alarm bells regarding any risks and fraud, enabling immediate correction at the business level [4]. Being able to create risk scenarios and test for financial resiliency is essential in a world of volatile economics. AI is more flexible and accurate than traditional risk models.

## 21.4 DIFFICULTIES IN PUTTING AI INTO PRACTICE

Adopting AI in financial management has many challenges, despite its potential, which need to be recognized and resolved.

### 21.4.1 Privacy and Data Security

Large amounts of private and sensitive financial data are used by AI systems, which raises questions about data breaches, misuse, and illegal access. According to Hidayat et al. [13] and Javaid [23], contemporary AI models frequently do not have proper data governance procedures. The innate dependence on third-party platforms and cloud systems makes security flaws even worse. AI systems must incorporate strong compliance criteria into their design in order to comply with data protection legislation like the GDPR in Europe and equivalent frameworks around the world. Without strong encryption, anonymization, and access control mechanisms, AI may turn out to be a liability rather than an asset, according to a number of academics, including Ochuba et al. [24].

### 21.4.2 Lack of Clarity Around Regulation and Compliance

The fast-moving nature of AI development has exceeded the pace of creating legal and regulatory structures. There are little to no clear guidelines on how to hold AI drive decisions accountable, specifically in finance [10]. Threats of regulation lead organizations to postpone the full realization of AI. Transparency and fairness are key areas of legal and ethical complexity in AI use for financial decision-making as noted by Javaid [23] and Adeyeri [12]. Multinationals face additional challenges implementing such policies, as inconsistent regulations between jurisdictions add complexity to the process.

### 21.4.3 Costly to Implement and Maintain

Starting with AI takes a lot of time and resources, setting up infrastructure, hiring programmers, having a training and recycling process. The cost of entry may be prohibitively high, especially for small and medium-sized enterprises (SMEs) [13]. This technology does not merely consist of obtaining arrangements yet also changing present processes for compatibility. As Mullangi [4] points out, the economic viability of cloud services, model training, integration with legacy systems, and continuous model updates can put a burden on budgets, particularly in developing economies.

### 21.4.4 Workforce Disruption

By automating tedious tasks, jobs that have historically been performed by finance employees are at risk of displacement. As Adeyeri [12] puts it, AI opens new pathways to a world of analytics and strategy but destroys many clerical positions. Hence, Hajj and Hammoud [10] highlight the need to design change management programmes, as well as reskilling of the workforce to enable smooth transitions. But those initiatives take time, investment and a cultural change that not all organizations may be able to immediately realize.

### 21.4.5 Ethical Bias and Algorithmic Transparency

Many AI systems encounter biases that are deceptive in their nature because the data they are trained on has those biases. As Adeyeri [12] elaborates on, this kind of algorithmic bias can implicate credit scoring, lending, and resources in a skewed way influenced by these technologies. According to Javaid [23], AI-based financial recommendations will not be trusted or accepted by stakeholders without transparency in AI decision logic that is also (black-box) systems. Such an ethical opacity makes it difficult to ascertain the accountability and fair nature of financial decision-making processes.

## 21.5 LIMITATIONS OF AI IN FINANCIAL MANAGEMENT

Other than implementation difficulties, there is a limit to what AI can actually do in finance:

a. *Absence of Emotional Intelligence*: AI is unable to act with the same empathy as human beings to create relationships with depth and complexity which are crucial in fields such as negotiations, client relationships, and crisis management [25].

b. *Challenge with Lack of Structure or Ambiguity in Data*: AI systems work best with inputs that are relatively structured. For the use case that included unstructured data (e.g., handwritten notes, nuanced emails), the need for human interpretation is there [26].
c. AI has inflexibility and flexibility problems: In situations that quickly evolve or are uncertain, humans are still a cut above [3].
d. *Updating Lifelong*: If any accounting standard, compliance requirements, or business process changes, the AI models need to be reprogrammed or retrained, which involves high maintenance costs for such systems.
e. *Low External Contextual Awareness*: Political, environmental, or global disruptions cannot be accounted for by AI outputs unless the AI is directly trained on such things. However, a more complete comprehension continues to require human oversight [3].

## 21.6 SUGGESTIONS FOR STRATEGY

Organizations must take a planned and well-rounded strategy if they want to fully utilize AI in financial management.

### 21.6.1 Make Data Protection Procedures Stronger

Strong cybersecurity frameworks that include multi-factor authentication, end-to-end encryption, and regular vulnerability assessments must be implemented by businesses [3]. According to Zhan et al. [3], protecting data is the first step in establishing trust with stakeholders.

### 21.6.2 Create Explicit Regulatory Structures

Uniform, open regulations for AI applications in finance should be established by governments and international organizations. To guarantee compliance and promote innovation, clear accountability standards, data usage regulations, and ethical norms are crucial [4, 13].

### 21.6.3 Make the Development of Human Capital a Priority

Programmes for upskilling and training must be funded. To manage digital systems, evaluate AI results, and participate in high-level strategic planning, finance professionals need to be prepared [4, 24]. AI should be used to supplement human labour, not to replace it.

### 21.6.4 Encourage Progress in Ethical AI

Businesses should use machine learning methods that include justice and demand algorithmic openness from AI providers. Third-party evaluations and ethical audits can aid in reducing algorithmic bias [13].

### 21.6.5 Encourage Innovation and Collaboration Worldwide

International cooperation in research and development can hasten the development of responsible AI. Cross-industry partnerships, open platforms, and common standards will increase the scalability and inclusivity of AI deployment [13].

### 21.6.6 Develop an Organizational Culture That Is Flexible

AI adoption should be closely linked to the overall culture of innovation and continuous improvement. Hajj and Hammoud [10] note that change management programmes should align to help employees adopt new workflows and technologies.

## 21.7 CONCLUSION

AI is leading the changes in the finance world. Be it predictive analytics, automated reporting, fraud detection, or customer personalization, its applications are transforming the financial landscape. AI eliminates most inefficiencies in traditional financial systems by providing much faster, more accurate, and more flexible services. That said, the transition does not come without challenges. The need for data privacy, ethical biases, expensive solutions, and the labour displacement that requires both intentionality and regulation. In addition to this, AI struggles with ambiguity and emotion, as well as with hyper-changing external factors; all areas where human judgement is irreplaceable. Overall, the place of AI in financial management is a question of not "if" but "how." Those organizations that adopt AI in a responsible manner while addressing the associated risks will find a significant competitive advantage. The secret is in using it wisely, aligning it with the type of strategy and adjusting your approach along the way because, as with everything else in high tech, things keep changing.

## REFERENCES

1. Robert CH, Jennifer LK, Todd M. *Analysis for financial management.* New York: McGraw-Hill Education; 2023.
2. Murugesan R, Manohar V. AI in the financial sector – A driver to financial literacy. *Shanlax Int J Commerce.* 2019;7(3):66–70.
3. Zhan JX, Ling Z, Xu Z, Guo L, Zhuang S. Driving efficiency and risk management in finance through AI and RPA. *J Adv Comput Syst.* 2024;4(5):1–9.
4. Mullangi K. Enhancing financial performance through AI-driven predictive analytics and reciprocal symmetry. *Asian Account Audit Adv.* 2017;8(1):57–66.
5. Weng B, Ahmed MA, Megahed FM. Stock market one-day ahead movement prediction using disparate data sources. *Expert Syst Appl.* 2017;79:153–63.
6. Jafar SH, Oyedele OM, Nawaah D, Bolanle AS. Exploring leadership challenges for adoption of digital innovation and sustainability. In: *Innovation ecosystems and sustainable technologies.* Bingley: Emerald Publishing Limited; 2025. p. 253–69.
7. Duan Y, Edwards JS, Dwivedi YK. Artificial intelligence for decision making in the era of Big Data – Evolution, challenges and research agenda. *Int J Inf Manag.* 2019;48:63–71.
8. Vesna BA. Challenges of financial risk management: AI applications. *Manag J Sustain Bus Manag Solut Emerg Econ.* 2021;26(3):27–34.

9. Bello OA, Olufemi K. Artificial intelligence in fraud prevention: Exploring techniques and applications challenges and opportunities. *Comput Sci IT Res J.* 2024;5(6):1505–20.
10. Hajj ME, Hammoud J. Unveiling the influence of artificial intelligence and machine learning on financial markets: A comprehensive analysis of AI applications in trading, risk management, and financial operations. *J Risk Financ Manag.* 2023;16(10):1–6.
11. Ahmadi S. A comprehensive study on integration of big data and AI in financial industry and its effect on present and future opportunities. *Int J Curr Sci Res Rev.* 2024;7(01):66–74.
12. Adeyeri TB. Economic impacts of AI-driven automation in financial services. *Valley Int J Digit Libr.* 2024;12(7):6779–91.
13. Hidayat M, Defitri SY, Hilman H. The impact of artificial intelligence (AI) on financial management. *Manag Stud Bus J (PRODUCTIVITY).* 2024;1(1):123–9.
14. Nawaah D, Asare PY, Quarshie MA. Climate finance and natural capital: Linking global initiatives with local impact. In: *Climate neutrality through smart eco-innovation and environmental sustainability.* Cham: Springer Nature Switzerland; 2025. p. 317–32.
15. Davenport TH. *The AI advantage: How to put the artificial intelligence revolution to work.* Cambridge (MA): MIT Press; 2018.
16. West DM. *The future of work: Robots, AI, and automation.* Washington (DC): Brookings Institution Press; 2018.
17. Challoumis C. The evolution of financial systems – AI's role in reshaping money management. In: *XVI international scientific conference*; 2024. p. 128–51.
18. Quarshie MA, Akhtar S, Nawaah D. Barriers to breakthroughs: The crucial role of support services in advancing accounting practices, financial literacy and performance in disability-led SMEs. *Qual Quant.* 2025;59:1–23.
19. Malik MY, Jafar SH, Dixit A. Efficiency analysis and macroeconomic determinants of non-tax revenues: Evidence from special category states of India. *Indian Econ J.* 2025:00194662251330385.
20. El Abiad Z, Abraham R, El-Chaarani H, Skaf Y, Binsaddig RO, Jafar SH. The impact of CEO characteristics on the financial performance of family businesses listed in the Euronext Exchange. *J Risk Financ Manag.* 2024;17(3):129.
21. Hemachandran K, Rodriguez RV, editors. *The business of the metaverse: How to maintain the human element within this new business reality.* Boca Raton (FL): CRC Press; 2023.
22. Quarshie MA, Djimatey R, Akhtar S, Nawaah D. Maximizing financial efficiency through technological synergy: Unleashing ICT for enhanced cash management in SMEs. *J Int Counc Small Bus.* 2025:1–31.
23. Javaid HA. The future of financial services: Integrating AI for smarter, more efficient operations. *MZ J Artif Intell.* 2024;1(2):1–10.
24. Ochuba NA, Adewunmi A, Olutimehin DO. The role of AI in financial market development: Enhancing efficiency and accessibility in emerging economies. *Finance Account Res J.* 2024;6(3):421–36.
25. Jiang J. A study on the digital transformation trends in financial management for small and micro enterprises. *Int J Glob Econ Manag.* 2024;3(1):355–63.
26. Kumar V, Garg ML. Predictive analytics: A review of trends and techniques. *Int J Comput Appl.* 2018;182(1):31–37.

# 22 Case Studies and Future Directions for AI in Finance

*Donkor Nawaah*

## 22.1 INTRODUCTION

In the financial industry, artificial intelligence (AI) has become a disruptive force that is transforming conventional business structures, increasing productivity, and improving decision-making [1, 2]. AI-driven technologies are changing how financial institutions function, from algorithmic trading and fraud detection to risk management and customer service. In addition to analysing current trends that will shape the next stage of AI-driven financial innovation, this chapter looks at actual case studies of AI applications in the financial industry. Although the financial sector has always been at the forefront of technical advancement, the introduction of AI has caused it to advance at a never-before-seen pace [3–5]. Machine learning (ML), natural language processing (NLP), and deep learning are examples of AI techniques that are revolutionising a variety of fields by boosting productivity, automating difficult processes, and producing previously unheard-of predicted insights. Examples of these applications include:

a. *Improved Risk Management and Fraud Detection*: By examining transaction patterns, user behaviour, and anomalies, financial institutions are using AI to detect fraudulent activity in real time. Compared to conventional rule-based models, AI-driven fraud detection systems can handle enormous volumes of data much more quickly, reducing false positives and enhancing fraud protection.
b. *Algorithmic Trading and Investment Strategies*: By allowing algorithmic trading, AI has changed the financial markets. In this approach, ML models examine past data and market trends to execute transactions at the best moments. As a result, market efficiency has increased, and businesses are now able to make data-driven investment decisions.
c. *Financial Services and Customer Experience*: Chatbots and virtual assistants driven by AI are improving customer service by offering immediate, tailored financial advice. By automating repetitive client contacts, financial institutions may save operating costs and increase user happiness.
d. *Credit Scoring and Alternative Lending*: AI algorithms are being used to evaluate creditworthiness by utilising non-traditional data sources including

 DOI: 10.1201/9781003611646-22

transaction history, social media activity, and behavioural patterns. As a result, underprivileged groups can now obtain credit without depending entirely on traditional credit ratings, creating new opportunities for financial inclusion.

e. *Regulatory Compliance and Anti-Money Laundering (AML)*: For financial institutions, regulatory compliance is still a major problem. AI-powered compliance solutions employ ML algorithms to track transactions, identify questionable activity, and guarantee compliance with intricate legal requirements. This improves financial integrity and lowers compliance expenses.

These developments show that AI is a key force behind the financial sector's transformation rather than just an additional tool. However, a thorough analysis of real-world applications using case studies is necessary to comprehend AI's influence in the real world.

### 22.1.1 Importance of Case Studies in Understanding AI's Real-World Applications

a. *Real-World Case Studies*: Case studies offer concrete insights into how AI is used in financial institutions, even though theoretical understanding of the technology's potential is crucial. Case studies accomplish several important goals.
b. *Illustrating Successes and Failures*: The use of AI in finance has brought forth both significant obstacles and ground-breaking achievements. Practitioners and scholars can find optimal practices and steer clear of potential problems by analysing real-world situations.
c. *Illustrating Industry-Specific Uses*: AI has varying applications in regulated compliance, banking, investment management, and insurance. Case studies demonstrate the flexibility of AI in financial services by highlighting use cases particular to a certain industry.
d. *Being Aware of AI's Limitations and Ethical Issues*: AI is not perfect. Risks still include algorithmic bias, data privacy issues, and regulatory obstacles. Analysing real-world examples enables one to pinpoint areas where regulatory action and human supervision are necessary for AI.
e. *Educating Future AI Development Strategies*: Case studies offer important insights into how financial institutions may improve and optimise AI strategies by examining the effects of AI on operational effectiveness, customer happiness, and financial success.

This chapter offers case studies from top international financial organisations that have effectively incorporated AI into their operations, demonstrating the importance of AI in the financial industry. For researchers, policymakers, and financial professionals looking to comprehend the real-world applications of AI in the sector, these stories provide insightful lessons.

### 22.1.2 Future Directions of AI in Financial Technology and Strategy

AI in finance is expected to change in the future because to changes in market demands, legal changes, and computer power improvements. Key topics that are anticipated to propel AI's development include:

a. *Quantum Computing and AI in Finance*: Financial modelling, risk analysis, and portfolio optimisation may undergo a radical change as a result of the convergence of AI and quantum computing. It may be possible to simulate market dynamics more quickly and accurately with quantum-enhanced AI models.
b. *Frameworks for Governance and Ethics in AI*: Regulatory agencies will keep creating frameworks to guarantee accountability, equity, and transparency in AI-driven financial services as the technology's use grows. Explainable AI (XAI) will be essential to fulfilling legal obligations.
c. *AI and Decentralised Finance (DeFi)*: AI will play a key role in the developing DeFi ecosystem, guaranteeing automated decision-making, fraud detection, and security for blockchain-based financial services. Predictive analytics and AI-powered smart contracts have the potential to completely alter the financial scene.
d. *Hyper-Personalised Banking and Financial Advisory Services*: By providing dynamic pricing models, customised investment strategies, and AI-assisted financial planning based on real-time data analysis, AI-driven personalisation will continue to influence financial services.
e. *Autonomous Financial Agents*: AI-powered autonomous financial agents that can manage risk, optimise portfolios, and carry out transactions with little assistance from humans may be a thing of the future. Trading and asset management might be revolutionised by these intelligent agents.

To effectively use AI as it develops, financial institutions need to keep ahead of new trends. The sections that follow will look at actual case studies that show how top multinational companies are using AI to spur innovation and gain competitive advantages in the finance industry.

## 22.2 CASE STUDIES OF AI IN FINANCE

AI is changing the face of finance all over the world [6]. Be it risk management or investment strategy; AI has redefined the ways we process everything from efficiency and accuracy to decision-making. This part contains case studies from different financial institutions that implemented AI successfully. The case studies comprehensively present the nature, impact and learning of AI implementation.

### 22.2.1 JPMorgan Chase (USA, 2017): AI for Fraud Detection and Risk Management

#### 22.2.1.1 Background

As the largest bank in America and processor of trillions of dollars in transactions every day, JPMorgan Chase is a prime target for financial fraud [7]. Traditional fraud detection systems based on rule-based algorithms were unable to cope with advanced cyber threats. Secondly, inefficient processing of legal and financial documents was causing delays, errors, and compliance risks for the bank.

#### 22.2.1.2 AI Implementation

To counter these threats, JPMorgan implemented ML tools that analyse transaction behaviour as and when it occurs and then highlight any transactions that reacted in a way that was inconsistent with their previous behaviour; an indicator of possible fraud [8]. The AI system is based on deep learning models and learns from a wide range of transaction data to constantly improve the detection of fraud. In addition, COiN (i.e., Contract Intelligence) is a NLP system by JPMorgan that utilises AI to automatically review legal contracts, loan agreements, and financial statements [9–12].

#### 22.2.1.3 Impact

a. Fraud-loss prevention has saved $150 million a year through AI.
b. Cut fraud alert false positives by 40% for better customer experience.
c. About 360,000 man-hours of legal review have been saved annually as COiN reviewed 12,000 legal contracts in seconds.

#### 22.2.1.4 Key Lessons

While AI-driven fraud detection and document processing are an exciting evolution for the financial services sector, ethical considerations, bias, and regulatory compliance are paramount for ensuring the technology is safe and equitable.

### 22.2.2 BlackRock (USA, 2018) Artificial Intelligence, Powered by Investment Scientists

#### 22.2.2.1 Background

BlackRock, the largest asset manager in the world, needed sophisticated risk analytics to aid investment decision-making and portfolio management with more than $9 trillion in assets. Old financial models failed in the complexity of and volatility of modern markets, thus the need for AI [13].

#### 22.2.2.2 AI Implementation

BlackRock deployed Aladdin AI, a ML driven predictive analytics portfolio risk management platform that assists in determining which investments to evaluate for possible risk. The AI model combines live financial data, geopolitical developments and market indicators to offer investment guidance and asset allocation advice. In addition to the previous baggage, deep learning models evaluate stock trends, investor sentiment, and past performance to improve trading decisions [14].

#### 22.2.2.3 Impact

- Portfolio losses were reduced by 15% during downturns using AI-enabled risk analysis [15].
- Compared to traditional models, returns improved by 18% when automated investment decision-making was implemented [13].

- The costs of operation decreased by 20%, since its Automated workforce supervised the assets [16].

#### 22.2.2.4 Key Lessons

While AI can improve investment accuracy and risk prediction performance, it also raises dependency risk and creates some systemic risk due to over-reliance on the automated trading models, so human oversight is still very necessary.

### 22.2.3 Ant Group (China, 2019): AI as an Alternative Model for Credit Scoring

#### 22.2.3.1 Background

The traditional scoring paradigm of China excluded millions of people who do not have a credit history, which hampers the provision of financial services to them. Eventually, the idea of Ant Group was to use AI-based credit assessment models based on non-traditional financial behaviour to broaden financial inclusion.

#### 22.2.3.2 AI Implementation

AI models from Ant Group rely on various factors such as e-commerce transactions, mobile payment behaviour, and social media interactions, to determine creditworthiness. AI uses these alternative data points to assess an individual's creditworthiness and repayment ability. Moreover, MYbank, a subsidiary of Ant Group focused on digital banking, put into action an AI-based risk assessment system that utilises real-time transaction data in order to block fake loan requests [17, 18].

#### 22.2.3.3 Impact

a. Alternative credit scoring using AI helped over 10 million people get access to financial services.
b. Using AI-based predictions to set individualised interest rates led to a 30% drop in loan defaults.
c. In response, Chinese regulators released guidelines to make AI-driven lending more transparent.

#### 22.2.3.4 Key Lessons

While AI can help broaden the boundaries of financial inclusion, lending should be regulated to curb the risk of unethical lending in the form of algorithmic bias.

### 22.2.4 HSBC (UK, 2020): AI in Anti-Money Laundering (AML) Compliance

#### 22.2.4.1 Background

HSBC, one of the largest multinational banks in the world, became the subject of various regulatory fines of over $2 billion, due to failures in meeting AML regulations. The bank needed an AI-powered compliance system that was more efficient in monitoring suspicious transactions and controlling the bank's exposure to financial crime risk.

#### 22.2.4.2 AI Implementation

To combat this issue, HSBC deployed graph-based AI models capable of analysing complex flows of transactions in order to uncover hidden patterns from a variety of transactional data samples that indicate potential money laundering. Using NLP tools, the AI system analyses regulatory filings, customer communications, and financial news to detect possible compliance risks. It further automated how it submits Suspicious Activity Reports (SARs) to regulators, so less manual review needed to be done by staff [19].

#### 22.2.4.3 Impact

a. Operational inefficiencies were reduced as 40% of false positive AML alerts were reduced.
b. About 60% reduction of time-to-compliance with AI-based transaction monitoring and real-time fraud detection.
c. Enhanced AML compliance and avoided regulatory fines of $100 million.

#### 22.2.4.4 Key Lesson

While AI will boost compliance efficiency, it must be continuously trained and retrained to respond to the ever-changing methods of financial crime.

### 22.2.5 Goldman Sachs (USA, 2021): AI in Algorithmic Trading

#### 22.2.5.1 Background

Goldman Sachs, another top investment bank, wanted to improve their trade execution efficiency and lower their market risks by using AI-based algorithmic trading models.

#### 22.2.5.2 AI Implementation

Goldman Sachs incorporated deep-learning models to gauge market sentiment based on news, social media, and financial reports [20]. Based on probabilistic risk assessments, the AI-driven trading platform executes real-time stock trades, sensing high return investment opportunities.

#### 22.2.5.3 Impact

a. About 90% faster trade execution by eliminating manual trade processing.
b. Portfolio returns were 20% better with AI-assisted projection model stock picks.
c. The predictive model gave an indication of possible risk, which enabled the traders to anticipate market movement risk.

#### 22.2.5.4 Key Lesson

Even though AI enhances speed and efficiency in markets, overreliance on automated trading may induce flash crashes and systemic instability in markets, calling for regulatory protection.

### 22.2.6 Wells Fargo (USA, 2022): AI in PERSONALISED BANKING

#### 22.2.6.1 Background

As one of the largest banks in the United States, Wells Fargo was also facing customer engagement and retention issues, which are typical with traditional banking businesses that offer very little personalisation. The customers required AI-focused financial advisory services that had personalised, instantaneous recommendations based on spending patterns.

#### 22.2.6.2 AI Implementation

Wells Fargo launched an AI-powered personal finance assistant directly inside its banking app. Using ML algorithms to learn from the transaction history, savings habits, and prevailing market trends, the assistant provided tailored suggestions for budgeting, investment, and debt or credit management [21]. The bank also employed NLP-based chatbots for customer support 24/7.

#### 22.2.6.3 Impact

a. Customer engagement improved by 35% due to more personalised satisfaction with AI-generated recommendations.
b. About 15% increase in customer savings rates contributed to personalised financial insights.
c. About 20% reduction in operational costs as AI handled repeat, standard inquiries for customers.

#### 22.2.6.4 Key Lesson

While hyper-personalisation powered by AI can cultivate customer loyalty, organisations must first resolve issues surrounding privacy of data collection and transparency of AI decisions.

### 22.2.7 Citigroup (USA, 2021): AI in Loan Underwriting

#### 22.2.7.1 Background

Faced with stiff competition from fintech lenders deploying AI-based risk assessment models, Citigroup needed to revamp lending under-writing. For a long time, traditional credit scoring methods were slow and inefficient, causing rejection rates to skyrocket for borrowers with limited credit histories.

#### 22.2.7.2 AI Implementation

Citigroup implemented a ML-based loan underwriting system that assessed borrower risk using algorithms rather than just traditional credit scores. Alternate-data credit-scoring systems looked to utility payments, online shopping behaviour, social media activity, and other information more generally related to credit-worthiness [22, 23].

#### 22.2.7.3 Impact

a. A 25% rise in previously ineligible borrowers receiving loans means more people included.
b. Lending profits surged as AI-powered underwriting led to 18% fewer loan defaults amid greater accuracy in risk assessment.
c. The processing time for loans was reduced from 3 days to 2 hours thus streamlining operations.

#### 22.2.7.4 Key Lesson

While AI has improved loan accessibility, regulatory authorities need to set clear guidelines around the transparency of AI lending systems, and how to mitigate their potential for bias.

### 22.2.8 Barclays (UK, 2019): AI in Cybersecurity

#### 22.2.8.1 Background

Phishing attacks, data breaches and other cyber threats posed a growing risk to customer security for Barclays. They required AI-based Cybersecurity Solutions to monitor fraud activity and stop it before it progressed.

#### 22.2.8.2 AI Implementation

Barclays used a system powered by AI, which analysed behavioural patterns and biometric authentication tokens. This AI model learned the normal patterns of customer logins, the transaction behaviours, and how each device interacted with the platform to detect an anomaly behaviour that was a sign of fraud [24, 25].

#### 22.2.8.3 Impact

a. About 45% fewer fraudulent transactions imply less financial loss.
b. Improved rate in the detection of cyberattacks by 60%, enhancing security.
c. Account hacks diminished by 70%, because of AI-fuelled voice and facial acknowledgment verification.

#### 22.2.8.4 Key Lesson

While AI can bolster cybersecurity, it must constantly learn and evolve with human supervision to face ever-evolving cyber threats.

### 22.2.9 PayPal (Global, 2020): AI in Transaction Fraud Prevention

#### 22.2.9.1 Background

Millions of transactions are processed daily through PayPal, which makes it an easy target for fraud like identity theft, chargebacks, and money laundering. With high false positives, traditional fraud detection systems reported low performance, and this resulted in delays in payments and angry customers [26].

#### 22.2.9.2 AI Implementation

PayPal used deep learning or neural networks to detect anomalies in real-time transaction behaviour. Using information about what and where customers tend to spend money, geolocation data, and whether customers are using other devices on the same network, the AI analyses an overall profile of behaviour over time to flag unusual activities before a transaction is ever approved [27, 28].

#### 22.2.9.3 Impact

a. About 80% improvement in fraud detection accuracy, with a reduction of false positives.
b. AI saved $1 billion in fraudulent transactions each year.
c. About 30% reduction in chargeback disputes ensuring merchant confidence.

#### 22.2.9.4 Key Lesson

Though AI-based fraud detection surely improves both security and efficiency, it will need to evolve with new tactics that fraud experts apply.

### 22.2.10 Deutsche Bank (Germany, 2021): AI in Risk Forecasting

#### 22.2.10.1 Background

Deutsche Bank had a hard time coping with erratic market swings and then needed sophisticated risk forecasting models to protect its investments [29, 30]. Changes in macroeconomic landscape and geopolitical threats evolved more rapidly than traditional financial modelling could capture.

#### 22.2.10.2 AI Implementation

Deutsche Bank implemented AI-powered risk analytics that incorporate live financial data, global sentiment analysis and historical market trends [31, 32]. It worked with an AI model to produce predictive risk scores for data, facilitating proactive decision-making.

#### 22.2.10.3 Impact

a. Risk projections were 35% more accurate, making the portfolio safer.
b. During market downturns, AI-driven investment rebalancing cut losses by 22%.
c. Improved turnaround times as Market risk assessments were finished 50% faster.

#### 22.2.10.4 Key Lesson

While AI leads to enhanced financial resilience, human intervention is crucial in validating the AI-generated risk assessments.

### 22.2.11 Square (USA, 2019): AI in Small Business Lending

#### 22.2.11.1 Background

Due to insufficient credit history, small company loans were frequently declined by traditional banks. Square offered AI-powered company loans based on transaction history in an effort to democratise financing.

#### 22.2.11.2 AI Application

Square introduced a loan approval system driven by AI that assesses creditworthiness by looking at cash flow patterns, merchant sales, and seasonal income variations [33, 34]. Without the need for human documentation, AI allows for rapid loan approvals.

#### 22.2.11.3 Impact

a. By increasing loan approval rates by 40%, entrepreneurship was encouraged.
b. AI-driven financing reduced default rates by 25% by personalising repayment conditions.
c. The time needed to process loans decreased from weeks to minutes, speeding up access to funds.

#### 22.2.11.4 Key Learning

Although AI makes it easier for small businesses to obtain finance, unscrupulous lending practices must be prevented by regulatory control.

### 22.2.12 Mastercard (Global, 2020): AI in Payment Security

#### 22.2.12.1 Background

Mastercard required AI-driven fraud protection solutions to safeguard its clients as digital payments increased.

#### 22.2.12.2 Application of AI

Mastercard created real-time fraud detection models driven by AI that examine billions of transactions [34, 35]. To identify irregularities, the system analyses cardholder behaviour, transaction locations, and purchase trends.

#### 22.2.12.3 Impact

a. A 50% decrease in fraudulent chargebacks decreased monetary losses.
b. AI reduced transaction declines by improving the accuracy of payment authorisation.
c. MasterCard improved efficiency by processing transactions 40% quicker.

#### 22.2.12.4 Key Learning

Although AI increases transaction security, banks still need to strike a balance between fraud detection and client convenience.

### 22.2.13 UBS (Switzerland, 2022): AI in Wealth Management

#### 22.2.13.1 Background

For high-net-worth clients, UBS needs insights driven by AI to offer individualised wealth management plans [36].

#### 22.2.13.2 AI Application

UBS has put in place AI-powered financial advising tools that customised portfolio recommendations by examining asset performance, market trends, and customer investing preferences.

#### 22.2.13.3 3 Impact

a. AI-powered wealth management increased the returns on customer portfolios by 22%.
b. Due to AI's ability to automate data processing, operational efficiency rose by 30%.
c. As financial personalisation was improved by AI, client engagement increased by 25%.

#### 22.2.13.4 Key Learning

While AI makes wealth management more efficient, human financial advisers are still essential for fostering relationships.

### 22.2.14 Revolut (UK, 2021): AI in Expense Management

#### 22.2.14.1 Background

AI was required by Revolut in order to identify inefficiencies in budgeting and enhance consumer spending insights [37, 38].

#### 22.2.14.2 Application of AI

The AI-powered cost tracking solution from Revolut examines spending patterns and generates automatic fraud warnings and budget advice.

#### 22.2.14.3 Impact

a. AI-driven notifications avoided overspending, resulting in a 20% monthly savings increase for customers.
b. Fraudulent transactions decreased by 40%, enhancing financial security.

#### 22.2.14.4 Key Learning

The use of AI improves financial literacy, but consumers must have faith in the suggestions made by AI [39]. Overall, these case studies illustrate how AI is revolutionising the financial industry in areas such as fraud detection, risk management, compliance, investing, and customer service. Transparency, ethical issues, and legal frameworks will all play a part in how AI is used in banking in the future.

## 22.3 FUTURE DIRECTIONS FOR AI IN FINANCE

The case studies demonstrate how AI is revolutionising a number of financial industries, including credit scoring, personalised banking, risk management, and fraud detection. The financial sector will be shaped by several key future trends as AI develops further:

a. AI-Powered Autonomous Finance and Hyper-Personalisation.
b. AI systems of the future will build highly customised financial ecosystems, going beyond simple financial advice. With little assistance from humans, AI-powered autonomous banking platforms will handle budgeting, bill paying, and investment management for customers.

c. Financial Services and Generative AI.
d. As large language models (LLMs) become more popular, generative AI will improve contract analysis, automated financial reporting, and regulatory compliance. Conversational banking, which enables voice-activated financial transactions in real time, will also be powered by AI.
e. Integrating Blockchain and AI for Safe Transactions.
f. Blockchain and AI integration will improve smart contract automation, fraud detection, and transaction transparency. Blockchain transactions will be tracked by AI for real-time risk assessment, guaranteeing unchangeable financial records.
g. Quantum Finance with AI.
h. Financial modelling will undergo a revolution thanks to quantum computing, which will allow AI to execute intricate risk analyses and market simulations in a matter of seconds. This will result in fraud detection algorithms and trading methods that are incredibly accurate.
i. AI Ethics and Regulatory Monitoring.
j. Financial organisations need to concentrate on ethical AI development and regulatory compliance as AI's role grows. To preserve transparency and confidence, future AI models will require explainability, fairness, and bias prevention.

## 22.4 CONCLUSION

With AI continuing to reshape the financial sector, the case studies discussed in this chapter illustrate the promise and the paradigm shifts that AI-powered finance brings. Over the past five years alone, banks have begun leveraging technology such as JPMorgan Chase using AI-driven fraud detection, BlackRock using Aladdin system, Ant Group using alternative credit scoring, Goldman Sachs using AI-powered trading and HSBC using AI-enabled AML compliance, which all serve as real-world examples of banks capitalising on how financial institutions are leveraging AI to improve risk management, enhance financial decision-making, and create hyper-personalised financial experiences. Financial services have been transformed by AI, but there are important lessons to be learnt from its deployment. These include the necessity of regulatory compliance, the ethical ramifications of AI-driven decision-making, and the significance of strong risk management systems. In light of these lessons, the conclusion highlights the necessity of ongoing innovation, responsible AI governance, and the long-term effects of AI on the financial industry.

## REFERENCES

1. Met İ, Kabukçu D, Uzunoğulları G, Soyalp Ü, Dakdevir T. Transformation of business model in finance sector with artificial intelligence and robotic process automation. In: *Digital business strategies in blockchain ecosystems: Transformational design and future of global business*. Cham: Springer International Publishing; 2019. p. 3–29.

2. Malik MY, Jafar SH, Dixit A. Efficiency analysis and macroeconomic determinants of non-tax revenues: Evidence from special category states of India. *Indian Econ J.* 2025:00194662251330385.
3. Neti H, Parte S. Riding the tech wave: Exploring tomorrow's landscape of information technology. *Int J Innov Res Technol.* 2023;10(7):42–51.
4. Ţîrcovnicu GI, Haţegan CD. Integration of artificial intelligence in the risk management process: An analysis of opportunities and challenges. *J Financ Stud.* 2023; 8(15):198–214.
5. Jafar SH, Kashid AU, Ghosh S, Srividhya S, Sharma D, Bodhankar A. An enhanced performance optimization of ATM networks for cross-border money transfers. In: *2024 15th International Conference on Computing Communication and Networking Technologies (ICCCNT).* Piscataway, NJ: IEEE; 2024. p. 1–5.
6. Nawaah D, Asare PY, Quarshie MA. Climate finance and natural capital: Linking global initiatives with local impact. In: *Climate neutrality through smart eco-innovation and environmental sustainability.* Cham: Springer Nature Switzerland; 2025. p. 317–32.
7. Tett G. *Fool's gold: How the bold dream of a small tribe at JP Morgan was corrupted by Wall Street greed and unleashed a catastrophe.* New York: Simon and Schuster; 2009.
8. McPhail LL, McPhail JE. Machine learning implications for banking regulation. In: *The Routledge handbook of FinTech.* London: Routledge; 2021. p. 395–415.
9. Robson J, Hutton S. Reports and surveys. *Polit Q.* 1969;40(1):103–12.
10. Mason AC. *Artificial intelligence cybersecurity threats: Determining strategy and decision-making effects* [dissertation]. San Diego, CA: Northcentral University; 2020.
11. Mansfield CL. It takes a thief … and a bank: Protecting consumers from fraud and scams on P2P payment platforms. *Univ Mich J Law Reform.* 2023;57:351.
12. Laplaza NV. AI integration in the banking industry: A case study of JP Morgan. Morgan [bachelor's thesis]. Madrid: Universidad Pontificia Comillas; 2024. Available from: https://repositorio.comillas.edu/xmlui/bitstream/handle/11531/79448/TFG-%20Vasco%20Laplaza%2C%20Natalia.pdf
13. Roger JDD. AI-driven financial modeling techniques: Transforming investment strategies. *J Appl Bus Econ.* 2024;26(4):63–74.
14. Lagna A. Asset manager capitalism and the political economy of artificial intelligence. *Rev Int Polit Econ.* 2025;32(2):512–28.
15. Byrum J. AI in financial portfolio management: Practical considerations and use cases. In: *Innovative technology at the interface of finance and operations: Volume I.* Springer Cham; 2022. p. 249–70.
16. Nauman M. AI in sustainable investing: A dual-edged sword. In: *FinTech and robotics advancements for green finance and investment.* Hershey, PA: IGI Global Scientific Publishing; 2025. p. 383–416.
17. McDonald T, Dan L. Alipay's 'Ant Credit Pay' meets China's factory workers: The depersonalisation and re-personalisation of online lending. *J Cult Econ.* 2021;14(1):87–100.
18. Li Y, Chen W. Entropy method of constructing a combined model for improving loan default prediction: A case study in China. *J Oper Res Soc.* 2021;72(5):1099–109.
19. Naheem MA. AML compliance–a banking nightmare? The HSBC case study. *Int J Disclosure Gov.* 2015;12(4):300–10.
20. Urban MA, Pažitka V, Ioannou S, Wójcik D. The financial geography of resilience: A case study of Goldman Sachs. *Ann Am Assoc Geogr.* 2022;112(6):1593–613.
21. Gigante G, Zago A. DARQ technologies in the financial sector: Artificial intelligence applications in personalized banking. *Qual Res Financ Mark.* 2023;15(1):29–57.
22. Sakthivel K. *An industry study of best practices in life insurance automated and accelerated underwriting models* [dissertation]. Little Rock, Arkansas: University of Arkansas at Little Rock; 2023.

23. Holtzen S, Williamson A, Sherman K, Douglas M, Ruane SG. Corporate policy or CEO activism? Citigroup's stance on reproductive healthcare in the USA. *CASE J.* 2024;20(6):1398–422.
24. Mehra S, Singh G. Revolution through artificial intelligence in context to financial services. In: *Applications of artificial intelligence in business and finance.* Palm Bay, FL: Apple Academic Press; 2021. p. 87–111.
25. Ainous R, Nouichi Y. Corporate digital responsibility and artificial intelligence in Banking sector. *Les Cahiers du Mecas.* 2024;20(2):1–12.
26. Khurana R. Fraud detection in ecommerce payment systems: The role of predictive AI in real-time transaction security and risk management. *Int J Appl Mach Learn Comput Intell.* 2020;10(6):1–32.
27. Chatterjee P. AI-powered real-time analytics for cross-border payment systems. *East Eur J Eng Technol.* 2022;1(1):1–14.
28. Dayalan P, Sundaramurthy B. Exploring the implementation and challenges of AI-based fraud detection systems in financial institutions: A review. In: *Creating AI synergy through business technology transformation.* IGI Global; 2025. p. 25–38.
29. Scheffmann T. Bank management of risk dynamics. In: *The 23rd international conference of the system dynamics society*; 2005. p. 17–21.
30. Buehler K, Freeman A, Hulme R. The risk revolution. Limits to value in electronic commerce related IT investments. *McKinsey Working Papers on Risk*, No. 1. McKinsey & Company; 2008, p. 59–80.
31. Villar AS, Khan N. Robotic process automation in banking industry: A case study on Deutsche Bank. *J Bank Financ Technol.* 2021;5(1):71–86.
32. Schmitz K. Artificial intelligence in credit scoring: Digitalization in the banking landscape in Germany [master's thesis]. Lisbon, Portugal: Universidade Catolica Portuguesa; 2023.
33. Cornelli G, Frost J, Gambacorta L, Jagtiani J. The impact of fintech lending on credit access for US small businesses. *J Financ Stab.* 2024;73:101290.
34. Patra GK, Rajaram SK, Boddapati VN, Kuraku C, Gollangi HK. Advancing digital payment systems: Combining AI, big data, and biometric authentication for enhanced security. *Int J Eng Comput Sci.* 2022;11(8): 25618–31.
35. Burugulla JKR. The future of digital financial security: Integrating AI, cloud, and big data for fraud prevention and real time transaction monitoring in payment systems. *MSW Manag J.* 2024;34(2):711–30.
36. Wittmann X, Lutfiju F. Adopting AI in the banking sector–The wealth management perspective. In: *Society 5.0: First international conference, society 5.0 2021, virtual event*, June 22–24, 2021, Revised Selected Papers 1. Cham: Springer International Publishing; 2023. p. 151–62.
37. Singh C. Artificial intelligence and deep learning: Considerations for financial institutions for compliance with the regulatory burden in the United Kingdom. *J Financ Crime.* 2023;31(2):259–66.
38. Supriadi I. The audit revolution: Integrating artificial intelligence in detecting accounting fraud. *Akunt Teknol Inf.* 2024;17(1):48–61.
39. Jafar SH, Oyedele OM, Nawaah D, Bolanle AS. Exploring leadership challenges for adoption of digital innovation and sustainability. In: *Innovation ecosystems and sustainable technologies.* Bingley: Emerald Publishing Limited; 2025. p. 253–69.

# Index

For Product Safety Concerns and Information please contact our EU
representative GPSR@taylorandfrancis.com
Taylor & Francis Verlag GmbH, Kaufingerstraße 24, 80331 München, Germany

www.ingramcontent.com/pod-product-compliance
Ingram Content Group UK Ltd.
Pitfield, Milton Keynes, MK11 3LW, UK
UKHW021721240926
475702UK00029BA/1750
*9781041007876*